The History
and
Families of Unije

A compiled history and family
Genealogies for the Island of Unije, Croatia

Grant Karcich

Llumina Press

Printed in the United States of America

Cataloging-in-Publication Data

Karcich, Grant.
   The history and the families of Unije: a compiled history and family genealogies for the Island of Unije, Croatia / Grant Karcich.
      p.   cm.
Includes bibliographical references.

 ISBN 978-1-62550-460-9

   1. Genealogy   2. Unije Island (Croatia).   3. Lošinj Island (Croatia).
4. Croatia–History–1527-1918.   5. Croatia–History–1918-1945.   6. Migration, Internal–Adriatic Coast (Croatia).   7. Emigration and immigration–United States.   I Title.
   DR 1637 U54 K37   2008
   949.72–dc22

Cover images:

- Island of Unije, published in Giuseppe Rieger's *Costa occidentale dell'Istria disegnata per ordine del Lloyd austriaco*, (Trieste, Litografia di B. Linassi e C.), 1845.
- Glagolitic script on 1676 stone basin; published in Branko Fucić's *Glagoljski Natpisi*, 1982.

Contents

GENEALOGIES

APPENDICES / SUPPLEMENTAL MATERIAL

SOURCES

To the memory of my mother.

Acknowledgments

I thank my father for instilling in me a love of history by recounting his stories of war and adventure. I wish to acknowledge my gratitude to those who provided genealogical information for the families from Unije. Among the first to collect genealogical data which contributed to the genealogies in this book are Andrew Karcich of New York, Antonio Rerecich (1912-1996), and his son Tony. Special thanks to Andrija Depikolvane for his assistance with Unije church records in Krk.

The author wishes to thank Enzo Valencich and Fiorella Rivera for translating the Italian text. The author also thanks Anton Angelich, Dorothy Buffington, Silvana Borrelli (Nicolich), Maria Carcich, Marina Carcich, Ted Carcich, Milka Fatović (Nikolić), Maria Gelinas, Vlakto Janeković, Dominic Karcic, Gary Loverich, Adrijano Nikolić, Irene Nicolich, Gaudent Radoslovich, Joanne Rasco, Fred Scopinich, Letizia Valic, and Ron Weddle for contributing photographs. Photographs not attributed to a source are from the author. This volume contains some of the verbal history passed down from my parents, other relatives, and inhabitants of Unije, to whom I am indebted.

Preface

In October 2005, workmen in Unije discovered documents in the rubble of a house being refurbished. The documents turned out to be parish records from the 19th Century written in Italian and Latin. They included a mouse-riddled registry of deaths and a census for the island both of which had remained hidden inside the walls of a kitchen for up to one hundred years. The records yielded important genealogical data and shed light on Unije's history from the previous centuries. During the transition to Italian rule in 1919-1921, priests in Unije and the nearby islands were forced to leave,[1] and though it is only speculation, the hidden documents might be a result of the transition to Italian rule. Like the hidden records, much of the history of Unije has remained hidden because no one had sought it out. Unije in the 18th Century had parish records written in an ancient Slavic script[2] but these records no longer exist. This volume attempts to reveal part of the hidden history of Unije's past.

Given names and surnames used in this text come from various sources, written in a variety of scripts, including Croatian, Italian, and Latin, and therefore the same names may appear in different forms. Data used to compile this history and family genealogies comes from a number of historical sources, including parish records (birth/baptismal, marriage, and death records), legal records, censuses, ship records, and family histories.

Book of the Dead 1815, Unije Parish Church discovered in 2005

Introduction

Unije (pronounced uni-ye) is written as Unie in Italian and Nia in Latin is a Croatian island in the northern Adriatic Sea (14 45'E – 44 38'N), and measures 9 kilometres north to south and from half to 2 kilometres east to west. Located in the Kvarner Gulf it is a part of Primorsko-Goranska County.

Except for Brijuni, off the coast of Istria, Unije is the most westerly island in the chain of Croatian Adriatic islands. Pula is 36 km to the north-west and Rimini, Italy some 100 kilometres due west. The important centers of Rijeka and Trieste lie to the north. At its south-eastern corner lies Unije's closest neighbour, the small island of Vele Srakane, with the island of Susak 9 kilometres further to the south. Immediately east of Unije lies the larger island of Losinj, with the town of Mali Losinj, also known as Lussinpiccolo in former times. On the island of Cres, adjacent to the northern end of the island of Losinj, is the village of Osor the former medieval center of the region.

This historical outline of Unije includes an overview based on the written sources that have been preserved. The earliest prehistoric pottery period, the early Liburnian period, and the succeeding Roman period are noted in the appendix along with the archaeological evidence in association with the island.[3] The impact of the Roman period is detected in the place names of the island and in some of the nautical vocabulary used by the Cakavian dialect spoken in Unije and in the eastern Adriatic region and also incorporated into standard Croatian. A variety of old Latin-related loan words have become part of the modern language used by Istrian and Dalmatian communities along the Adriatic Sea, attesting to the presence of the preceding population which inhabited the region prior to the commencement of the Slavic migration in the 7th Century.

The history of the people of Unije goes back a long way and illustrates the long genealogical sequence that connects the people of Unije to the neighbouring islands. Over the centuries, the families of nearby Losinj have contributed substantially to the makeup of the families in Unije. Also, other inhabitants from Cres, Krk, and the mainland contributed to families on the island community. The majority of the families that settled in Unije were of Slavic background and the slow movement of families to Unije over several hundred years is indicative of how the Adriatic islands were settled.

5

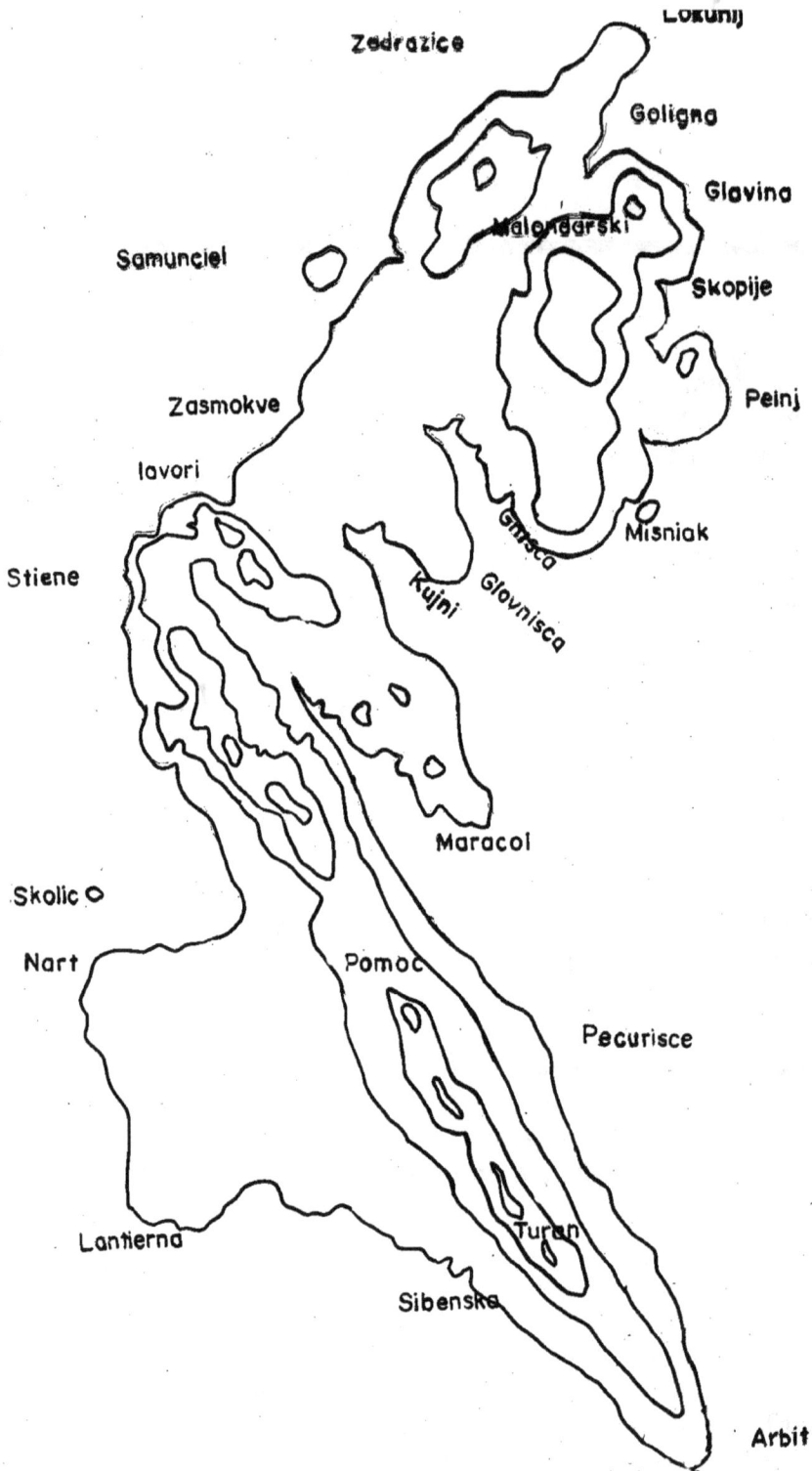

Lo*unij

Zedrazice

Goligna

Glavina

Samunciel

Malondarski

Skopije

Peinj

Zasmokve

Iavori

Gnisca

Misniak

Stiene

Rujni

Glovnisca

Maracol

Skolic ○

Nart

Pomoc

Pecurisce

Lantierna

Turan

Sibensko

Arbit

Middle Ages: early beginnings

There is archaeological evidence for an occupation in Unije at Mirišće Bay between the 1st and 4th Centuries A.D.; however, the absence of such evidence during the 6th to 8th Centuries attests to the lack of a permanent human habitation on the island of Unije during the early Medieval period. [4] Between the 6th and 11th Centuries Unije and the other Kvarner islands were depopulated for a variety of reasons, including diseases and a weak political administration. After the end of the Roman Empire, Slavic people began to migrate into coastal Croatia. Slavic peoples came into the Balkans in the 6th Century, but their migration to the Kvarner islands occurred some time later. Although a monastery existed on the neighbouring island of Susak in 1071, Unije was probably inhabited some time afterwards. [5]

Definitely by the 15th Century Unije was inhabited, for in 1477 there is evidence of retaining walls on the island[6] which strongly suggests a permanent settlement. The modern-day population of the southern Kvarneric islands (Losinj, Ilovik, Susak, Srakane, and Unije) begins with the settlement of Veli Losinj in 1280 by Obrado Harnovich (Harvojić) and twelve families newly arrived from Dalmatia. [7,8] Gradually the families in Losinj created a second settlement. These two settlements were known as Velo Selo and Mali Selo and eventually developed into the towns of Veli Losinj (Lussingrande) and Mali Losinj (Lussinpiccolo) respectively. The neighbouring islands of Ilovik and Unije were most likely settled soon after the initial settlement on the island of Losinj and possibly by families from Losinj. One of the early families from Losinj, the Rerecich family, established itself in Unije at an early date.

Various people from the island of Losinj owned the *polje* or the flat fields in Unije on the western end of the island, where they grew grapes. Women would tend and guard the vineyards. The inhabitants of Unije drove their oxen over the hills to till their small plots of land, tended their vines, and sowed their fields on the other side of the island. Though Losinj families continued to own plots of land in Unije, the *polje* lands were later purchased by the residents of Unije, a process that was uncompleted until the early 20th Century. Early on, family members grouped together, shared their workload and lived in extended families. In mediaeval times, Slavic families would live and work together in *zadrugas*, forming large extended families often run by brothers.

THE HISTORY AND FAMILIES OF UNIJE

Zadrugas were common in ancient Croatia, Bosnia, Serbia, and Montenegro, and based on an old social structure, dating from the arrival of first Slavic peoples to Croatia. In a peasant economy, cash is not a major component and peasants are dependent primarily on what they can obtain from their cultivated fields and livestock. In such a society, a *zadruga* was an advantage because it pooled agricultural produce and equipment from a number of related families and shared these resources in a communal economy. A *zadruga* was usually composed of a number of related brothers or uncles. The houses in a *zadruga* had married brothers with separate rooms with their own hearths, but usually sharing one roof. Property was inherited equally between brothers and father's siblings. In Unije the brothers of the Nicolich (Agatin) family built four adjoining houses, which still stand today. Oral tradition states that these houses were built with the proceeds of a hidden cache of money. Another set of houses were erected by the Carcich (Bravarof) families using tithes collected for the church.

Zadrugas continued to operate in Croatia up to the 19th Century when they began to decrease in importance from the influence of private property and a cash economy. Unije early on had some families that operated in a *zadruga* type economy and other families operated only as nuclear or single families. This would explain why Unije has a number of extended families living side-by-side in some cases, and others living in single family homes. Any influence that the *zadrugas* had in Unije was gone by the beginning of the 20th Century, though its influence had begun to decrease substantially in the previous century.

The residents of a *zadruga* recognized a common ancestor and carried a common name. This was known by a lineage (*bratstvo*) name. The lineage came from one founder, usually a male, but when a widow settled and formed a separate family with her sons, it could be a female founder. Such lineages had group names ending in –ić, –ović, or –ičić. Other family lineages also took on a patronymic based on the father's name and ending in –ov, –ev, –ef, or –in. Some lineage names also developed from these patronymics. Such lineage names were used in addition to surnames, so that families would have both a surname and lineage name. In Unije a third of the families carried the surname Carcich or Karčić, but a large number of lineages distinguished the different Carcich / Karčić families. The Carcich lineages include: Andricev, Baldić/Baldich, Bardar, Bravarof, Cicola (found in Cunski), Gevin/Jevin, Pasquić/Pasquich, Prussian, Rocov, and Zburkin.

The 16th and 17th Centuries

Unije is referred to as Nia on maps from the 16th and 17th century, while documents from the 18th century add an initial vowel resulting in the variations *onia* and *unij*. At the end of the 16th Century a small settlement existed on the island. By 1588 a number of farmers and vine cultivators flourished in Unije[9], and they probable brought their families to live on the island. A decade later the islands of Losinj, Ilovik, Susak, and Unije had a population of about 1000 individuals, with 600 to 700 residing in Losinj and the remainder living in Unije, Susak, and Ilovik. [10] Taking into account that Susak, Unije, and Ilovik account for 300 or 400 inhabitants, and since Susak normally had as many people as Unije and Ilovik combined, the population of Unije in 1600, plausibly was between 75 and 100 inhabitants.

The early modern history of Unije has been turbulent due to the population movements caused by Turkish incursions on the mainland. The Uskok pirates plundered the islands using Unije as a base of operations by sheltering in the cove at Gnišća on the north end of the island. The Uskoks were displaced persons that had been uprooted from Dalmatia and the interior by the Turkish occupation of the Balkans. They settled on the Adriatic coastal mainland with their main base at Senj some 57 kilometres northeast of Unije. Initially, they carried out attacks in the Turkish areas of Dalmatia, but later began attacking and plundering the communities on the Istrian peninsula and the islands of the Kvarner. Attacking in large numbers, the Uskoks stole livestock and other goods. In 1543 they plundered Cres, Osor and burned settlements on the island of Losinj. The Venetian authorities built a tower on the island of Veli Srakane, to the south of Unije, in 1573 to protect the inhabitants of the area from pirates. To pay for the construction of the tower and for other defensive measures the local population was taxed. [11] However, repeated attacks against Osor occurred in 1573, 1575, and 1605. Susak was attacked in 1579, while Mali and Veli Losinj were again attacked in 1580.

During August of 1612, fourteen Uskok ships used Unije as a base to attack shipping in the area. [12] While war raged between Venice and Austria from 1614 to 1617, the Uskoks again plundered the Kvarner islands and Istria, but in 1617 Austria, which administered the Uskok stronghold at Senj, signed a peace treaty with Venice and agreed to resettle the Uskoks in the interior, thereby ending the long reign of Uskok piracy around Unije and the neighbouring islands. Unsubstantiated stories claimed that some of the Uskoks settled in Unije. [13] However, robbery of livestock did not cease after the Uskoks were disbanded, because sporadic raids by recent colonists from Istria continued to plague the islands into the 18th century.

In 1588 the names of individuals who farmed in Unije are recorded in a transaction regarding the sale of vineyards between Zorzem Pracin and Tomic Susnačić, son of Jakov. These surnames are no longer found on any of the islands, but Pracin may have been related to Pagien (Pajcen), a surname found in the first half of the 17th Century in Mali Losinj. In 1591 other vineyards in Unije were cultivated by Mikula Dalgčić, Mikoli Posibelić, Mikula Skrivanić, Marko Dorčić, and Matic Digčić. Documents of wills show other cultivators with land holdings in Unije. The Scrivanich (Skrivanić) family rented the neighbouring island of Veli Srakane, and also had vineyards in Unije. In 1608 Petar Gojaković sold his vineyard to Martin Žižić, while in 1618, Antonic Skrivanić willed his vineyard in Unije to the brothers of Saint Anthony, and two years later, Anton son of Anton Raguzinić deeded his vineyard to them. [14] Members of the Ducich and Radoslovich[15] families lived in Unije in the 1620's and 1630's. Some of these families would have worked as tenants, providing a portion of their produce to the landowners.

Maračol and Mišnjak coves with the island of Losinj in the background

The surnames found in Unije during the 16th and 17th Centuries originated from three different areas and are an indication of the migration routes of the early families coming to Unije. One migrating group consisting of the surnames Halić, Ragusinić, Rerecich, Skrivanić and Nicolich (Mikulić) appear in the early 16th Century church records for Mali Losinj and their origins may stem from the initial colonization of that island from the south. Another related group consisting of surnames includes Ducich, Zurich, and Žižić also come from the south, particularly from Dalmatia. The other major group comprises of surnames from the region north of Unije. This group includes Dorcich, Gojaković, Zuanich (Ivanić), and Matiasich found in Istria, Raguzinić (Raguzin) on the island of Krk, Dedich from Rab, and Radoslovich and Velcich from the island of Cres. It is interesting to note that the surnames such as Radoslovich and Rerecich, can be found on the island today, while others, such as Matiasich and Dedich have not been retained on the island.

Some of surnames that are later associated with Unije, make their appearance in the region at an early date. A Radoslovich family was in Unije in 1624. The Rerecich families in Unije are believed to have originated from two brothers Jerić and Sime (Simon) from Veli Losinj from which developed the two main Rerecich clans of Unije, the Jercich and the Simef lineages. The Rerecich surname came to the island of Losinj during the 13th Century. In 1684 the surname Karčić (Carcich) appears in connection with Unije along with the surname of Nadalin. The surname Nadalin dates back to the 16th Century Mali Losinj where it occurs in the form, Nadalinić. A Luka Karčić is found in association with the town of Vrbnik, Krk in 1490 and in 1497. [16] In the 15th and 16th Centuries, the Karčić surname and its related derivations of Kerčić and Karsić are found on the island of Krk. [17] and later the version, Chercich, appears in the town of Cres. One Karčić (Carcich) lineage, the Bravarof lineage, dates at least back to the early18th Century and may extend back even further. The general term *bravari* is used for lock-keepers or herders. Genetic data can illustrate that, the Carcich (Karčić) families may have been in the region near Unije for a longer time period than the historical documents can show. The author, who is a Carcich, carries paternal DNA that closely matches the Y-chromosomal markers that are commonly found in the population of Primorko-Goranska County[18] to which Unije and Losinj belong.

The inhabitants of Unije lived off the proceeds of the land, usually raising sheep, goats, pigs, and cattle, and growing grapes, olives, and various grain crops. Although settlers of the neighbouring islands, such as Susak and Losinj occupied themselves with fishing and with the maritime trade, the farmers on Unije had little inclination to do so. Sheep were one of the main-stays of Unije's economy, and provided milk, cheese, and meat. Most families tended their own herd of sheep with each having a unique brand or *belezi* of owernship which was incised on the ears of the sheep.[19] These *belezi* were passed down from

Sheep Brands

father to son. It is credible these shepherds lived a transitory, physically hard life moving from place to place in order to make a living. In 1631 there is mention of, "parish cattle herders bravara from the island of Unije [that] animals which were entrusted to their care, weren't sufficiently fattened", and "on the island of Unije in the waters of the Kvarner we have 20 cattle, 100 head of sheep, and 5 cows, also a number of their young Heifers which still suckle." [20]

The Roman Catholic Church played a large role in the community. Documents for 1650 mention the inhabitants of Unije paid 400 Venetian liras in church tithes. Confirmation records for Unije in 1677 show a Martin Chercich (Carcich), Antonia Radoslovich, Antonio Susovich, Antonia Picinich, Antonia Guslomanich, and Maria Dedich. [21]

The island of Unije was owned and administered by the Bishop of Osor. The farmers on Unije had a subservient existence to the Church on the island. In September of 1679 the local residents sought to be relieved from paying a third of their produce to the Bishop of Osor and the Abbey of Saint Peter. In their litigation of 13 June 1680 against the Church, the plaintiffs were the Bravari (or shepherds) of Unije and the following named individuals: Kasper Zuanich, Luke Robcich, Zane Matiasich, Anton Velcich, Nickolas Dedich, Anton Radoslovich, Frane Zauncich, Nicholas Rerecich, Luke Rerecich, Anton Zurich. The plaintiffs questioned their payments to the Church. However, the residents of Unije lost their case against the Church for the judgment ordered the inhabitants of Unije to:

> "better attend to their cultivation of vineyards and other
> products... [and to provide] every year the full third, and free
> of tithe, of all the yield of grains, wheat, oats, millet, rye,
> legumes of all sorts, and alfalfa, that will be harvested on the
> island, without detracting the *zobure* and *potkupje* and *mast*,
> of the wine products and wines of all the qualities grown on
> the island....One full fifth of these products from every
> vineyard shall be divided between the Osor's Abbey of Saint
> Peter and the Bishopry, as also the tithe, which the colons
> shall pay on the above products, from the fourth part which
> shall be the *terratico*. They shall pay the tithe on newborn
> livestock, as the young born yearly to sheep and goats of these
> flocks belong to the Abbey and Bishop's office. This will
> apply also to the shepherds own animals when the young are
> begotten. [22]

This one-sided agreement was enforced for several generations afterwards since the litigation mentions, that all inhabitants "of Onije, and their successors, [are] to maintain and inviolably observe never to oppose under any pretext, tithe, or colors imaginable: by that, to obligate both sides and their inheritors in the most ample form possible." [22] The inhabitants had to pay a part of their produce to the church as a form of rent, plus they had to pay the normal tithe to the church, and the taxes to the state, for construction of defences that the Venetians built around Unije. This left the inhabitants as little more than serfs, tied to the land and not able to sustain themselves during times of drought and famine.

Milling Stones in Unije

The migratory trickle of families to Unije, as well as to other neighbouring islands, follows both a northern and southern course. This pattern continues throughout the centuries down into the 19th century. Usually, families move in from neighboring islands, but as time goes on more families arrive from the mainland. Up until 1943 there was some migration from Italy, due to the trade routes between Italy and the islands of Cres and Losinj. It is only in the last century that the traditional north and south migrations were supplanted by mainland Yugoslavia, and today from the interior of Croatia, and from Bosnia, and Macedonia.

The Church in Unije

The first church in Unije, Saint Andrew the Apostle, was built in 1680 outside of the settlement and adjacent to the cemetery. The Roman Catholic Church in Unije was represented by a local priest, who reported to the bishop of Osor. One of the earliest dated artefacts found in the Nicolich (Agatin) household of Unije was commissioned by the local priest, Matthew Brnić. It was a stone basin used to hold olive oil, and it contains an inscription by Brnić dating to 1676. The inscription reads:

1676 na dan 24 miseca ijulja ja pop Matij Brnić ucinih tu kamenicu[23] (1676 on the 24th of the month of July, I Father Matthew Brnić made this stone basin). The text is in Croatian and written in the ancient Glagolitic script, a special Slavic alphabet that pre-dates the use of the Cyrillic alphabet commonly in use today in Slavic speaking regions of eastern Europe.

Much of the religious life of the inhabitants would have been administered by Glagolitic priests, such as Matij Brnić from Krk. Masses were conducted in Church Slavonic, and records of baptisms, marriages, and deaths would be recorded in the Glagolitic script. These practices are known from the neighbouring communities of Cunski and Mali Losinj, and such practices were also employed in Unije.

The use of Glagolitic in Unije indicates that the island parish had the right to have church services conducted in Croatian. Because this right extended back to before the split of the Roman Catholic church with the Greek Orthodox church, the Croatian church continued to operate with some autonomy when it came to the use of the native vernacular. While the Roman Catholic Church traditionally employed Latin in the cathedrals in Osor, Krk and in parts of Istria, the Kvarner islands and other parts of Istria used the Croatian language and the Glagolitic script in church services. Most churches in northwestern Croatian maritime communities did not use Latin in their church services but rather used an archaic form of Croatian thereby predating the use of the vernacular in Protestant churches by several hundred years.

The Glagolitic alphabet was brought to the northern Adriatic islands by Slavic immigrants. The script was devised by the Slavic missionaries Saint Cyril and Methodius, who converted the Slavic tribes of Moravia, Slovenia and Croatia in the ninth century. The Glagolitic script was retained by the Slavic clergy on the island of Krk and in Dalmatia and it was used by Roman Catholic parishes in books of worship, such as missals, hymnals, and breviaries. Later, legal texts were written in Glagolitic using the local Cakavian dialect as spoken in coastal Croatia.

1676 Olive Stone Basin with Inscription in Unije

Glagolitic books were used in Church services in Unije by 1744 for in that year, the Church of Saint Andrew in Unije is listed as having a *Carte Gloria nuove in illirico* and a *Missale nuovo illirico* (New Glagolitic Missal). A hundred years earlier, the priest in Unije 1647 was Don Marcus Petrina. The local bishop in Osor together with the Abbey of Saint Peter, also of Osor, administered the island of Unije, and the bishop regularly visited the island, usually on an annual basis, a tradition which is still carried out to this day. During the bishop's visits in 1670, 1671, and 1674, several Glagolitic church books are mentioned, such as a Ritual *Illirico*, a *Schavetto o Euvangelistario*, as well as several Glagolitic missals, and a Latin missal. At this time the parish priest is listed as Thadeo

Vitcouich (Tadija Vitković, in Croatian). As late as June 1785 a *Messale Illirico* is listed in the Church of Saint Andrew suggesting that Glagolitic was in use in Unije during the closing decades of the 18th century.[24] However, due to a scarcity of Glagolitic church books and the lack of priests skilled in reading them, the use of Croatian in the church services was abandoned. By 1803 the use of Church Slavonic and the Glagolitic script in Unije was replaced by the Italian language and the Roman script.

The first Church rectory in Unije was built in 1753 according to the inscription over the door jam which reads, "1753 D.T.R." This house is reputed to be the first house in Unije with roof tiles instead of hatch in the roof construction, and its walls were constructed of clean cut limestone. The bell tower of St. Andrew's Church was built in 1857, while the public fountain in front of the church was erected in 1886. The bells of the bell tower used during Austrian rule were melted down for munitions in WWI. These were replaced by a couple of bells in 1921, and finally replaced again with electronic-activated bells in the early 1990's. Though begun in the late 18th century, St. Andrew's was later enlarged, acquiring its present form in 1911, and a few repairs were completed in the early 1960's, in the 1980's, and again in 2006. The painting of Our Lady of Carmel, above the main altar and the marble columns are in the baroque style.

Church Rectory, Unije 1753

St. Andrew's church in the cemetery – exterior

St. Andrew's church in the cemetery - interior

18th Century

Several new family surnames appear in association with 18th Century records for the island. These are Bellanich, Haglich, Galosich, Giurich, Mancich, Nicolich, Ragusin, and Valich. Confirmation records show that a number of Carcich families lived in Unije in the first few decades of the 18th Century since in 1715 confirmations occur for Christoforo, Biaso, and Paulo Carcich.[25]

Some of the oldest families in Unije can trace their origins directly back to an ancestor in the early part of the 18th Century. During this period family lineage names became established based on *bratstvo* lineages. Lineage names (also know as *nadimak* in Croatian and *soprannome* in Italian) are commonly used to distinguish a particular family. Often a surname may contain several lineage names. Lineage names are based on, either a personal given name, a locality, or an occupation, and often originate as a nick-name that later is formerly adopted by future generations of a family. The previously mentioned Carcich (Bravarof) dates back to the early 18th Century and several family branches of this lineage developed in Unije and in Cunski. The Radoslovich (Kalcich) family lineage dates back to Martin Radoslovich (1715-1750), though it is unclear when this lineage name was first adopted.

A number of families were well established in Unije in the early decades of the 18th Century that their surnames begin to appear in the marriage records for Mali Losinj.[26] The names that appear in the Losinj records between 1710 and 1740 include: Biaso Bellanich, Karstić Karčić, Martin Karčić, Matteo Karcich, Matteo Giurich, Matij Halić, Gasparo Nicolich, Martin Nicolich, Franić Radoslović, Gaspar Radoslovich, Karstić Radoslović, Martin Radoslović, Mattio Radoslovich, Simun Radoslović, Augustin Rerečić, Martin Rerečić, Matij Rerečić Mikula Rerečić, and Jivan Valčić. The Mali Losinj records show that there were at least 24 families in Unije. These were Bellanich (1 family), Carcich (5 families), Galosich (1 family), Giurich (1 family), Haglich (1 family), Mancich (1 family), Nadalin (1 family), Nicolich (2 families), Radoslovich (5 families), Ragusin (1 family), Rerecich (3 families), Valich (2 families).

Based on the minimum number of individuals for which records exist there were at least 68 individuals residing in Unije between 1720 and 1730. Since the individuals listed also had additional children for which we do not have records, and some families such as the Bellanich and Nicolich are underrepresented, it is a fair assumption that the minimum

18

record count is not sufficient to give a total number of residents in Unije. A more realistic population figure for Unije at this time would need to double this number to 136 individuals.

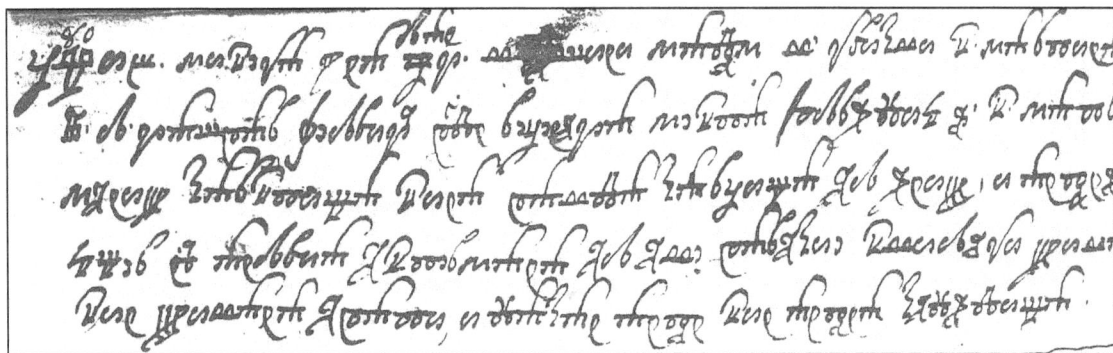

Marriage record for Karstić Karčić (Christofolo Carcich), Mali Losinj, June 14,1722 (*1722. miseca juna dan 14 v Lošini Malom... Karstić sina Pavla Karčića od Unij i Antonu hćer po. Andrija Ostermana*)

In the early part of the 1700's there would have been a bottleneck in terms of viable marriage partners. During the early 18th Century a considerable number by people who lived in Unije married in Mali Losinj. It can be speculated that this represents the first adult generation which was ready to marry after the influx of new settlers in the late 17th or early 18th Centuries. With such a small population in Unije at this time, those seeking to marry would have had to look to other communities for spouses and Mali Losinj would have been a natural source for spouses, since it was close and had a much larger population than Unije.

Other surnames no longer found in Unije occur in various records from 1740 to 1783 and include Jurić (Giurich), Ivancich, Marcich or Mancich, Ragusin, Riezo, and Sepcich. [27, 28] Mattio Giurich raised a family in Unije after 1740 and though his descendents died out in Unije in the 19th Century, his family comes from a 17th Century Losinj family. The genealogy of this Giurich family is found in this volume. Likewise, one of the Nicolich families in Unije is descendent from 17th Century Mali Losinj families. Some surnames may have died out while their descendents intermarried with other families on the island. Some surnames did not increase in number. For example the Valich family remained in Unije in small numbers. Jivan Valić, son of Anton, married in 1722, and Maria Valić of Jivan married in 1726. The small number of modern day Valić families from Unije can be attributed to the large number of females versus male births to families with this surname over the last couple of hundred years. Early in the 18th Century several Radoslovich families descendent from Unije got established in Mali Losinj. Later in the same century Carcich families from Unije transplanted to Cunski to raise their families.

The Radoslovich families from Mali Losinj and the Carcich families from Cunski are listed with the genealogies found in this volume.

In the later part of the 1770's, Alberto Fortis (1741-1803) an Italian natural scientist, travel writer, and friar, visited the islands of Cres and Losinj, and his published account of the visit was written in English to John Strange the Bishop of Londonderry. By the time Alberto Fortis passed by Unije, the island must have had a stable population, perhaps numbering 150 to 200 individuals. However to the outside world, the inhabitants of Unije seemed of little importance, so that Fortis was able to write,

> [Unije] has few inhabitants, and those excessively poor. It's principal product is fire wood, great part of it being woody. It might produce honey and wax in abundance [sic], and cattle likewise; but it yields little of any thing, for those reasons which are well understood in our days, especially by those who apply themselves to the study of publick [sic] economy. The fishing round about Onie [Unije] is a considerable product; it consists chiefly in tunny, mackrel, and *Sardelle* [sardines]; but the poor inhabitants have not the means of profiting by it, and strangers come and reap all the advantage under their eyes.[29]

Fishing when it occurred, would have been done from shore with line and hook, and would have provided a good source of protein in times of hunger. Farming and herding was the main livelihood in the island. With a large section of the north of the island forested, Unije contained firewood for export. Fortis mentions that, "firewood is also a considerable article of active trade.... The trees commonly used for fire wood are the common and evergreen oak, the elm and ash, besides wild vines, the arbutus, pheleaea, juniper, &c." A couple of inhabitants of Mali Losinj, whose fathers were from Unije transported firewood from Cres and Mali Losinj to Venice in the 18th Century. Mattio Carcich son of Paolo, and Cristoforo Radoslovich, son of Simon were involved in the firewood export trade. [30]

Shipping in the Kvarner had an opportunity to recover from its loses, after the demise of the Uskoks. However, loses continued to occur due to natural disasters. There are several shipwrecks around Unije. One occurred in May of 1757 at Mezzo on Unije when a Segnese ship encountered difficulties. Another shipwreck occurred during November of 1764, between the island of Unije and Srakane, as the ship, the *San Giuseppe*, captained by Andrea Sreglich, while en route to Corfu and Salonica broke up on the south end of Unije. In October 1786 on the small island of Misgnač, off the east coast of Unije two small boats got stuck and lost some of their cargo of lumber. [31] A old shipwreck, which divers have discovered, lies just off the coast of the small islet of Skolic, which is passed regularly by the ferry as it comes into the main wharf in Unije. Closer to our era, the

Anton Milan went aground on the north cape of Lokunji in 1929 losing its load of cement.

Fortis provides insights into the agricultural practices that were common on the Kvarner islands. He mentions that, "every house has its little garden", with women being "extremely robust and accustomed to carry very heavy burdens on their head, as well up hill as down", and the "children of the low people are employed from their tenderest age, either in cultivating the land, fishing, or attending the cattle....many are employed in the manufacture of Rascia which is a coarse kind of woolen stuff". Oxen were not often used to till, but that was:

> almost wholly performed by the laborious and sturdy arms of the men, who are generally well paid for their labour, in proportion to the scarcity of hands. These workmen indeed do a great deal more than ours. They are obliged first of all to clear the spot appointed for culture from the moveable stones, and that is continual employment...and these stones they dispose in little walls wherewith they surround the field by way of fence and boundary. Generally these artificial fields are of a circular or elliptical figure, and are called *coronale* by the islanders. [32]

Fortis also indicates that cultivation was predominantly of olives and grape, with large herds of sheep for husbandry. Although most of Fortis' observations were made while at Cres, they would apply to Unije and the other Kvarner islands as well. Limited amounts of corn were sown and potatoes were unknown in these islands. Figs were the primary fruit, while peaches, pears, and apricots were scarce. A certain root of the Arus plant was used to make bread, though Fortis deemed it not to be nutritious. Olive oil was a mainstay on the island and was produced from three varieties of olives, called *slatke, starovijerke,* and *istrionke.* "Oil is exported out of the island; but almost all the value is required for the purchase of corn of which the inhabitants do not raise enough to maintain them four months of the years....The wine … is not of a perfect quality in proportion to the oil. This is probably owing to the little knowledge and care they have in gathering and pressing the grapes, and in fermenting the wine." [33]   Fortis describes the care used in tending grapevines, when he states that,

> the islanders use to lay a heap of earth about every vine, which is kept very low, and almost totally divested of sprigs every year, and these heaps keep the roots fresh in the dry season and in the winter, and during the windy season of spring serve to cover the vines entirely. They commonly plant vines as tick as we do Indian corn. [34]

T R A V E L S

I N T O

D A L M A T I A;

C O N T A I N I N G

GENERAL OBSERVATIONS ON THE NATURAL HISTORY OF THAT COUNTRY
AND THE NEIGHBOURING ISLANDS; THE NATURAL PRODUCTIONS,
ARTS, MANNERS AND CUSTOMS OF THE INHABITANTS.

I N A

S E R I E S   O F   L E T T E R S

F R O M

ABBE   A L B E R T O   F O R T I S,

T O   T H E

EARL OF BUTE, THE BISHOP OF LONDONDERRY,
J O H N   S T R A N G E,   Esq. &c. &c.

TO WHICH ARE ADDED BY THE SAME AUTHOR,

O B S E R V A T I O N S   O N   T H E   I S L A N D

O F

C H E R S O   AND   O S E R O.

TRANSLATED FROM THE ITALIAN UNDER THE AUTHOR's INSPECTION.

W I T H   A N   A P P E N D I X,   AND OTHER CONSIDERABLE

A D D I T I O N S,   N E V E R   B E F O R E   P R I N T E D.

I L L U S T R A T E D   W I T H   T W E N T Y   C O P P E R   P L A T E S.

————MODO EXUSTIONE, MODO ELUVIONE TERRARUM
DIUTURNITATI RERUM INTERCEDIT OCCASUS.————
MACROB. IN SOMN. SCIP. L. 2. C. 10.

L O N D O N:

PRINTED FOR J. R O B S O N, BOOKSELLER,
NEW B O N D S T R E E T.
M DCC LXXVIII.

Travels into Dalmatia by Alberto Fortis, 1778

"Sheep are the most numberous species of quadrupeds on the island; oxen, beast of burden, and hogs being in no great number.... Every proprietor of flocks, or several together, entrust them to a shepherd, each marking his own sheep by different cuts in their ears." [35] The unique sheep brands or *belezi* have been passed down in families and were only recently discarded.

The 18th century witnessed livestock robberies on the islands of Cres. Fortis states that "the Morlack robbers, and particularly those of the Istrian colonies, Castelnovo,

Carnizza, Medolino, and Altura, too often land on the island and carry off all the animals of every species that they can collect together, and that frequently before the eyes of the keepers themselves, who are not in a condition to oppose armed plunders." [36] Stories have come down to us in Unije of inhabitants keeping watch for robbers, as evident by the remains of snail shells eaten while standing watch on the hilltops of the island.

Stone House in Unije

Many of the houses in Unije at this time would have been small stone huts with thatched roofs and lacking windows. While visiting the island of Susak, Fortis[37] describes these houses as having "only one aperture in those cottages, which serves for door, window, and outlet for the smoke; there are no division in the inside; not even a floor, excepting what the ordinary ground furnishes, and it is lower than the outside". Such living conditions, with large families residing in a small house with little ventilation, were not healthy. In Fortis' time the population of Mali Losinj had suffered an outbreak of small pox, while dysentery was evident in the town of Cres, [38] and the health of the towns people of Osor was often stressed by malaria, that even the bishop of that town stayed away part of the year. The lines of communication to Unije went through Osor and Losinj and it is, therefore, highly plausible that the inhabitants of Unije also suffered from these diseases, being in contact with the inhabitants of these towns.

Though the local Croatian dialect was used by the common people, the influence of Italian was increasing due to contact and trade with other islands and with merchants from the mainland. Fortis[39] indicates that the Croatian language, or the Sclavonian, as he called it on Cres and Losinj "is more widely diffused than any of the other European dialects, is commonly used by the people, and the peasants of the island". When referring to the speech of S. Vito (Rijeka) Fortis states that, "the language of the country is the Croatian but all the genteel [sic] people of both sexes speak good Italian". The same would be true for the languages spoken on the islands of the Kvarner.

The Roman Catholic Church still maintained a strong influence on the islands in the later part of the 18th Century. Fortis writes that,

> The tithes of the island of Cherso and Oser are distributed in four parts. One part is assigned to the poor... the second is allotted to the church for reparations, ornaments, &c.[sic], The third belongs to the Canons of Cherso and Osero, Lubenice, and Caisole; and the fourth is assigned to the bishop over all the diocese. In the two Lossins [sic] the portion of the poor was long ago given to the parish priest and curates, who have no certain funds for their maintenance.[40]

19th Century

The beginning of the 19th Century ushered in a new period with a rise of nationalism and a new political administration. After the Napoleonic Wars, Venice no longer ruled the Kvarner islands. Austria took over the civil administration from 1814 to 1918, and the development of Croatian and Italian political factions in Unije, probably dates from this period.

The 1815 census for Unije [41] shows 222 inhabitants and 45 dwellings on the island, while the census of 1819 lists 49 dwellings, which indicates that four new structures were constructed on the island in the four years up to 1819. The populations in both Unije and Susak were increasing rapidly at this time, and this put pressure on finding more arable land. In Fortis' time the population of Susak numbered about 300 inhabitants. Soon its population increased rapidly, as the town developed an extension in the 1820's towards the seaside. Due to the population pressures and possibly to the inability of the Susak soil to sustain olive trees, some inhabitants of Susak began to build in Unije, on the eastern side of the island. This settlement was abandoned around 1850 due to resistance from the other inhabitants of Unije, who at time harassed these new settlers from Susak.

The population of Unije began to increase in the first half of the 19th Century which continued to rise into the next century with a population peak of 783 inhabitants in 1921. This was due to a decrease in mortality as a result of better health resources. Mali Losinj had a doctor in the 18th and 19th Centuries, and Unije would have benefited by its close proximity to the town. The death register for Unije from 1815 to 1880 shows that the islanders died from a variety of illnesses including famine, fevers, and epidemic diseases. Life expectancy at birth, based on a sample of 243 deaths in Unije for the period from 1815 to 1850, was 35 years of age. This is similar to other European communities and those found in North America at this time period. Many children died in the first 10 years of life suggesting that various diseases contributed to such deaths. However, if one survived the early childhood years, that person stood a good chance of living into their 70's, or 80's. Health improvements in the latter half of the 19th Century pushed life expectancy up. Certain families in Unije had individuals living into their 90's during the late 19th Century.

Life Table for Unije based on Deaths from 1815 to 1850		
Interval of Years	Number of Deaths	Life Expectancy
0-1	50	35.4
1-10	60	42.8
11-20	15	47.1
21-30	17	41.3
31-40	15	36.1
41-50	14	30.1
51-60	20	23.5
61-70	22	18.3
71-80	19	13.8
81-90	11	10.0

Several Unije families are known to have a high number of individuals with cancer. Cancer rates for Unije, likely were high due to genetic causes. Cancer rates on the islands of Krk, Cres, and Losinj are known to be higher than on the Croatian mainland. 42 These islands have an excessive occurrence of prostate, stomach, and pancreatic cancers in men, and ovarian, breast, stomach, bowel, and brain cancer in women compared to the rates on the mainland. Historic migration between the islands of Unije, Krk, Cres, and Losinj help explain why cancer rates are higher on the islands.

The 19th Century ushered in new families to Unije. Lovro Segota with origins in Jalanac had six children born at the beginning of the century. Cecco and Pillepich families settled on the island during the middle to late 19th Century. Cecco is said to have originated from Dubrovnik, though this may be based on their family lineage name Raguseo while the first records of the family show up in the records for Mali Losinj during the early part of the 19th Century. The Pillepich's arrived in Unije from Rijeka as did other Pillepich's which settled in Mali Losinj. Other families came to Unije from Mali Losinj. One was the family of Joannes (Ivan) Radoslovich of the clan Mattesinich, born in Mali Losinj, and later settling with his parents in Unije raising a large family whose descendants are now scattered world-wide. The Mattesinch family from Mali Losinj dates back to a Simon Radoslovich, originally from Unije, who died before 1749.

Although, the Carcich (Bravarof) family dates back to the 18th Century or earlier, some new Carcich families are derived from this older family lineage. The family of Antonio Carcich (Bravarof) and two other (Bravarof) families are known from this time period. Two of these families lived in Unije. One Bravarof, Martin son of Martin married and started a family in Cunski on the island of Losinj. In fact several Carcich families, just prior to this period settled in Cunski. The Bravarof, Ciadic, Cicuola, Pasquic, and Vlasich branches of the Carcich families in Cunski originated from these early settlers.

Other Carcich families in Unije between 1810 and 1820 where the Jevin, Pasquich, Rocov, Andricev, and Zburkin lineages. The Zburkin clan dates back to Mikula Carcich who married a Stefanich from north of Martinscica on the island of Cres and settled in Unije with two sons, Mikula and Gaudenzio, born in 1786 and 1795 respectively.

Joseph Rieger published a panorama image of the coast line of Istria and Dalmatia in 1845. The representation of Unije shows the town and part of the island from the west end of the island, though there is no view of the polje or flat land that juts out to the west of the island. Rieger's image agrees with structures that are currently in existence. The image shows several paths or roads. One goes around the edge of Kris, the hill above the town, and the other heads up Kris to fields with retaining walls, which are still visible today. A number of houses are discernable as are several multi-storey buildings.

As a young conscript during the Prussian-Austrian War in 1866, Ivan Nicolich (1842-) from the Sancich branch of Unije witnessed the naval attack on the island of Vis. Several other men from Unije were in the Austrian navy during the 19th Century, often stationed at the naval station in Pula, to the northwest of Unije.

In 1885 the inhabitants of Unije asked the government to allow the teaching of Italian in the school on the island. [43] Perhaps a Croatian school had been established earlier, as it was in Susak, which had a school by 1845. Joseph Rieger's 1845 illustration depicts a building similar to the latter school building next to the church.

Unije 1845, published by Joseph Rieger

Definitely, by 1888 a school existed on the island [44] and students were taught to learn the catechism, to read, write, and calculate by Father Anton Andrijčić. The school year lasted from October to July with exams twice a year. [45] The teacher in 1911-1912 was Marija Fučić. The following year Fučić taught 39 students in the Croatian school. Lino Nicolich (Niccoli) (1894-1964) who went on to found a bank in the United States and Andric Karčić (1888-1972) who became a lawyer in Karlovac, both began their schooling in Unije. Giovanni Radoslovich (1879-1973) from Unije became a school teacher on the island of Ilovik before WWI. Later Andrea Carcich (1921-2004), also from Unije became a school teacher in Cunski before WWII.

During 1893 and subsequent years phylloxera (Daktulosphaira vitifoliae), a grapevine insect pest began destroying the vines in Unije. Introduced from America, it decimated the grapevines on the island, until a variety of American vine was planted that was resistant to the disease, and then grafted with the common vines (Vitis Vinifera) of Unije. The varieties of grapes planted in Unije were *suščan, bjelikuć, troviśćina, plavac* (zinfandel*), jiakuć, belćina, boldun,* and *muskat.* The first three varieties were the most productive in Unije.

Unije School Group 1911/1912: On the floor - Andrija Radoslović 1845-1935 (Girica), Anton Šegota (Toni Šegota od Luovre), First row – Marija Fučić, teacher, Anton Radoslović 1886-1976 (Udovac). Anton Nikolić (Toni Marketa), Anton Nikolić 1891- (Markovca), Ivo Gršković, Priest; Second row – name unknown, Agata Radoslović 1890-1971 (Matešiniča), Marija Radoslović 1895-1993 (Matešiniča -Divojčina), Andrija Karčič 1888-1972, lawyer from Unije; Last row – Ana Karčič 1901-1967 (Cota Juriča), Ana Belanič (Čikuoljeva), Marija Nikolič (Marketa).

Pozdrav iz UNIJA

Unije Circa 1900

20th Century

The 20th Century brought great changes to Unije in the form of war, language, and immigration. On the census for 1900 Unije is listed as containing 176 houses and 696 inhabitants. The census divides the residents into Italian and Croatian speakers with 446 for the former and 250 for the latter. This linguistic and cultural divisions into Italians and Croatians played a large role in shaping the community, especially following the breakup of the Austrian Empire after WWI and the establishment of an Italian administration.

Two cooperatives were set up in Unije based on national identity. The result was the building of separate olive mills for the Italian and Croatian factions. Of the two mills in the harbour, the one at the head of the pier was the Italian mill, and the one in the southern end of the harbour was the Croatian mill. The Croatian mill was started in 1900 and the Italian mill began around the same time. A list of the Italian mill members is listed in the appendix. A sardine factory was also started near the southern edge of town.

Italian became more commonly used on the island during the 19th Century. Italian loan words appear in the pre-1945 dialect of Unije. Some Italian words that entered the everyday language of the islanders include, *liber* (free) from the Italian *libero*, *mul* (dock, Italian *molo*), *libar* (book, Italian *libero*), *fermat* (to stop, Italian *fermare*), and *funiestra* (window, Italian *finestra*). A compilation of words used in Unije is found in *Unije: kuzelj vaf sarcu*.[44] The Unije dialect also contains many old Latin words that came into the language over a long period of time and are also found in standard Croatian and in the dialects spoken on the Adriatic coast. Even some Slovenian nouns may be found in the dialect of Unije that are more common in Slovenian than in Serbo-Croatian. Alberto Fortis noted Slovenian words in use on the island of Krk in the 1770's, where several villages "speak a mixt[sic] jargon of Carnian Sclavonic [Slovenian], Latin and Italian"[46]. A similar observation was made at the turn of the 19th century by the Slovenian linguist, Oblak also on Krk. The growing use of Italian at this time may be a recent cultural phenomenon but the link to Slovenian may be both a cultural, as well as genetic link dating back to the first Slavic immigrants to the islands as is evident by a strong genetic correlation between the population of western Croatia and that of Slovenia. [47]

During WWI, eight men from Unije died fighting in the Austrian army, mainly on the Galician front. These included Mate Nicolich (1894-1915), Zaccaria Nicolich (1875-1917), Andrea Nicolich, Ivan Carcich (died 1917), Andrea Carcich, Antonio Carcich (1898-1917), Sime Nicolich (1885-1915), and Toni Radoslovich (died 1915). The Austrian destroyer, *Viribus Unitis* was lying off the Italian coast near Ancona, when Italy entered WWI on the side of Britain and France. It shelled the coastal railway causing severe damage. On board at the time was Tucich Segota (1880-) from Unije. Another resident of Unije, Luca Carcich, was on the Austrian destroyer *Tegetthof* when they encountered and shot down an Italian aircraft.

Croatian Mill in Unije

Italian Mill in Unije

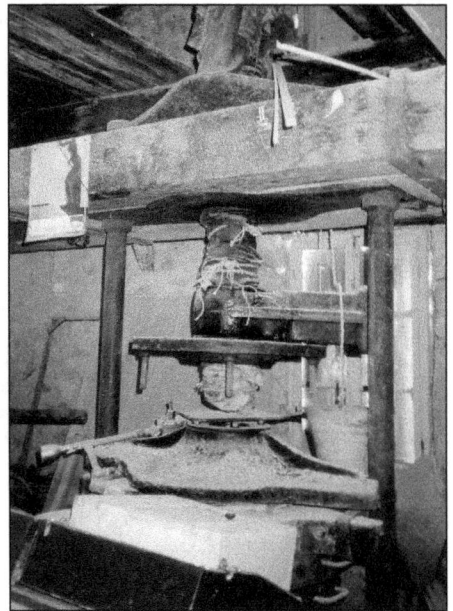

Milling Stone and Press, Croatian Mill, Unije

A major incident occurred in Unije in WWI over Nazario Sauro, an Austrian citizen who joined the Italian Navy. On August 1st, 1916 Sauro was in command of the submarine, *Pullino*, as it took on water near the small island of Galiola, eight km north-west of Unije. Sauro brought the submarine to rest at Galiola and fearing the Austrian authorities he and his crew set course for Italy in several other boats. Galiola, at that time had a lighthouse, and four families lived on the island one of which was the Nicolich family of Unije. The head of this family, Antonio Nicolich (1879-), and another man, made for Unije after Nazario left. They managed to reach the lighthouse in Unije, and informed the authorities of the incident. Using the telephone at the lighthouse, they contacted the Austrian Navy in Pula, which dispatched a ship that picked up the crew of the submarine and Nazario before they were able to reach Italy. Nazario was hanged in Pula as a traitor on August 10th, 1916. Later, in WWII, the German Navy levelled the lighthouse on Galiola but it was rebuilt after the war.

From 1919 to 1943 only the Italian language and history were taught in school. Kindergarten was introduced to Unije for children of four years of age. Grades one to five and some high school classes were taught. In addition to the subjects taught in the Austrian period, were the subjects of geography, history, and physical science. [48] In 1929 a military barracks was built next to the school.

Cosulich family at No.66, Unije   circa 1910: Dominicus Cosulich 1836-1913; Justo Ferluga, Giovanni Ferluga 1871-1921, Irene Radoslovich 1908-1995, Irene Ferluga 1874-1942, Maria Carcich-Ferluga 1898-1942, Luca Cecco, Maria Nicolich (Sancich), Toni Nicolich (Paliermo), Dumica Nicolich (Agatin) 1878- , Dumica Nicolich 1907-2001, Olga Ferluga 1895-1952, Margarita Cecco 1876-1969, Ita Nicolich 1882 -1963; manager of Sardine factory is seated on donkey.

An electric generating station was in operation by 1932 and provided several hours of electricity during the day. This station was used previously as a temporary fish-packing site. A new fish-packing building went up in Maracol cove run by the Arrigoni company, and the earlier factory in town was closed. The factory employed many of the women on the island as seasonal labourers. Tuna was shipped in from the Black Sea and sardines from local catches. The factory closed in 1943, but was reopened briefly by the Yugoslav authorities after WWII.

Arrigoni Factory, Unije

During WWII, it was a somewhat more complicated story since many families had, at that time, immigrated to the United States. Therefore, men of families from Unije fought in the armies of Italy and the United States. On the American side, several men fought in Europe and the Pacific. John Nicolich, born 1922 in Unije, was parachuted into Florence, Italy, during the war by the Americans where he operated as a spy. There was Andric Nicolich (1921-1944) who died in Europe in the American armed forces, while several others served in the Pacific theatre of war. Lino Nicolich (1894-1964), who had gone on to study at the Maritime Academy in Losinj, skippered the *Henry Meigs*, an American Liberty ship in the Pacific. Earlier, Lino had served in the WWI and was awarded the second highest citation in the Austrian army by Emperor Franz Joseph. Andric Karčić (1888-1972) served in the Ustash administration, as liaison to the Italian Army in Croatia. He had an office in Susak, next door to Fiume (Rijeka) and had others from Unije working as guards. Towards the end of the war, Andric worked in the Consulate-General's office in Vienna, and after the war he lived in the United States.

St. Andrija Church 1930-31: Carabiniere (military policeman), Andrea Radoslovich –Gartljic (1871 -1947), Soldier, Jovanin Pillepich (1886-1948), mayor, Antonio Braiko (1922-), Nicolo Radoslovich (1921-1945), Giovanni Radoslovich (Kalcic), Soldier, Don Andrea Virla, Luigi Miceleti, Antonio or Marco Bellanich (Preruc) (1912-), Francis Ferrara (1925-), Gasparo Carcich (1924-), Joseph Nicolich (1921-), Soldier, Osip Nicolich (Sancich) (1909-1993), Carabiniere.

Most young men from Unije, drafted into the Italian armed forces, served in the navy. There was Andrea Radoslovich (1913-1942) who died after his ship was struck and sunk between Italy and Valona, Albania. And there was Rufino Niccoli (Nicolich), who was captain of an Italian submarine which was lost in the first days of Italy's entry into WWII. Andrea Valic who fought in the Italian Army, lost his life in 1943 fighting near the Don River in the Soviet Union.

When Italy capitulated to the Allies in September 1943, in quick succession the military arsenal in Mali Losinj was occupied first by the Četniks, then the Partisans, and the Germans. Each in turn sent patrols to Unije. The Partisan occupation of Mali Losinj didn't last long, as the German army attacked and took the town keeping control until the closing months of WWII. Luca Karcich (1889-1945), had been on the *Tegetthof* during WWI and worked in the US in the intervening years, was in Unije during the war. When the Germans occupation occurred they sought out people like Luca, who had American citizenship. He was arrested, taken to Germany and disappeared.

Shortly after the Četniks left Unije, the Partisans made an appearance on the island. Usually they stayed hidden on the island, especially during the following period of German occupation. However, Partisans at this time were executing perceived Italian and

German sympathizers. Andrea Radoslovich (1898-1950), from the Popich branch of the Radoslovich family of Unije, came to the island when Italy capitulated in September of 1943. He wanted to arrange the murder of five island families who were claimed to have Italian sympathies. He was dissuaded from carrying out his plan by Mati Carcich (Jevin). Andrea, himself, suffered from throat cancer, and died shortly after the end of the war.

During the night of January 14th, 1945 three German patrol boats, the S33, S58, and S60 measuring some 30 metres, ran aground near the lighthouse in Unije. The boats had left Pula and were on their way to Losinj. The Germans immediately set upon extracting themselves from the beach, but they had come up too far to be able to haul themselves back into the water under their own power. They cordoned off the south-western part of the island and sent patrols into town. On January 15th, an English squadron, consisting of three ships, came up broadside to the grounded patrol boats and began to shell them. Some of the shells fell into the bay beside the town, while one shell fell into the town near house number 124. The bombardment was brief, and after five or more minutes, the English ships turned around and sped back toward Italy. The next day the Germans abandoned the patrol boats and set them on fire. Later in 1945, the commander of German forces in Losinj, Platzcomandir Fischer, surrendered himself to the Partisans and, though hidden in Unije, he was executed by the Partisans near Split.

At the end of WWII the 639 residents of Unije registered themselves as 421 Croatians and 216 Italians. [49] The number of families, at that time, is given as: Belanić 7, Busanić 1, Čeko 4, Citcović 1, Delconte 1, Deroia 1, Galošić 1, Haljić 1, Karčić 59, Nadalin 5, Nikolić 43, Picinić 1, Pilepić 3, Poljanić 1, Radoslović 18, Rerečić 15, Segota 6, Valić 2, Verbora 1, Vidulić 1.

The coming of the Communist regime brought forced internment within the post-war Yugoslavia and emigration was heavily curtailed after the initial exodus of Italians and Italian-leaning families. Movement was restricted and examples of murder were known to be used to intimidate individuals and families from fleeing across the Adriatic Sea. The remains of John Carcich of Unije along with three others were discovered in a cove near Cunski in 1996. John and his companions were known to be planning to sail across the Adriatic and were last see alive in 1956. From 1945 to 1960 six families and a total of 30 individuals from Unije made the clandestine crossing of the Adriatic.

The population of Unije remained stable up to WWII and then steadily declined thereafter. The population structure in 1980 had a high proportion of inhabitants aged 70 and older. [50] Today about 70 people make Unije their home year-round, but many more stay here during the summer months. Mostly Croatian vacationers from the mainland, others from Slovenia, Italy, and overseas have homes or rent during the summer. In the winter pheasant hunters come to the island. The families that settled in Unije over the last three hundred years are still found here, except their numbers have diminished and the majority of them have resettled in North America, Italy, and Australia. The new arrivals to Unije in the last fifty years have been mainly Croatians and a few Bosnians, from the mainland.

Unije School Children 1927-1931 Standing in Centre: Teaching couple, Pifani?, Matteo Rerecich (1919-) Dominic Valic (1917- 1981), Andrea Nicolich (Niccoli) (1919-1997), Tonic Carcich (Rocov); First row seated: Letizia Carcich (1921-), Irma Radoslovich (1918-), Felicita Carcich, Christina Rerecich, Maria Carcich (Bravarof), Maria Segota (1921-1992), Jolanda Carcich (1921-), Julie Carcich (1920-). Second row seated: Stefania Radoslovich, Domenica Carcich, Anita Carcich (1914-1996), Lydia Rerecich (1914-) Palmira Carcich (1921-), Rosaria Carcich (Jevin) (1914-2006), Maria Radoslovich, Maria Nicolich, Felicita Carcich, Margarita Radoslovich; Third row: Maria Carcich, Maria Carcich, Antonia Radoslovich (1921?-), Caterina Rerecich (1914-1996), Maria Nicolich (1913-), Sofia Carcich (1914-1998), Domenica Valic (1916-2007), Antonia Nicolich (1919-2001)

Over the last four hundred years many of the smaller islands in Dalmatia have had a gradual increase in population, followed by a sharp decrease in the middle of the last century. Unije follows this pattern and when its population is compared with Susak the similarities and differences become apparent. Unije started with a smaller population in the 1600's and therefore grew more slowly. Susak's population began a steeper rate of growth at the beginning of the 1800's, while Unije's rate increase began in the mid-1800's. Increases in health and longevity helped increases in population on both islands, while the addition of new families in Unije, such as the Cecco, Pilepic, Radoslovich (Matesinich), and Segota, also helped increase the population in Unije. Both Unije and Susak decline in population in the first half of the 1900's, though Unije begins its decline about two decades sooner, due to earlier immigration to America.

Population for Unije 1600 - 2000			
Year	Population	Year	Population
1600	75-100*	1921	783
1730	136*	1931	717
1770	150-200*	1945	649
1815	222	1948	457
1818	220	1953	402
1869	520	1961	273
1880	630	1971	113
1890	678	1981	85
1900	696	1990	82
1910	758	2000	70
*estimated			

Agriculture production waned on the island after 1965 as many inhabitants left. To revive agriculture, the Jadranka company of Mali Losinj brought over 125ha back into production between 1984 and 1991, cultivating alfalfa, barley, corn and legumes. In addition, 1200 sheep and 600 goats were raised on the island. Jadranka ceased operation after the breakup of Yugoslavia. Pheasant hunting has been undertaken in Unije with 2,000 pheasants and 5,000 partridges being released annually on the island. Various beekeeping experimentation has been carried out in Unije. In 1996, an airstrip for small single engine planes was built on the flat plain south of town and is operated by the Croatian government.

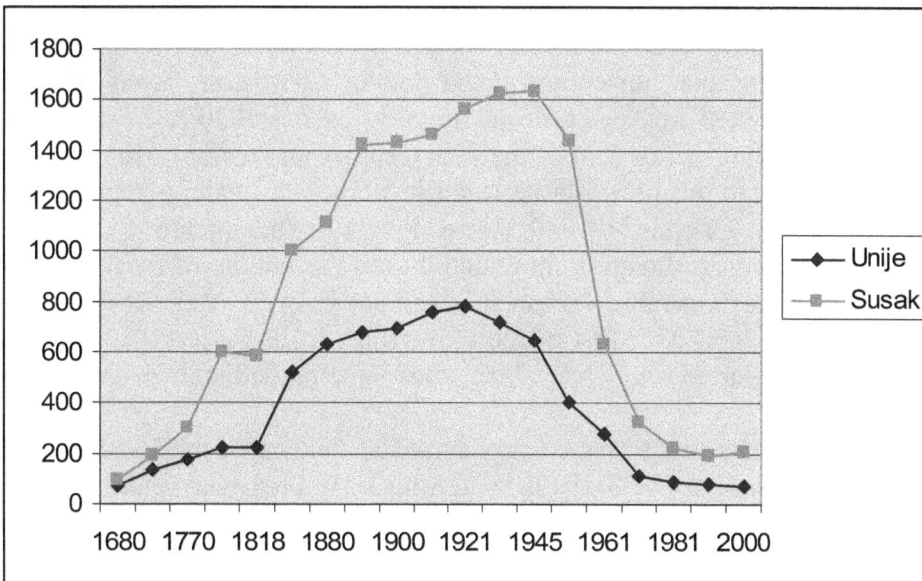

Population Graph for Unije and Susak 1680 to 2000

Immigration

Before immigration to the Americas became available in the later part of the 19th Century, the inhabitants of Unije were limited to travel and employment in the neighbouring islands and towns of the Kvarner and sometimes further afield to cities, such as Venice. In the 18th Century, several individuals sold firewood which was shipped to Venice. Travel to Osor, Mali Losinj, Cunski and the island of Cres allowed some individuals from Unije to settle in these locations. The genealogies of the families from Unije which settled in Mali Losinj and Cunski are listed in this volume.

The story of immigration is tied to the maritime history of Losinj. From the 17th Century onwards, the people of Losinj gravitated towards the sea and many became sailors in the Adriatic and Mediterranean regions. The sailors from Losinj were some of the first Croats to visit the Americas. In 1779 Peter Budinić from Veli Losinj sailed the *Santo Domenico* to the Caribbean. Others continued the maritime trade to the Americas and Gasparo Budinich, of Veli Losinj, died in Kingston, Jamaica in 1792. In 1834, Petar Jakov Leva, also from Veli Losinj, sailed the *Ferdinando V Re d'Ungheria* around Cape Horn to Valparaiso, Chile. [51] Another Losinj captain by the name of Martinolich sailed the *Amalia Giuseppina* to pick up cotton at the port of Galveston, Texas in 1844. A Croatian community existed in New Orleans as early as the 1820's. Losinj Captains began to sail to this port in the first half of the 19th Century and many Losinj immigrants arrived in America through this port. Marko Ragusin from Veli Losinj is reputed to have entered America via New Orleans by 1849. Ragusin went to Sacramento, California, and later to San Jose. Others from Losinj immigrated during the middle of the 19th Century to the United States and Australia. Fortunato Corsano, born in Mali Losinj in 1841, immigrated to Australia in 1867. Most of the immigrants from Unije to Australia came after WWII, except for Matteo Carcich (1878-), who came immediately prior to the war.

The bulk of Losinj immigration to America occurred at the end of the 1870's and early 1880's. Venanzio Martinolich (1848-1913) from Mali Losinj but with relatives in Unije, came through New Orleans and lived for a time in Colorado in 1888 where his brother Benjaminus (1849-) had settled two years previously. In 1891, Venanzio moved his family to Port Guichon, in the Vancouver area of British Columbia. Others, like John A. Martinolich (1877-), also came to British Columbia in 1893, but by 1902 he was operating a shipbuilding firm in Dockton, Washington. Both communities in Vancouver and Dockton became small centres of Croatian immigrants with a number of families from the islands of Losinj and Unije. Other families from Mali Losinj, continued to come to the area such as Giuseppe Nicolich (1864-1934) of the Muscardin lineage with distant relatives in Unije, who married Elvira Ivancic (1871-1942), raised two sons, Eugene and Joseph L. (1896-1973) in Vancouver and Seattle.

During the second half of the 19th Century, many islanders from Unije traveled to the east coast, the west coast and Colorado in the United States to find work. Antonio Carcich (1860-) from Unije is listed in New York City in 1874. Other individuals from Unije were known to be in New York from 1885 onwards. A list of these individuals from Unije, who worked in New York City, is found in the Appendix. During the 1890's and the first decade of this century practically every family in Unije had one or more members working in America.

Several families from Unije came to British Columbia and Washington State. A typical immigrant from Unije was Andrea Domenico Galosich (1866-1948). Andrew came to Delta, British Columbia in 1890 and in 1900 he brought over his wife Thomasina Nicolich (1869-). Andrea's brother, Giovanni Galosich (1964-1918), a sailor, was in New York City in 1888 and it is likely Andrea came to the west coast via New York. By WWI Andrea and Thomasina later lived in the Seattle area and in the early 1920s they moved to California. There was a sizeable number of people from Unije in the Seattle area during WWI. Benjamin Carcich (1864-1919) and Dominic Ferluga (1896-1993) lived there until their deaths. Matteo Nicolich (1888-1959) and his wife Mary Simicich (1893-1978) lived in Seattle and their sons, Mathew (1918-) and Lawrence (1921-) were born in Seattle. The family of Giuseppe Nicolich (1879-1945) and Mattea Karcich (1890-1963) lived in Seattle and their son Joseph (1913-1990) was born there. Antonio Carcich (1876-) came to the United States in 1905 and, two years later, married and brought over his wife Antonia (1880-). Antonio and Antonia raised two children in the Seattle area, Stella (1908-) and Matt (1910-1978).

Others from Unije came to the Seattle area as individuals. Domenico Simeone Carcich (1858-1925) worked in the region and Giovanni Andrea Nicolich (1875-1961) was registered for military service in Seattle in 1917. A Rose Carcich (1915-1990) also lived in the Seattle area. Theodore Carcich (1905-1988) born in Unije, later to become vice-president of the Seventh Day Adventist church, moved to Seattle shortly after 1942. His family settled in Colton, Washington.

Early on, some individuals from Unije went to work in the coal mines of south eastern Colorado. After the building of the Santa Fe railroad to Trinidad in 1879, the coal mines were exploited with cheap immigrant labour. These people worked in the mines of Forbes and Tobasco, then newly-built mining communities. An influx of immigrants from Croatia brought 500 workers to the Trinidad area of Colorado by 1900. Miners came from Cunski and Mali Losinj and by the turn of the century, there were at least three men from Unije among this group. Andro Karcich from Unije, and his wife

Suzanna Mihlik lived and worked here around 1908. Also around this time, Mat Karcich, from Cunski, whose father was from Unije, and his wife Anna Galecich, lived here and stayed until 1915. Andrea Carcich, from Unije, lived in Trinidad. Several others from Unije worked here for a short time and returned to New York or moved elsewhere. Many miners left the area during and after the 1913-14 strike, which saw large-scale violence and disruptions. In 1914, Forbes, where several men from Unije worked, was burnt to the ground and several guards and miners were killed. At least one family from Unije remained in Forbes in the following years.   Today nothing remains of the town and it had a similar fate as the neighbouring town of Hastings, which declined in population in the twenties and thirties and was abandoned by 1952. Hastings had a tragic mine explosion in 1917 where 121 miners lost their lives. Matt P. Carcich, originally from Cunski and later of Trinidad, Colorado, was appointed administrator to the estates of the survivors of the mine explosion.

The descendants of these families from Forbes, Tabasco, and Trinidad, Colorado, now live in Colorado, New Mexico, California, and New York. Some remained in the region a while longer, but by 1920 most had left for other places, some going to New York where there were now several established families from Unije. One family of Carcich's from Cunski stayed behind in Trinidad, Colorado and their descendants are now found in the western United States. A few moved to other centres, such as San Pedro (Los Angeles), California.

Before 1903, most immigrants had to travel to ports in Italy, Holland, Havre, France, Bremer or Hamburg, Germany to find passenger ships to America. Some of the ship's workers from Unije crossed the Atlantic Sea in ships such as the *La Champagne, La Touraine, Aquitaine*, and the *Spartan Prince*. After 1902 a closer route opened up from Trieste to New York on the Austro-Americana (Cosulich) Line, and the Cunard Line. New York was the first port of call for most travelers from Unije. Some came through the Port of New York and moved to the west coast. From 1885 onward there is a steady stream of individuals from Unije arriving in the United States as documented in passenger ship's records and federal censuses. Most stayed in New York City.

Many immigrants from Unije worked in Manhattan on the docks. They chose to live in Midtown Manhattan between West 42nd and 50th Streets, and between 9th and 12th Avenues a region called "Hell's Kitchen". This part of Manhattan bordered the Hudson River and had many docks where the newcomers worked. At 42nd Street there was a slaughterhouse, one of many which extended down to 35th Street. On the river at 42nd Street there was a ferry connecting with New Jersey and also on the river at 54th St. and 12th Ave. was a city dump. A railway yard in Manhattan was located at 60th St. and 11th Ave. and another yard was at 30th Street. A train track ran down 11th Ave. The New York Central Railroad was a major employer for the men who came to New York. Other employers were Schraft's restaurant and Horn and Hardart where several women from Unije worked in their commissaries.

The earlier residents of "Hell's Kitchen" from 1851 onward were the Irish. Later Italians settled there, and a small Black population extended from 59th St. to 65th St. The newly-arrived from Unije were men, both single and married. They usually lived in groups, with a brother, cousin, uncle or friend from the old country, sharing expenses and meals. Some families from Unije continued to live in Hell's Kitchen until the 1950s. Though a relative few reside today in Manhattan, the bulk of families of Unije ancestry moved to the adjoining regions of New York and New Jersey.

There were two grocery stores frequented by people from Unije who lived in Manhattan. One store was operated by the Angelich family and the other by the family of Andrea Vallich at 544 West 45th Street which until 1914 was a gathering place for those from Unije. Gaudentio Radoslovich of Unije first operated a taxi cab company in Manhattan and later ran a restaurant at 807 Greenwick Street from 1922 to 1950. It was near the New York Central Railroad's St. James Park freight operation.

The original Croatian church in Manhattan, attended by the new immigrants from Unije, was Saints Cyril and Methodius at West 50th Street and 10th Avenue. Over a dozen children and several adults of families from Unije were baptised and married in this church. Saints Cyril and Methodius existed at this location from 1913 to the 1974, when it was relocated to 502 West 41st Street. Several societies were founded to help the immigrants both in Unije and in the United States. The *Società di Mutuo Soccorso* was formed in Unije on Aug. 9, 1897, and the Istrian Benevolent Association was founded in New York City on December 28, 1922. The directors of the Association were John Carcich of 557 11th Ave., Dominick Carcich of 557 11th Ave., Andrew Nicolich of 636 45th St., Bortolo Rerecich of 597 11th Ave., and Paul Rerecich of 552 W 45th St., all from New York City. [52] Also formed to assist Unije was the Sveti Andrija Society of New York. Both the *Società* and the Association were established to help those who need financial assistance. Later they became social gathering clubs. The Benevolent Association started with 32 members, and before it folded in 1994, it had up to 72 members. [53]

807 Greenwick Street, Manhattan, N.Y.
circa 1935

Saints Cyril and Methodius at West 50th Street
in 2007

Unije – povijest i obitelji:
sabrana povijest i obiteljske genealogije otoka Unije, Hrvatska

U sjećanje na moju majku.

Zahvaljujem svojem ocu što je u mene usadio ljubav prema povijesti prepričavajući mi priče o ratu i avanturama. Želim izraziti zahvalnost svima onima koji su mi pružili genealoške podatke o obiteljima s Unija. Među prvim sakupljačima genealoških podataka, a koji su priloženi genealogijama u ovom djelu su Andrew Karcich iz New Yorka, Antonio Rerecich (1912–1996) i njegov sin Tony. Posebno se zahvaljujem Andriji Depikolvaneu za pomoć s unijskim crkvenim zapisima koji se nalaze na otoku Krku.

Autor se želi zahvaliti Enzu Valencichu i Fiorelli Rivera za prijevod teksta na talijanski jezik. Također se zahvaljuje Antonu Angelichu, Dorothy Buffington, Silvana Borrelli (Nicolich), Maria Carcich, Marina Carcich, Ted Carcich, Milka Fatović (Nikolić), Maria Gelinas, Vlakto Janeković, Dominic Karcic, Garyju Loverichu,, Adrijanu Nikoliću, Ireni Nicolich, Gaudent Radoslovichu, Joanne Rasco, Fred Scopinich, Letizia Valic i Ron Weddle na pomoći s fotografijama. Fotografije koje nisu pripisane određenom izvoru potječu od samog autora. Ovo djelo sadrži nešto od usmene povijesti koju su mi prenijeli moji roditelji, rodbina te stanovnici Unija kojima se zahvaljujem na pomoći.

Predgovor

U listopadu 2005. jedan je radnik prilikom obnavljanja ruševne kuće na Unijama otkrio određene dokumente. Ispostavilo se da su ti dokumenti župni zapisi s Unija iz 19. stoljeća pisani talijanskim i latinskim jezikom. Uključivali su knjigu umrlih i popis stanovništva otoka, a ostali su skriveni u kuhinjskim zidovima gotovo stotinu godina. Zapisi su pružili važne genealoške podatke i rasvijetlili prošlost otoka. Prelaskom pod vladavinu Italije (1919 -1921) svećenici s Unija i okolnih otoka bili su prisiljeni otići[1], te iako možemo samo nagađati, postoji mogućnost da bi skriveni dokumenti mogli biti rezultat prijelaza pod talijansku vlast. Poput ovih skrivenih dokumenata mnogo od povijesti Unija ostalo je sakriveno jer je nitko nije istraživao. U 18. stoljeću postojali su crkveni zapisi s Unija pisani staroslavenskim pismom, no oni više ne postoje[2]. Ovo djelo želi pokušati razotkriti djelić skrivene povijesti otoka Unije.

Imena i prezimena navedena u ovom tekstu dolaze iz različitih izvora, pisana su različitim pismima, uključujući hrvatski, talijanski i latinski zbog čega se isto ime može pojaviti u različitim oblicima. Podaci korišteni u kompilaciji ove povijesti i obiteljskih genealogija potječu iz brojnih povijesnih izvora, uključujući župne zapise (matične knjige), pravne dokumente, popise stanovništva, brodske isprave te obiteljske povijesti.

Uvod

Unije (piše se Unie na talijanskom i Nia na latinskom) su hrvatski otok u sjevernom dijelu Jadranskog mora (14 45'E – 44 38'N), dužine 9 kilometara u pravcu sjever – jug i širine od pola do 2 kilometra u smjeru istok – zapad. Smješten u Kvarnerskom zaljevu, otok je dio Primorsko-goranske županije.

Izuzev Brijuna koji se nalaze pred istarskom obalom, Unije su najzapadniji otok u lancu hrvatskih jadranskih otoka. Pula je smještena 36 kilometara sjeverozapadno, a Rimini, Italija nekih 100 kilometara zapadno. Sjeverno su važni centri kao Rijeka i Trst. Na jugoistočnom rubu otoka smjestio se najbliži susjed Unija, maleni otok Vele Srakane, a otok Susak leži još 9 kilometara južnije. Odmah istočno od Unija nalazi se veći otok Lošinj, s gradom Malim Lošinjem, nekad poznatim i pod imenom Lussinpiccolo. Na otoku Cresu, koji se smjestio uz sjeverni kraj Lošinja, nalazi se selo Osor, nekadašnje srednjovjekovno središte regije.

Ovaj kratki povijesni prikaz Unija uključuje pregled zasnovan na očuvanim pisanim izvorima. Opaska o najranijem prethistorijskom periodu iz kojeg datira keramika - ranom liburnijskom periodu, te rimskom razdoblju koje je uslijedilo nakon njega navedena je u dodatku zajedno s arheološkim dokazima vezanima uz otok.[3] Utjecaj rimskog razdoblja vidljiv je u imenima mjesta na otoku te donekle u nautičkom vokabularu čakavskog dijalekta kojim se govori na Unijama i istočnoj jadranskoj regiji, a koji je postao dijelom standardnog hrvatskog jezika. Cijeli niz starih latinskih posuđenica postao je dijelom suvremenog jezika kojim govore istarske i dalmatinske zajednice duž Jadranskog mora, što potvrđuje prisutnost stanovništva koje je u ovoj regiji obitavalo prije početka seobe Slavena u 7. stoljeću.

Povijest stanovništva otoka Unije je daleka i ilustrira dugačak genealoški slijed koji povezuje stanovnike Unija sa susjednim otocima. Kroz stoljeća, obitelji s obližnjeg Lošinja znatno su utjecale na strukturu obitelji na Unijama. Također, svoj doprinos otočnim zajednicama dali su i stanovnici Cresa, Krka i kopnenog dijela obale. Većina obitelji koje su naselile Unije slavenskog je porijekla, a njihovo sporo kretanje prema Unijama u vremenu od nekoliko stotina godina ukazuje koliko je jadranskih otoka bilo naseljeno.

44

Srednji vijek: rani počeci

U zaljevu Mirišće pronađeni su arheološki dokazi o okupaciji Unija u periodu između 1. i 4. stoljeća, međutim, odsutnost takvih dokaza u vremenu od 6. do 8. stoljeća potvrđuje nepostojanje stalnih ljudskih naselja na otoku Unije u ranom srednjem vijeku.[4] Između 6. i 11. stoljeća Unije i drugi kvarnerski otoci bili su suočeni s depopulacijom. Uzroci su bili raznoliki, a uključivali su različite bolesti i slabu političku upravu. Nakon pada Rimskog Carstva, slavensko stanovništvo započelo je s naseljavanjem priobalne Hrvatske. Iako su Slaveni na Balkan došli u 6. stoljeću, njihova seoba na kvarnerske otoke započela je nešto kasnije. Premda je na susjednom otoku Susku 1071. postojao samostan, naseljavanje Unija vjerojatno je uslijedilo nešto kasnije.[5]

Unije su sigurno bile naseljene do 15. stoljeća – postoji dokaz o postojanju potpornih zidova na otoku koji datira iz 1477. godine[6] što jasno ukazuje na postojanje stalne naseobine. Suvremeno nastanjivanje južnih kvarnerskih otoka (Lošinja, Ilovika, Suska, Srakana i Unija) počinje svoju povijest 1280. godine kad su Obrado Harnovich (Harvojić) i dvanaest obitelji upravo pristiglih iz Dalmacije utemeljili Veli Lošinj.[7,8] Postupno, obitelji na Lošinju osnovale su i drugo naselje. Ova dva naselja bila su poznata kao Velo Selo i Mali Selo te su se na kraju razvila u gradove Veli Lošinj (Lussingrande) i Mali Lošinj (Lussinpiccolo). Naseljavanje susjednih otoka Ilovika i Unija najvjerojatnije je započelo ubrzo nakon tog početnog naselja na otoku Lošinju i vjerojatno od strane obitelji s Lošinja. Obitelj Rerecich, jednu od ranih lošinjskih obitelji, već vrlo rano nalazimo na Unijama.

Razni stanovnici s otoka Lošinja posjedovali su polja na zapadnom kraju Unija gdje su uzgajali grožđe. Žene su održavale i čuvale vinograde. Stanovnici Unija tjerali su volove preko brda kako bi izorali svoje male zemljišne parcele, brinuli se za vinovu lozu i sijali svoja polja na drugoj strani otoka. Iako su lošinjske obitelji i dalje posjedovale zemljišta na Unijama, polja su kasnije kupili stanovnici Unija, a taj proces dovršen je tek u ranom 20. stoljeću. Već vrlo rano članovi obitelji su se počeli grupirati, dijeliti teret posla i živjeti u proširenim obiteljima. U srednjem vijeku slavenske obitelji običavale su živjeti i raditi zajedno u zadrugama, formirajući tako velike proširene obitelji na čijem čelu su često bila braća.

Zadruge su bile uobičajene u drevnoj Hrvatskoj, Bosni, Srbiji i Crnoj Gori. Temeljile su se na staroj društvenoj strukturi još iz vremena dolaska prvih slavenskih naroda u Hrvatsku. U seoskoj ekonomiji novac nije osnovna komponenta i seljaci prvenstveno ovise o onome što mogu dobiti od svojih kultiviranih polja i stoke. U takvom društvu zadruga je predstavljala prednost zato što je udruživala poljoprivredni proizvod i opremu nekoliko srodnih obitelji koje su te resurse dijelile unutar svoje zajedničke ekonomije. Zadrugu je obično činilo nekoliko braće ili ujaka. Kuće u zadruzi bile su takve da su oženjena braća imala zasebne sobe, svaku sa svojim ognjištem, ali obično je postojao jedan zajednički krov. Imovina se jednakomjerno nasljeđivala među braćom i očevom braćom ili sestrama. Na Unijama, braća iz obitelji Nicolich (Agatin) izgradila su četiri kuće koje su graničile jedna s drugom, a koje postoje još i danas. Usmena tradicija kazuje da su te kuće sagrađene prihodom od novca skrivenog na tajnom mjestu. Jedan drugi sklop kuća podigle su obitelji Carcich (Bravarof) od desetine namijenjene crkvi.

Zadruge su u Hrvatskoj djelovale sve do 19. stoljeća kada počinju gubiti na važnosti pod utjecajem privatnog vlasništva i novčane ekonomije. Vrlo rano, na Unijama su postojale obitelji koje su djelovale u tipu zadružne ekonomije te obitelji koje su postupale kao nuklearne ili pojedinačne obitelji. Ta činjenica mogla bi objasniti zašto na Unijama u nekim slučajevima određeni broj proširenih obitelji živi jedna pored druge, dok druge žive u zasebnim obiteljskim kućama. Sav utjecaj koji su zadruge imale na Unijama nestao je do početka 20. stoljeća, iako je taj utjecaj počeo znatno opadati već u prethodnom stoljeću.

Stanovnici zadruge priznavali su zajedničkog pretka i nosili zajedničko ime koje je bilo poznato kao bratstvo (loza). Obiteljska loza potjecala je od jednog osnivača, obično muškarca, ali kad bi se nastanila udovica i osnovala zasebnu obitelj sa svojim sinovima, osnivač loze je mogla biti i žena. Takve obiteljske loze imale su grupna imena koja su završavala ma –ić, –ović ili –ičić. Druge obiteljske loze također su uzimale patronime zasnovane na imenu oca koji su završavali na –ov, –ev, –ef ili –in. Neka imena bratstava također su se razvila od tih patronima. Takva imena koristila su se kao dodatak prezimenima tako da su obitelji imale i prezime i ime bratstva. Na Unijama, trećina obitelji nosila je prezime Carcich/Karčić, ali velik broj obiteljskih rodova razlikovao je različite obitelji Carcich/Karčić. Rodovi obitelji Carcich uključuju: Andrićev, Baldić/Baldich, Bardar, Bravarof, Cicola (iz Ćunskog), Gevin/Jevin, Pasquić/Pasquich, Prussian, Rocov i Zburkin.

16. i 17. stoljeće

Na zemljovidima iz 16. i 17. stoljeća Unije se spominju kao Nia, dok dokumenti iz 18. stoljeća dodaju jedan početni vokal što rezultira varijacijama Onia i Unij. Do kraja 16. stoljeća na otoku je postojalo maleno naselje. Do 1588. na Unijama je prosperirao određen broj zemljoradnika i vinogradara[9] koji su vjerojatno sa sobom doveli svoje obitelji. Desetljeće kasnije na otocima Lošinju, Iloviku, Susku i Unijama živjelo je oko 1000 ljudi - 600 do 700 živjelo je na Lošinju, a ostali na Unijama, Susku i Iloviku.[10] Uzevši u obzir da je na Susku, Unijama i Iloviku živjelo 300 ili 400 stanovnika te da je na Susku obično živjelo onoliko ljudi koliko na Unijama i Iloviku zajedno, 1600-te godine je populacija Unija vjerojatno brojala između 75 i 100 stanovnika.

Rana moderna povijest Unija bila je turbulentna zbog kretanja stanovništva uzrokovanog turskom najezdom na kopnu. Uskočki gusari pljačkali su otoke koristeći Unije kao bazu svojih operacija, skrivajući se u zaljevu Gnišća na sjevernom kraju otoka. Uskoci su bili osobe razmještene iz Dalmacije i unutrašnjosti zbog turske okupacije Balkana. Naselili su jadransko kopneno priobalje, a glavna baza bio im je Senj, smješten nekih 57 kilometara sjeveroistočno od Unija. U početku su napadali područja u Dalmaciji pod turskom okupacijom, ali kasnije su počeli napadati i pljačkati zajednice na istarskom poluotoku i kvarnerskim otocima. Napadajući u velikim skupinama, Uskoci su otimali stoku i druga dobra. 1543. godine opljačkali su Cres, Osor i spalili naselja na Lošinju. 1573. venecijanske vlasti sagradile su utvrdu na otoku Veli Srakane, južno od Unija kako bi stanovnike tog područja zaštitile od gusara. Da bi se platila izgradnja utvrde, kao i za druge obrambene mjere, lokalno stanovništvo bilo je oporezivano.[11] Međutim, napadi na Osor nastavili su se 1573, 1575. i 1605. godine. Susak je napadnut 1579, dok su Mali i Veli Lošinj ponovno napadnuti 1580. godine.

U kolovozu 1612. godine četrnaest uskočkih brodova koristilo je Unije kao uporište za napade na brodove u tom području,[12] za vrijeme dok je bjesnio rat između Venecije i Austrije od 1614. do 1617. Uskoci su ponovno pljačkali kvarnerske otoke i Istru, ali 1617. godine Austrija, koja je upravljala uskočkim uporištem u Senju, potpisala je mirovni sporazum s Venecijom i pristala raseliti Uskoke u unutrašnjost, tako prekidajući dugu vladavinu uskočkog piratstva na Unijama i okolnim otocima. Nepotvrđene priče tvrdile su da su se neki Uskoci nastanili na Unijama.[13] Međutim, krađa stoke nije prestala nakon raspuštanja Uskoka – sporadičnim upadima novi kolonisti iz Istre nastavili su harati po otocima sve do 18. stoljeća.

Zaljevi Maračol i Mišnjak s otokom Lošinjem u pozadini

1588. godine imena pojedinaca koji su obrađivali zemlju na Unijama zabilježena su u poslovnoj transakciji između Zorzema Pracina i Tomice Susnačića, sina Jakova, a koja se odnosila na prodaju vinograda. Ova prezimena više se ne mogu naći niti na jednom otoku, ali postoji mogućnost da je prezime Pracin u srodstvu s Pagien (Pajcen), prezimenom koje se je u 17. stoljeću moglo naći u Malom Lošinju. 1591. godine druge vinograde na Unijama obrađivali su Mikula Dalgčić, Mikoli Posibelić, Mikula Skrivanić, Marko Dorčić i Matic Digčić. Dokumenti oporuka ukazuju na postojanje i drugih zemljoradnika koji su posjedovali zemlju na Unijama. Obitelj Scrivanich (Skrivanić) uzela je u najam obližnji otok Veli Srakane te posjedovala vinograde na Unijama. 1608. godine Petar Gojaković svoj vinograd je prodao Martinu Žižiću, dok je 1618. Antonic Skrivanić oporučno svoj vinograd na Unijama ostavio braći Svetog Antuna, isto kao i Anton, sin Antona Raguznića, dvije godine kasnije.[14] Članovi obitelji Ducich i Radoslovich[15] živjeli su na Unijama 1620-ih i 1630-ih. Neke od tih obitelji mora da su radile kao zakupci i davale određeni dio svojih proizvoda zemljoposjednicima.

Prezimena koja pronalazimo na Unijama za vrijeme 16. i 17. stoljeća potječu s tri različita područja te ukazuju na migracijske rute kojima su prve obitelji dolazile na Unije. Jedna migracijska grupacija koja uključuje prezimena Halić, Ragusinić, Rerecich, Skrivanić i Nicolich (Mikulić) javlja se u ranom 16. stoljeću u crkvenim zapisima za Mali Lošinj, a njihovo porijeklo vjerojatno vuče korijen od prvih kolonizatora tog otoka iz smjera juga. Druga grupa srodnika s prezimenima kao što su Ducich, Zurich i Žižić također dolazi s juga, posebice iz Dalmacije. Još jedna velika grupacija uključuje prezimena iz regije sjeverno od Unija - Dorcich, Gojaković, Zuanich (Ivanić) i Matiasich koje pronalazimo u Istri, Raguzinić (Raguzin) na otoku Krku, Dedich s otoka Raba te Radoslovich i Velcich s otoka Cresa. Zanimljivo je da prezimena kao što su Radoslovich i Rerecich možemo i danas naći na otoku, dok se druga poput Matiasich i Dedich nisu održala.

Neka od prezimena koja se kasnije vezuju uz Unije javila su se u toj regiji već vrlo rano. Obitelj Radoslovich bila je na Unijama 1624. godine. Smatra se da su otočke obitelji Rerecich proistekle od dvojice braće, Jerica i Sime (Simona) iz Velog Lošinja od kojih su se na Unijama razvila dva glavna klana Rerecicha – linije Jercich i Simef. Prezime

Rerecich na otok Lošinj došlo je u 13. stoljeću. 1684. godine prezime Karčić (Carcich) javlja se u vezi s Unijama zajedno s prezimenom Nadalin. Prezime Nadalin datira iz Malog Lošinja 16. stoljeća gdje se javlja u formi Nadalinić. Neki Luka Karčić spominje se u vezi s gradom Vrbnikom na Krku 1490.[16] te 1497. godine. U 15. i 16. stoljeću prezime Karčić te njegove izvedenice Kerčić i Karsić mogu se naći na otoku Krku,[17] dok se kasnija verzija Chercich javlja u gradu Cresu. Jedna linija Karčića (Carcicha), linija Bravarof, datira barem iz ranog 18. stoljeća, a možda još i ranije. Opći pojam bravari upotrebljava se za imenovanje čuvara ustava ili pastira. Genetski podaci mogu ukazivati na mogućnost da su obitelji Carcich (Karcic) živjele u regiji blizu Unija puno duže nego što to govore povijesni dokumenti. Začetnik, koji je Carcich, nosilac je očinske DNK koja je usko kompatibilna s markerima za Y kromosom koji su uobičajeni kod populacije Primorsko-goranske županije,[18] a kojoj pripadaju i Unije i Lošinj.

Sa sjevera i juga obitelji su na Unije i na obližnje otoke dolazile malo-pomalo. Taj uzorak nastavlja se kroz stoljeća sve do 19. stoljeća. Obitelji su se obično doseljavale sa susjednih otoka, ali s vremenom sve više ih je dolazilo s kopna. Do 1943. postojala je određena seoba iz Italije uzrokovana trgovačkim putevima između Italije i otoka Cresa i Lošinja. Tek u prošlom stoljeću tradicionalne migracije sa sjevera i juga istisnule su one iz kopnenih područja Jugoslavije, prvenstveno Hrvatske i Bosne.

Stanovnici Unija živjeli su od zemlje, većinom od uzgoja ovaca, koza, svinja i stoke, te uzgoja grožđa, maslina i različitih žitarica. Premda su se stanovnici susjednih otoka kao što su Susak i Lošinj bavili ribarstvom i pomorskom trgovinom, zemljoradnici na Unijama nisu bili skloni tim aktivnostima. Ovce su bile jedno od glavnih uporišta otočne ekonomije; osiguravale su mlijeko, sir i meso. Većina obitelji brinula se za vlastito stado ovaca i svaka je imala jedinstven žig ili «beleg/beleh» vlasništva koji je bio urezan u uši ovaca.[19] «Belezi» su se prenosili s oca na sina. Pastiri su vjerojatno živjeli kratko, fizički zahtjevnim životom, seleći se s jednog mjesta na drugo kako bi preživjeli. 1631. spominju se «pastiri župne stoke bravari s otoka Unije [te da] životinje koje su im bile povjerene na brigu nisu bilo dovoljno utovljene», kao i da «na otoku Unije u vodama Kvarnera imamo 20 grla stoke, 100 ovaca i 5 krava, također i nešto njihovih mladih junica koje još sišu.»[20]

Rimokatolička crkva odigrala je važnu ulogu u zajednici. Dokumenti iz 1650. spominju da su stanovnici Unija platili 400 venecijanskih lira crkvene desetine. Krizmeni zapisi za Unije u godini 1677. bilježe Martina Chercicha (Carcicha), Antoniu Radoslovich, Antonia Susovicha, Antoniu Picinich, Antoniu Guslomanich i Mariu Dedich.[21] Otok Unije bio je u vlasništvu i pod upravom biskupa iz Osora. Zemljoradnici s Unija bili su podložni crkvi na otoku. U rujnu 1679. lokalno stanovništvo tražilo je oslobođenje od davanja trećine proizvoda osorskom biskupu i opatiji Svetog Petra. U parnici koju su 13. lipnja 1680. pokrenuli protiv Crkve, tužitelji su bili Bravari (ili pastiri) s Onia te sljedeći imenovani pojedinci: Kasper Zuanich, Luka Robcich, Zane Matiasich, Anton Velcich, Nickolas Dedich, Anton Radoslovich, Frane Zauncich, Nicholas Rerecich, Luka

Rerecich, Anton Zurich. Tužitelji su stavili pod znak pitanja svoja davanja crkvi. Međutim, stanovnici Unija izgubili su u sporu protiv crkve i u presudi im je naređeno da:

Žigovi na ovcama

«se radije posvete kultiviranju svojih vinograda i drugih proizvoda … [te da osiguraju] svake godine punu trećinu, i slobodnu od desetine, od cijelog prinosa žitarica, pšenice, zobi, prosa, raži, mahunarki svih vrsta i alfalfe, koji će se pobirati na otoku, bez uskraćivanja zobura i potkupja i masti, od vinskih proizvoda i vina svih kvaliteta uzgojenih na otoku ….Jedna puna petina ovih proizvoda iz svakog vinograda bit će podijeljena između osorske opatije Svetog Petra i biskupije, kao i desetina, koju će naseljenici plaćati na gore spomenute proizvode, od četvrtog dijela koji će biti *terratico*. Plaćat će desetinu na novorođenu stoku, jednako kao što mladunčad rođena godišnje ovcama i kozama ovih stada pripada opatiji i biskupskom stanu. Ovo će se odnositi također na vlastite životinje pastira kad se rode mladi.»[22]

Ovaj jednostrani ugovor provodio se kroz nekoliko generacija s obzirom da se u parnici spominje da svi stanovnici «Onija, i njihovi nasljednici [trebaju] ga održavati i brinuti da se nikad, ni pod kojom izlikom ne suprotstave desetini: time, obvezati obje strane i njihove nasljednike najdalekosežnije moguće.»[22] Tako su stanovnici morali platiti dio svojih proizvoda crkvi u obliku rente, i dodatno su morali platiti normalnu desetinu crkvi, poreze državi za izgradnju obrambenih objekata koje su Mlečani sagradili oko Unija. Stanovnici Unija su stoga bili jedva nešto bolji od kmetova, vezani uz zemlju i nesposobni da prežive u vremenima suše ili gladi.

Crkva na Unijama

Prva crkva na Unijama, crkva Svetog Andrije Apostola sagrađena je 1680. godine izvan naselja i uz groblje. Rimokatoličku crkvu na Unijama predstavljao je lokalni svećenik koji je odgovarao biskupu iz Osora. Jedan od najranijih artefakata pronađen u domaćinstvu Nicolich (Agatin) naručio je lokalni svećenik Matija/Matej Brnić. Bila je to kamena plitica za čuvanje maslinovog ulja s natpisom koji je urezao Brnić 1676. Natpis napisan hrvatskim glagoljičkim slovima kazuje:

(1676. godine, 24. dana mjeseca srpnja, ja, otac Matija/Matej Brnić napravih ovu kamenu pliticu).[23] Tekst je na hrvatskom jeziku i napisan starim glagoljičkim pismom, posebnim slavenskim alfabetom koji je prethodio upotrebi ćiriličnog alfabeta, danas u općoj upotrebi u slavenskim regijama istočne Evrope.

Većinu vjerskog života stanovnika obavljali su glagoljski svećenici kao što je Matija Brnić s Krka. Mise su vođene na staroslavenskom, a zapisi o krštenjima i vjenčanjima pisani su glagoljičkim pismom. Ovakva praksa poznata je iz susjednih zajednica kao što su Ćunski i Mali Lošinj, a tako je bilo i na Unijama.

Upotreba glagoljice na Unijama ukazuje na činjenicu da su otočne župe imale pravo provoditi crkvene službe na hrvatskom jeziku.

Zbog činjenice da je to pravo bilo starije od raskola između Rimokatoličke i Pravoslavne crkve, crkva u Hrvatskoj nastavila je raditi jednakom autonomijom i kad je došlo do upotrebe narodnog jezika. Dok je Rimokatolička crkva tradicionalno upotrebljavala latinski u crkvama u Osoru, Krku i dijelovima Istre, kvarnerski otoci i Istra u crkvenim službama koristili su hrvatski jezik i glagoljičko pismo. Većina crkava u hrvatskim morskim zajednicama nije upotrebljavala latinski u crkvenim službama već arhaični oblik hrvatskog, te je stoga nekoliko stotina godina prije Protestantske crkve koristila govorni jezik.

Glagoljski alfabet su na sjeverne jadranske otoke donijeli slavenski doseljenici. Pismo su stvorili slavenski misionari Sveti Ćiril i Metod koji su u 9. stoljeću na kršćanstvo preobratili slavenska plemena u Moravskoj, Sloveniji i Hrvatskoj. Glagoljsko pismo zadržalo je slavensko svećenstvo na otoku Krku i u Dalmaciji te je korišteno u rimokatoličkim župama u bogoštovnim knjigama kao što su misali, pjesmarice i brevijari. Kasnije su glagolicom pisani i pravni tekstovi i to na lokalnom čakavskom dijalektu kakav se govorio u obalnim dijelovima Hrvatske.

Kamena plitica za masline s urezanim natpisom iz 1676, Unije

Glagoljske knjige korištene su u crkvenim službama na Unijama do 1744. jer se te godine navodi da crkva Svetog Andrije na Unijama posjeduje *Carte Gloria nuove in illirico* i *Missale nuovo illirico* (Novi glagoljski misal). Stotinu godina ranije, 1647. Don Marcus Petrina služio je kao svećenik na Unijama. Lokalni biskup u Osoru upravljao je otokom Unije (zajedno s opatijom Svetog Petra u Osoru), a biskup je redovno posjećivao otok, obično jednom godišnje (tradicija koja se provodi sve do danas). Za vrijeme biskupovih posjeta 1670, 1671. i 1674. spominje se nekoliko glagoljskih crkvenih knjiga poput *Ritual Illirico, Schavetto o Euvangelistario, kao i nekoliko glagoljskih* i latinskih misala. U to vrijeme kao župni sveenik spominje se Thadeo Vitcouich (Tadija Vitković). U lipnju 1785. *Messale Illirico nalazi se u crkvi Svetog Andrije što* pokazuje da je glagoljica na Unijama bila u upotrebi i u zadnjim desetljeima 18. stoljea.24 Međutim, zbog nedostatka glagoljskih crkvenih knjiga i malog broja sveenika koji su ih znali čitati upotreba hrvatskog jezika u crkvenog bogoslužju je napuštena. Do 1803. staroslavenski jezik i glagoljica na Unijama su zamijenjeni talijanskim jezikom i latinicom.

Prema posveti iznad dovratnika na kojoj piše «1753 D.T.R» prvi župni ured na Unijama izgrađen je 1753. godine. Ovo se smatra prvom kućom na Unijama s krovnim crijepom umjesto slame u krovnoj konstrukciji, a njeni zidovi konstruirani su od ravno rezanog vapnenca. Zvonik crkve Svetog Andrije sagrađen je 1857. dok je javna fontana ispred crkve podignuta 1886. Zvona zvonika koja su bila u upotrebi za vrijeme austrijske vladavine rastopljena su za potrebe izrade streljiva u Prvom svjetskom ratu. Zamijenjena su parom zvona 1921. godine i konačno ponovno zamijenjena elektronički pokretanim zvonima u ranim 1990-ima. Iako započet u kasnom 18. stoljeću Sveti Andrija je kasnije nadograđivan, svoj današnji oblik poprimio je 1911., a nekoliko popravaka izvedeno je u ranim 1960-ima, u 1980-ima te nanovo 2006. godine. Slika Naše gospe od Karmela iznad glavnog oltara i mramorni stupovi u baroknom su stilu.

Župni ured, Unije 1753

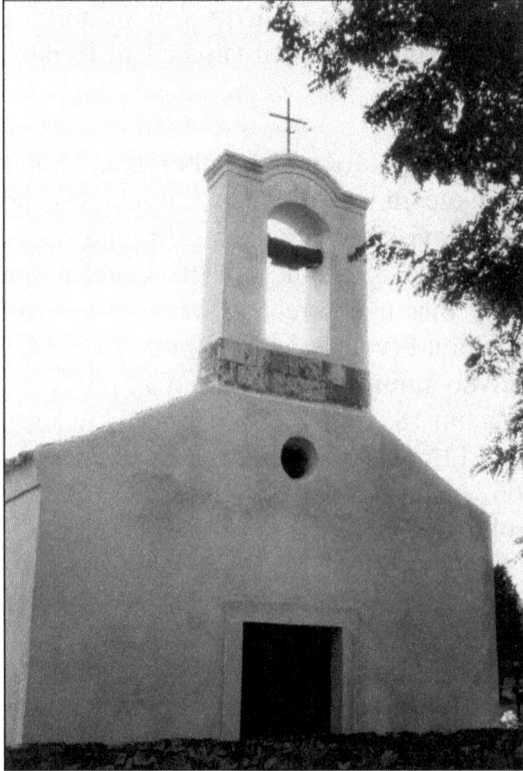

Crkva Sv. Andrije na groblju – izvana

Crkva Sv. Andrije

18. stoljeće

Nekoliko novih obiteljskih prezimena javlja se u otočkim zapisima iz 18. stoljeća. To su Bellanich, Haglich, Galosich, Giurich, Mancich, Nicolich, Ragusin i Valich. Podaci o krizmama pokazuju da je nekoliko obitelji Carcich živjelo na Unijama u prvih nekoliko desetljeća 18. stoljeća, budući da su 1715. godine krizmani Christoforo, Biaso i Paulo Carcich.[25]

Neke od najstarijskih otočkih obitelji mogu pratiti svoje porijeklo do pretka u ranom 18. stoljeću. U tom razdoblju obiteljska imena počela su se temeljeti na bratstvu. Obiteljska imena (također poznata kao nadimci na hrvatskom i *soprannome* na talijanskom) obično se koriste kako bi se razlikovala određena obitelj. Prezime često može sadržavati nekoliko obiteljskih imena. Obiteljska imena temelje se ili na osobnom imenu, lokalitetu ili zanimanju i često nastaju kao nadimak koji kasnije formalno usvajaju buduće generacije neke obitelji. Ranije spomenuti Carcich (Bravarof) datira iz ranog 18. stoljeća, a nekoliko obiteljskih linija te loze razvilo se na Unijama i u Ćunskom. Loza obitelji Radoslovich (Kalcic) potječe od Martina Radoslovicha (1715 -1750), iako nije jasno kada je to obiteljsko ime bilo usvojeno.

Određen broj obitelji tako se je dobro etablirao na Unijama u prvim desetljećima 18. stoljeća da su se njihova prezimena počela pojavljivati u knjigama vjenčanih u Malom Lošinju.[26] Imena koja se javljaju u zapisima s Lošinja između 1710. i 1740. su: Biaso Bellanich, Karstić Karčić, Matteo Karcich, Martin Karčić, Matteo Giurich, Matija Halić, Gasparo Nicolich, Martin Nicolich, Franić Radoslović, Gaspar Radoslovich, Karstić Radoslović, Martin Radoslović, Mattio Radoslovich, Simun Radoslović, Augustin Rerečić, Martin Rerečić, Matija Rerečić, Mikula Rerečić i Jivan Valčić. Popisi iz Malog Lošinja govore o barem 24 obitelji na Unijama: Bellanich (1 obitelj), Carcich (5 obitelji), Galosich (1 obitelj), Giurich (1 obitelj), Haglich (1 obitelj), Mancich (1 obitelj), Nadalin (1 obitelj), Nicolich (2 obitelji), Radoslovich (5 obitelji), Ragusin (1 obitelj), Rerecich (3 obitelji), Valich (2 obitelji).

Na temelju minimalnog broja osoba za koje postoji evidencija, na Unijama je između 1720. i 1730. godine živjelo najmanje 68 ljudi. Budući da su popisani pojedinci imali djecu o kojoj nemamo podatke, te da za neke obitelji poput Bellanicha i Nicolicha nisu navedeni svi članovi, postavlja se ispravna pretpostavka da je taj minimalan zapisan broj nedostatan da bi se odredio ukupan broj stanovnika Unija. Realniji broj stanovnika koji su tada živjeli na Unijama bio bi 136, odnosno duplo više.

U ranim 1700-ima mora da je postojala nestašica prikladnih bračnih partnera. U ranom 18. stoljeću znatan broj ljudi koji su živjeli na Unijama oženili su se u Mali Lošinj. Može se pretpostaviti da oni predstavljaju prvu odraslu generaciju spremnu na ženidbu nakon dolaska novih naseljenika u kasnom 17. i ranom 18. stoljeću. S obzirom na tako malu populaciju na Unijama tog vremena oni koji su bili spremni za brak bili su primorani bračne drugove tražiti u drugim u zajednicama, i Mali Lošinj je bio prirodan izbor s obzirom na svoju blizinu i brojnije stanovništvo.

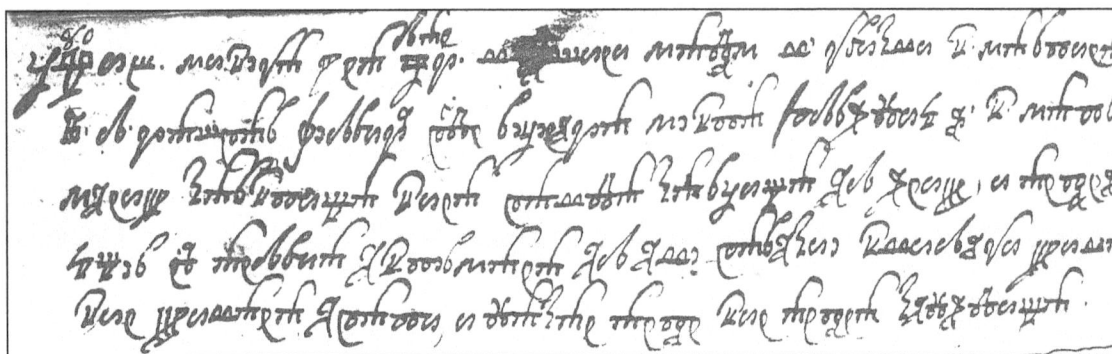

Knjiga vjenčanih za Karstić Karčić od Unij, 1722

Ostala prezimena kojih više nema na Unijama pojavljuju se u različitim zapisima od 1740 do 1783. Neka od njih su Juric (Giurich), Ivancich, Battin, Marcich ili Mancich, Ragusin, Riezo i Sepcich. [27, 28] Mattio Giurich podizao je obitelj na Unijama nakon 1740. te iako su njegovi nasljednici na Unijama izumrli u 19. stoljeću, njegova obitelj potječe od lošinjske obitelji iz 17. stoljeća. Genealogija ove obitelj Giurich dana je u ovom djelu. Jednako tako, jedna od unijskih obitelji Nicolich potječe od obitelji iz Malog Lošinja koje su tamo živjele u 17. stoljeću. Neka prezimena su izumrla, a njihovi nasljednici sklapali su brakove s drugim otočkim obiteljima. Neka prezimena nisu brojčana porasla. Na primjer, obitelj Valich zadržala se je na Unijama u malom broju. Jivan Valić, Antonov, oženio se 1722., a Maria Valić, Jivanova, udala se 1726. Mali broj današnjih obitelji Valić koje žive na Unijama može se pripisati velikom broju ženske djece u odnosu na broj muške djece koja su se rađala u obiteljima s ovim prezimenom zadnjih nekoliko stotina godina. U ranom 18. stoljeću nekoliko potomaka unijske obitelji Radoslovich naselilo se je u Malom Lošinju. Kasnije u istom stoljeću, unijske obitelji Carcich preselile su u Ćunski kako bi podigle svoje obitelji. Genealogije obitelji Radoslovich iz Malog Lošinja i obitelji Carcich iz Ćunskog također su navedene u ovom djelu.

U drugom dijelu 1770-ih Alberto Fortis (1741–1803), talijanski prirodoslovac, putnik, spisatelj i redovnik, posjetio je otoke Cres i Lošinj, a njegov objavljeni prikaz tog posjeta napisan je na engleskom za Johna Strangea, biskupa Londonderryja. Do vremena kad je Alberto Fortis prošao pored Unija, otok mora da je imao stabilnu populaciju, od možda 150 do 200 ljudi. Međutim, za vanjski svijet stanovnici Unija bili su od male važnosti, tako da je Fortis zapisao:

« [Unije] imaju malo stanovnika, i to izuzetno siromašnih. Njihov glavni proizvod je drvo za ogrjev s obzirom da je velik dio [otoka] pokriven šumom. Mogu [Unije] proizvoditi med i vosak obilato, jednako tako i stoku; ali daju malo ičeg drugoga, zbog razloga koje danas jako dobro razumijemo, posebno oni koji se bave javnom ekonomijom. Ribarenje oko Onia [Unija] je proizvod od znatne važnosti, lovi se najviše tuna, skuša i srdela; ali siromašni stanovnici nemaju sredstava da bi profitirali od njega pa stranci dolaze i ubiru svu tu prednost pred njihovim očima. »[29]

Kad se je vršilo, ribarilo se s obale uzicom i udicom što je osiguravalo dobar izvor proteina u vremenima gladi. Zemljoradnja i uzgoj stoke bili su glavni izvori sredstava za život na otoku. Kako je velik sjeverni dio otoka bio pod šumom, s Unija se je izvozilo drvo za ogrjev. Fortis spominje da «je drvo za ogrjev također važan artikl aktivne trgovine …. Drveće koje se obično koristi za ogrjev su običan hrast i crnika, brijest i jasen, uz divlje loze, planiku, pheleaea, borovnicu, itd.» Nekoliko stanovnika Malog Lošinja, čiji su očevi bili s Unija, u 18. se je stoljeću bavilo prijevozom drva za ogrjev s Cresa i Malog Lošinja u Veneciju, a među njima su bili i Mattio Carcich, sin Paola i Cristoforo Radoslovich, sin Simona.[30]

Nakon odlaska Uskoka brodarenje u Kvarneru dobilo je priliku oporaviti se od gubitaka. Međutim, gubici su se nastavili uslijed prirodnih katastrofa. Oko Unija pronalazimo nekoliko brodskih olupina. Jedan brodolom zbio se je u svibnju 1757. kod Mezza na Unijama kad je brod «Segnese» upao u poteškoće. Drugi brodolom desio se u studenom 1764. između otoka Unije i Srakane, kad se brod «San Giuseppe», pod kapetanom Andreom Sreglichem, na ruti za Corfu i Salonicu raspao na južnom kraju Unija. U listopadu 1786. na malom otoku Misgnaču, nešto dalje od obala otoka Unije dva mala broda zapela su i izgubila nešto od svog tereta koji je uključivao drvnu građu.[31] Stara brodska olupina na kojoj su ronioci otkrili jarbole leži samo malo dalje od obale malenog otoka, pored kojeg redovno prolazi trajekt na ulasku u glavno unijsko pristanište. Bliže našem dobu, 1929. brod «Anton Milan» potonuo je na sjevernom rtu Lokunji prevozeći cement.

Fortis daje uvid u poljoprivredne prakse koje su bile u upotrebi na kvarnerskim otocima. Spominje da «svaka kuća ima mali vrt», da su žene

«izuzetno čvrsto građene i naviknute nositi vrlo teške terete na glavi, uzbrdo i nizbrdo», te da «djeca niskog roda rade od najranije dobi, bilo u obradi zemlje, ribarenju ili brizi oko stoke…mnoga su zaposlena u manufakturi *rascie* što je gruba vrsta vunenog materijala.» Volovi se često ne koriste za oranje, nego su taj naporan posao «gotovo uvijek obavljale čvrste ruke muškaraca koji su općenito dobro plaćeni za svoj rad, u odnosu na manjak radne snage. Ovi radnici doista rade puno više od naših. Kao prvo, moraju mjesto određeno za neku kulturu očistiti od kamenja, a to je trajan rad…a to kamenje ulažu u male zidove kojima ograđuju polje kao nekom vrstom ograde ili granice. Općenito govoreći, ova umjetna polja kružnog su ili eliptičnog oblika, a otočani ih nazivaju coronale.»[32]

Nadalje, Fortis navodi da su glavne poljoprivredne kulture bile masline i grožđe, s velikim stadima ovaca u stočarstvu. Iako je Fortis svoja promatranja obavio na Cresu, ona su se isto tako mogla odnositi i na Unije i ostale kvarnerske otoke. Sijala se ograničena količina kukuruza, a krumpir je bio nepoznat na tim otocima. Glavno voće bile su smokve, dok je breskvi, kruški i marelica bilo vrlo malo. Određeni korijen biljke kozlac korišten je za pravljenje kruha, iako je Fortis smatrao da nema prehrambenu vrijednost. Maslinovo ulje bilo je glavno uporište otočke ekonomije i proizvodilo se iz tri varijeteta maslina - *slatke, starovijerke* i *istrionke*. «Ulje se izvozi s otoka, ali gotovo sav dobitak potreban je za kupovinu kukuruza kojeg stanovnici ne uzgajaju u dovoljnoj količini koja bi potrajala mjesecima ....Vino … nije izvrsne kvalitete u odnosu na ulje. Uzrok je vjerojatno nedovoljno znanje i briga koju posvećuju skupljanju i tiještenju grožda te fermentaciji vina.»[33] Fortis opisuje način brige o vinogradima kada govori da «otočani običavaju oko svake loze položiti hrpicu zemlje. Loza se održavala niskom i svake je godine lišavana izdanaka. Zemlja korijenje održava svježim za vrijeme sušne sezone i zimi, a za vjetrovita vremena u proljeće njome se loza pokriva u cijelosti. Obično lozu sade jednako gusto kao što mi sadimo indijanski kukuruz. »[34]

«Ovce su najbrojnija skupina četveronožaca na otoku; volova, teretnih životinja i svinja nema u velikom broju …. Svaki vlasnik stada, ili njih nekoliko zajedno, stada povjeravaju na brigu pastiru, a svaki obilježava svoje ovce različitim rezom na ušima.»[35] Jedinstveni žigovi na ovcama ili belezi prenosili su se unutar obitelji i napušteni su tek nedavno.

U 18. stoljeću na otoku Cresu dolazilo je do krađa stoke. Fortis navodi da su «morlački kradljivci, a osobito oni iz istarskih kolonija Castelnovo, Carnizza, Medolino i Altura prečesto pristajali na otok i odnosili životinje svake vrste koje su mogli skupiti, i to često pred očima samih vlasnika koji se nisu mogli suprotstaviti naoružanim pljačkašima.»[36] Do nas su došle priče s Unija o muškarcima koji su stražarili pred pljačkašima, što je vidljivo po ostacima puževih kućica koje su jeli dok su držali stražu na vrhovima brda.

Mnoge od kuća na Unijama u to vrijeme bile su male kamene kolibe sa slamnatim krovovima i bez prozora. Prilikom posjeta otoku Susku Fortis[37] opisuje kuće koje imaju «samo jedan otvor u tim kolibama, koji služi kao vrata, prozor i izlaz za dim; unutrašnjost nema raspodjelu, čak niti pod, osim što ga pokriva obična zemlja, te je niže nego vani». Takvi životni uvjeti gdje velike obitelji obitavaju u malenoj kući s vrlo malo ventilacije nisu bili zdravi. U Fortisovo vrijeme populaciju Malog Lošinja pogodile su velike boginje, dok je dizenterija vladala u gradovima na Cresu,[38] a zdravlje građana Osora često je ugrožavala malarija te je čak i gradski biskup dio godine izbivao iz grada. Komunikacija prema Unijama išla je preko Osora i Lošinja te je stoga vrlo vjerojatno da su stanovnici Unija također bolovali od istih bolesti, s obzirom da su bili u kontaktu sa stanovnicima spomenutih gradova.

Premda je obično stanovništvo govorilo lokalnim hrvatskim dijalektom, sve više je rastao utjecaj talijanskog kao posljedica kontakata i trgovine s drugim otocima te trgovcima s kopna. Fortis[39] ukazuje da je hrvatski jezik, ili sklavonski kako ga zove na Cresu i Lošinju «puno rasprostranjeniji od bilo kojeg drugog evropskog dijalekta, koriste ga svakodnevno obični ljudi i seljaci na otoku.» Govoreći o govoru S. Vito (Rijeka) Fortis navodi da «je jezik sela hrvatski, ali uglađeni [sic] ljudi oba spola govore dobrim talijanskim.» Jednako se može reći i za jezike koji su se govorili na kvarnerskim otocima.

U drugom dijelu 18. stoljeća Rimokatolička crkva još je imala jak utjecaj na otocima. Fortis piše da

«se desetine s otoka Cresa i Osora dijele na četiri dijela. Jedan dio se dijeli sirotinji ... drugi je za crkvene popravke, ornamente, itd., treći pripada kanonicima sa Cresa, iz Osora, Lubenica i Caisole; a četvrti se dodjeljuje biskupu iz cijele biskupije. U dva Lošinja dio za sirotinju već se odavno daje župnom svećeniku i kapelanima koji nemaju sigurna sredstva za zivot. »[40]

19. stoljeće

Početak 19. stoljeća označava novi period karakterističan porastom nacionalizma i novom političkom administracijom. Nakon napoleonskih ratova Venecija više nije vladala kvarnerskim otocima. Od 1914–1918 civilnu upravu preuzela je Austrija, a razvoj hrvatskih i talijanskih frakcija na Unijama također vjerojatno datira iz tog razdoblja.

Popis stanovništva iz 1815. [41] pokazuje da je na otoku živjelo 222 stanovnika u 45 naselja, dok popis iz 1819. popisuje 49 naselja, što ukazuje na nastanak četiri nova naselja u četiri godine. Populacija na Unijama i Susku u to vrijeme je brzo rasla posljedica čega je bila veća potražnja za obradivom zemljom. U Fortisovo doba Susak je imao 300 stanovnika. Ubrzo je taj broj porastao te se grad 1820-tih proširio prema morskoj obali. Zbog pritiska broja stanovnika i vjerojatno zbog nemogućnosti uzgoja maslina na tlu otoka Suska neki njegovi stanovnici počeli su graditi na Unijama, na istočnoj strani otoka. Ovo naselje napušteno je oko 1850. zbog otopora ostalih stanovnika Unija koji su uznemiravali nove naseljenike sa Suska.

Broj stanovnika na Unijama počeo je rasti u prvoj polovici 19. stoljeća, a porast se je nastavio i u sljedećem stoljeću. Vrhunac je dosegnut 1921. sa 783 stanovnika. Bila je to posljedica smanjenja stope smrtnosti kao rezultat bolje zdravstvene njege. Mali Lošinj imao je liječnika u 18. i 19. stoljeću, a i Unije su vjerojatno profitirale blizinom tog grada.

Registar umrlih za Unije od 1815. do 1880. pokazuje da su otočani umirali od raznih bolesti, uključujući glad, groznice i epidemije. Očekivani životni vijek procijenjen na osnovu 243 smrtna slučaja na Unijama između godine 1815 i 1850 bio je 35 godina. Situacija je bila slična i u drugim europskim zajednicama, kao i onima Sjeverne Amerike tog doba. Mnoga djeca umirala su u prvih 10 godina života od različitih bolesti. Međutim, osoba koja bi preživjela rano djetinjstvo imala je dobre izglede do doživi 70-tu ili 80-tu. Unapređenje zdravstvenog sistema u drugoj polovini 19. stoljeća produžilo je očekivani životni vijek. U kasnom 19. stoljeću u nekim obiteljima na Unijama živjeli su i devedesetgodišnjaci.

Zna se da je veliki broj članova nekih unijskih obitelji bolovao od raka. Visoka stopa oboljelih raka na Unijama vjerojatno je uzrokovana genetikom. Poznato je da su stope za rak na otocima Krku, Cresu i Lošinju veće nego na hrvatskom kopnu.[42] Na ovim otocima velika je pojavnost raka prostate, stomaka i gušterače kod muškaraca, te raka jajnika, dojke, stomaka, crijeva i mozga kod žena u usporedbi sa stopama na kopnu. Povijesna migracija između otoka Unije, Krka, Cresa i Lošinja može objasniti visok postotak raka na tim otocima.

U 19. stoljeću na Unije se doseljavaju nove obitelji. Početkom stoljeća, Lovri Segoti porijeklom iz Jablanca rodilo se je šestero djece. Obitelji Cecco i Pillepich doselile su na otok od sredine do kraja 19. stoljeća. Smatra se da obitelj Cecco potječe iz Dubrovnika premda je ova tvrdnja možda zasnovana samo na njihovom obiteljskom imenu Raguseo, dok prve zapise o obitelji možemo naći u Malom Lošinju početkom 19. stoljeća. Obitelj Pillepich na Unije je stigla iz Rijeke kao i drugi Pillepichi koji su doselili u Mali Lošinj. Druge obitelji na Unije su stigle iz Malog Lošinja. Jedna on njih bila je obitelj Joannesa (Ivana) Radoslovicha iz klana Mattesinich, rođenog u Malom Lošinju koji je kasnije s roditeljima doselio na Unije i podigao velike obitelj čiji su potomci danas raseljeni diljem svijeta. Obitelj Mattesinch iz Malog Lošinja potječe od Simona Radoslovicha s Unija koji je umro prije 1749.

Tabela životnog vijeka na Unijama na temelju smrtnih slučajeva od 1815. do 1850		
Godišnji interval	Broj smrti	Očekivani životni vijek
0-1	50	35.4
1-10	60	42.8
11-20	15	47.1
21-30	17	41.3
31-40	15	36.1
41-50	14	30.1
51-60	20	23.5
61-70	22	18.3
71-80	19	13.8
81-90	11	10.0

Iako obitelj Carcich (Bravarof) potječe iz 18. stoljeća ili ranije, iz ove ranije obiteljske loze proizašle su neke nove obitelji Carcich. Obitelj Antonia Carcicha (Bravarofa) i druge dvije obitelji (Bravarof) poznate su upravo iz ovog vremenskog perioda. Dvije od ovih obitelji živjele su na Unijama. Jedan od Bravarofa, Martin, sin Martinov, oženio se i zasnovao obitelj u Ćunskom na otoku Lošinju. U stvari, nekoliko obitelji naselile su se u

Ćunski upravo prije ovog vremena. Ogranci Bravarof, Ciadic, Cicuola, Pasquic i Vlasich obitelji Carcich iz Ćunskog potječu od ovih ranih naseljenika.

Ostale obitelji Carcich koje su na Unijama živjele između 1810 i 1820 bile su linije Jevin, Pasquich, Rocov, Andricev i Zburkin. Klan Zburkin potječe od Mikule Carcicha koji je oženio ženu iz obitelji Stefanich iz sjeverne Martinšćice s otoka Cresa i doselio na Unije s dvojicom sinova, Mikulom i Gaudenzijem, rođenima 1786. i 1795. 1845. godine Joseph Rieger objavio je panoramsku snimku istarske i dalmatinske obale. Snimka Unija prikazuje grad i dio otoka od njegovog zapadnog dijela, mada nema pogleda na polje ili ravno zemljište koje strši van prema zapadnom dijelu otoka. Riegerov prikaz sukladan je strukturama koje i danas postoje. Prikazuje i nekoliko puteva ili cesta. Jedna ide oko ruba Krisa, brda iznad grada, a druga od Krisa prema poljima sa sačuvanim zidovima koji su vidljivi još i danas. Primjećuje se i nekoliko kuća kao i nekoliko višekatnica.

Kao mladi vojni obveznik za vrijeme prusko-austrijskog rata 1866. Ivan Nicolich (1842-) iz Sancicheve grane s Unija bio je svjedokom mornaričkog napada na otok Vis. Nekoliko drugih muškaraca s Unija služili su u austrijskoj mornarici u 19. stoljeću, a najčešće su bili stacionirani u mornaričkoj bazi u Puli, sjeverozapadno od Unija.

Unije 1845, izdavač Giuseppe Rieger

1885. stanovnici Unija tražili su vladu da dopusti poučavanje talijanskog u otočnoj školi.[43] Možda je već ranije utemeljena hrvatska škola, kao što je bio slučaj na Susku koji je školu imao do 1845. Ilustracija Giuseppe Riegera iz 1845. ocrtava zgradu jednaku kasnijoj školskoj zgradi koja se nalazila pored crkve. U svakom slučaju, do 1888. na otoku je sigurno postojala škola[44] a učenike je otac Anton Andrijčić poučavao katekizmu, čitanju, pisanju i računanju. Školska godina trajala je od listopada do srpnja, a ispiti su se održavali dva puta godišnje.[45] Od 1911 do 1912 učitelj je bio Marijo Fučić. Sljedeće godine Fučić je poučavao 39 učenika u hrvatskoj školi. Lino Nicolich (Niccoli) (1894–1964) koji je osnovao banku u Sjedinjenim Državama i Andric Karčić (1888–1972) koji je postao advokat u Karlovcu obojica su započeli školovanje na Unijama. Giovanni Radoslovich (1879–1973) s Unija postao je učitelj na otoku Iloviku prije Prvog svjetskog rata. Kasnije je Andrea Carcich (1921–2004), također s Unija, postao učitelj u Ćunskom prije Drugog svjetskog rata.

Za vrijeme 1893. i narednih godina filoksera, nametnik na vinovoj lozi, počela je uništavati vinovu lozu na Unijama. Unesena iz Amerike filoksera (*Daktulosphaira vitifoliae*) desetkovala je lozu na otoku, sve dok nije posađen jedan tip američke loze otporan na bolest i potom cijepljen s domaćim lozama (*Vitis Vinifera*) s Unija. Vrste grožđa sađene na Unijama bile su suscan, bjelikuc, troviscia, plavac (zinfandel), jiakuc, belcina, boldun i muskat. Prva tri varijeteta bila su najproduktivnija.

20. stoljeće

20. stoljeće donijelo je velike promjene na Unije – rat, jezičnu promjenu i iseljavanje. Na popisu stanovništva iz 1900. na Unijama je popisano 176 kuća i 696 stanovnika. Popis stanovništvo dijeli na talijanske i hrvatske govornike (446 prvih i 250 drugih). Ove lingvističke i kulturne podjele na Talijane i Hrvate odigrale su veliku ulogu u oblikovanju zajednice, osobito nakon raspada austrijskog carstva poslije Prvog svjetskog rata i upostave talijanske uprave.

Na Unijama su utemeljene dvije kooperative utemeljene na nacionalnom identitetu. Rezultat je bio izgradnja dva odvojena mlina za mljevenje maslina – za talijansku i hrvatsku frakciju. Od dva mlina u luci, onaj na početku lučkog nasipa bio je talijanski, a onaj na južnom kraju luke hrvatski. Hrvatski mlin započeo je s radom 1900, a talijanski otprilike u istom vremenu. Popis članova talijanskom mlina dan je u dodatku. U blizini južnog ruba grada započela je s radom i tvornica sardina.

Hrvatski mlin na Unijama

Talijanski mlin

Talijanski jezik počeo se je na otoku više koristiti u 19. stoljeću. Talijanske posuđenice u unijskom dijalektu javljaju se prije 1945. Neke talijanske riječi koje su ušle u svakodnevni govor otočana uključuju: liber (slobodan) od talijanskog *libero*, mul (dok, tal. *molo*), libar (knjiga, tal. *libero*), fermat (stati, tal. *fermare*) i funiestra (prozor, tal. *finestra*). Može se naći i kompilacija riječi: kuzelj vaf sarcu.[44] Unijski dijalekt također sadrži mnogo starih latinskih riječi koje su u jezik ušle kroz dugi vremenski period, a nalaze se i u standardnom hrvatskom jeziku i dijalektima koji se govore na jadranskoj obali. U unijskom dijalektu mogu se naći čak i neke slovenske imenice. Alberto Fortis zapazio je upotrebu slovenskih riječi na otoku Krku 1770-ih, gdje se u nekim selima «govori miješanim [sic] žargonom karnijsko sklavonskog [Slovenskog], latinskog i talijanskog.»[46] Slično je krajem 19. stoljeća primijetio i slovenski lingvist Oblak, također na Krku. Rastuća upotreba talijanskog u tom vremenu mogla je biti trenutni kulturni fenomen, ali veza sa slovenskim mogla je biti ujedno i kulturna i genetska veza iz vremena prvih slavenskih doseljenika na otoke što je vidljivo iz snažne genetske korelacije između populacije zapadne Hrvatske i Slovenije.[47]

U Prvom svjetskom ratu osmorica muškaraca s Unija poginula su boreći se u austrijskoj vojsci, većinom u Galiciji. Bili su to Mate Nicolich (1894–1915), Zaccaria Nicolich (1875–1917), Andrea Nicolich, Ivan Carcich (umro 1917.), Andrea Carcich, Antonio Carcich (1898–1917), Šime Nicolich (1885–1915) i Toni Radoslovich (umro 1915.). Austrijski razarač «Viribus Unitis» leži ispred talijanske obale pored Ancone, otkad je Italija ušla u Prvi svjetski rat na strani Britanije i Francuske. Bombardirao je obalnu željeznicu uzrokujući ogromnu štetu. Na njemu je bio i Tucich Segota (1880-) s Unija. Još jedan stanovnik Unija, Luca Carcich, služio je na austrijskom razaraču «Tegetthofu» kad je ovaj susreo i oborio talijanski avion.

Za vrijeme Prvog svjetskog rata na Unijama je došlo do velikog incidenta zbog Nazaria Saura, austrijskog građanina koji je pristupio talijanskoj mornarici. 1. kolovoza 1916. Sauro je zapovijedao podmornicom «Pullino» u koju je prodrla voda u blizini malog otoka Galiola, osam kilometara sjeverozapadno od Unija. Sauro je podmornicu zaustavio kod Galiolie *(Galiola)*, a u strahu od austrijskih vlasti on i njegova posada u nekoliko čamaca uputili su se prema Italiji. Galiola je u to vrijeme imala svjetionik, a na otoku su živjele četiri obitelji, od kojih i obitelj Nicolich s Unija. Glava obitelji Antonio Nicolich (1879-) i jedan drugi muškarac uputili su se prema Unijama nakon što je Nazario otišao. Od 1919. do 1943. u školi su poučavani samo talijanski jezik i povijest. Za djecu od četvrte godine uveden je vrtić. Postojali su razredi od prvog do petog i neki razredi

---

Uspjeli su doći do svjetionika na Unijama i obavijestiti vlasti o tom incidentu. Koristeći telefon u svjetioniku kontaktirali su austrijsku mornaricu u Puli. Poslan je brod koji je pokupio posadu podmornice i Nazaria prije nego su stigli do Italije. Nazario je obješen u Puli kao izdajnik 10. kolovoza 1916. Kasnije, u Drugom svjetskom ratu, njemačka mornarica sravnila je svjetionik na Galioli sa zemljom, ali je obnovljen nakon rata.

srednje škole. U austrijskom periodu poučavali su se i zemljopis, povijest i fizika.[48] 1929. pored škole je izgrađena vojarna.

Do 1932. počela je s radom i električna centrala koja je osiguravala nekoliko sati električne energije dnevno. Ta centrala je prije bila korištena kao privremeno mjesto za pakiranje ribe. Nova zgrada za pakiranje ribe podignuta je u zaljevu Maracol - vodila ju je kompanija «Arigoni» (*Arrigoni*), a nekadašnja gradska tvornica je zatvorena. Tvornica je zapošljavala mnoge otočke žene kao sezonske radnice. Iz Crnog mora je dopremana tuna, a srdele su bile iz lokalnog ulova. Tvornica je zatvorena 1943, ali je su je jugoslavenske vlasti ponovno otvorile nakon Drugog svjetskog rata.

Priča se je zakomplicirala za vrijeme Drugog svjetskog rata jer su mnoge obitelji emigrirale u Sjedinjene Države. Stoga su se muškarci iz unijskih obitelji borili u vojskama Italije i Sjedinjenih Država. Na američkoj strani nekoliko muškaraca borilo se je u Europi i na Pacifiku. Johna Nicolicha, rođenog 1922. na Unijama Amerikanci su spustili padobranom u talijansku Firencu, gdje je radio kao špijun. Bio je tamo i Andric Nicolich (1921–1944) koji je poginuo u Evropi u američkim oružanim snagama, dok je nekolicina drugih služila na Pacifiku. Lino Nicolich (1894–1964) koji je studirao na Pomorskoj akademiji na Lošinju bio je skiper na «Henryju Meigsu», američkom brodu tipa Liberty na Pacifiku. Ranije je Lino služio u Prvom svjetskom ratu, a car Franjo Josip odlikovao ga je drugim najvišim ordenom u austrijskoj vojsci. Andric Karcic (1888–1972) službovao je u ustaškoj administraciji kao časnik za vezu s tallijanskom vojskom u Hrvatskoj. Imao je ured na Susku, odmah do grada Fiume (Rijeke). Ljudi s Unija radili su kao njegovi čuvari. Pred kraj rata Andric je bio zaposlen u uredu generalnog konzula u Beču, a nakon rata živio je u Sjedinjenim Državama.

Većina mladih ljudi s Unija koje je unovačila talijanska vojska služili su u mornarici. Andrea Radoslovich (1913–1942) umro je nakon što mu je brod pogođen i potonuo između Italije i Valone u Albaniji. Rufino Niccoli (Nicolich) bio je kapetan talijanske podmornice koja je nestala prvih dana nakon talijanskog ulaska u Drugi svjetski rat. Andrea Valic koji se borio u talijanskoj vojsci poginuo je 1943. u borbama pored rijeke Don u Sovjetskom Savezu.

Nakon talijanske kapitulacije pred saveznicima u rujnu 1943. vojni arsenal u Malom Lošinju ubrzo su okupirali prvo četnici, potom partizani, a zatim Nijemci. Svaka strana je pritom slala svoje patrole na Unije. Partizanska okupacija u Lošinju nije dugo trajala jer su njemačke snage napale i osvojile grad kojeg su držale pod kontrolom do pred kraj Drugog svjetskog rata. Luca Karcich (1889 – 1945) koji je služio na «Tegetthofu» za vrijeme Prvog svjetskog rata i radio u SAD-u u godinama između ratova za vrijeme Drugog svjetskog rata bio je na Unijama. U vrijeme njemačke okupacije tragalo se je za osobama poput Luce koji je imao američko državljanstvo. Uhićen je i odveden u Njemačku gdje je i nestao.

Crkva Sv. Andrija 1930-31: Carabiniere, Andrea Radoslovich-Gartljic (1871 -1945), Giovanni Radoslovich (Kalcic), Vojnik, Jovanin Pillepich (1886-1948), Antonio Braiko (1922-), Nicolo Radoslovich (1921-1945), Giovanni Radoslovich (Kalčić), Voujnik, Don Andrea Virla, Luigi Miceleti, Antonio or Marco Bellanich (Preruć) (1912-)? ,Francis Ferrara (1925-), Gasparo Carcich (1924-), Joseph Nicolich (1921-), Vojnik, Osip Nicolich (Sancich) (1909-1993), Carabiniere.

Brzo nakon odlaska četnika s Unija došli su partizani. Obično su se skrivali na otoku, osobito u razdoblju njemačke okupacije. Međutim, partizani su u to vrijeme vršili pogubljenja navodnih talijanskih i njemačkih simpatizera. Andrea Radoslovich (1898 – 1950) iz ogranka Popich unijske obitelji Radoslovich na otok je došao nakon talijanske kapitulacije u rujnu 1943. Želio je organizirati ubojstvo pet otočkih obitelji za koje se je tvrdilo da imaju simpatije Talijana. Mati Carcich (Jevin) odvratio ga je od provođenja tog plana. Sam Andrea bolovao je od raka grla i umro je ubrzo nakon kraja rata.

U noći 14. siječnja 1945. tri njemačka patrolna broda - S33, S58 i S60 dužine nekih 30 metara nasukala su se u blizini unijskog svjetionika. Brodovi su isplovili iz Pule i kretali se u pravcu Lošinja. Nijemci su se odmah počeli izvlačiti s plaže, ali zašli su predaleko da bi se u more mogli vratiti vlastitim snagama. Ogradili su jugozapadni dio otoka i poslali patrolu u grad. 15. siječnja engleska eskadrila od tri broda došla je bočno od nasukanih patrolnih brodova i počela s bombardiranjem. Neke od granata pale su u zaljev u blizini grada, dok je jedna granata pala u grad blizu kuće na broju 124. Bombardiranje je kratko trajalo i nakon pet ili nešto više minuta engleski brodovi su se okrenuli i ubrzali natrag prema Italiji. Sljedeći dan Nijemci su napustili patrolne brodove i zapalili ih. Kasnije 1945. zapovjednik njemačkih snaga na Lošinju Platzcomandir

Fischer predao se partizanima te, iako se skrivao na Unijama, partizani su ga ubili u blizini Splita.

Tvornica Arrigoni

Koncem Drugog svjetskog rata od 639 stanovnika Unija 421 se izjasnio kao Hrvat a 216 su se izjasnili kao Talijani.[49] Brojčano stanje obitelji iznosilo je: Belanić 7, Busanić 1, Čeko 4, Citcović 1, Delconte 1, Deroia 1, Galošić 1, Haljić 1, Karčić 59, Nadalin 5, Nikolić 43, Picinić 1, Pilepić 3, Poljanić 1, Radoslović 18, Rerečić 15, Segota 6, Valić 2, Verbora 1, Vidulić 1.

S dolaskom komunističkog režima u poslijeratnu Jugoslaviju uvedeno je prisilno zatočeništvo, a iseljavanje je jako smanjeno nakon početnog egzodusa Talijana i njima sklonim obiteljima. Iseljavanje je bilo ograničeno i poznato je da su korištena sredstva zastrašivanja kako bi se obitelji i pojedinci odvratili od bijega preko Jandranskog mora. Posmrtni ostaci Johna Carcicha s Unija i još trojice drugih otkrivena su u malom zaljevu blizu Ćunskog 1996. Bilo je poznato da John i njegovi drugovi planiraju preplovili Jadran i posljednji put su viđeni živi 1956. Od 1945. do 1960. šest obitelji i ukupno 30 pojedinaca s Unija potajno su prešli Jadransko more.

Populacija na Unijama ostala je stabilna do Drugog svjetskog rata nakon kojeg je uslijedilo stalno smanjivanje. Populacijska struktura u 1980-ima pokazivala je velik udio stanovnika starih 70 i više godina.[50] Danas oko 70 ljudi na otoku živi tokom cijele godine, ali mnogo ih je više za vrijeme ljetnih mjeseci. Većinom su to hrvatski izletnici s kopna, te turisti iz Slovenije, Italije i prekomorskih zemalja koji na otoku posjeduju kuće ili ih ljeti unajmljuju. Zimi na otok dolaze lovci na fazane. Obitelji koje su se na Unije doselile u posljednjih tri stotine godina još uvijek se mogu naći na otoku, osim što su se brojčano smanjile i većina njihovih članova živi u Sjevernoj Americi, Italiji i Australiji.

68

Novopridošlice na otok u zadnjih pedeset godina većinom su Hrvati i nešto Bosanaca s kopna.

Populacija na Unijama 1600 - 2000

Godine	Populacija	Godine	Populacija
1600	75-100*	1921	783
1730	136*	1931	717
1770	150-200*	1945	649
1815	222	1948	457
1818	220	1953	402
1869	520	1961	273
1880	630	1971	113
1890	678	1981	85
1900	696	1990	82
1910	758	2000	70

*procjena

Zadnjih četiri stotine godina na mnogim manjim dalmatinskim otocima populacija se je postepeno povećavala, nakon čega je sredinom prošlog stoljeća uslijedio nagli pad.

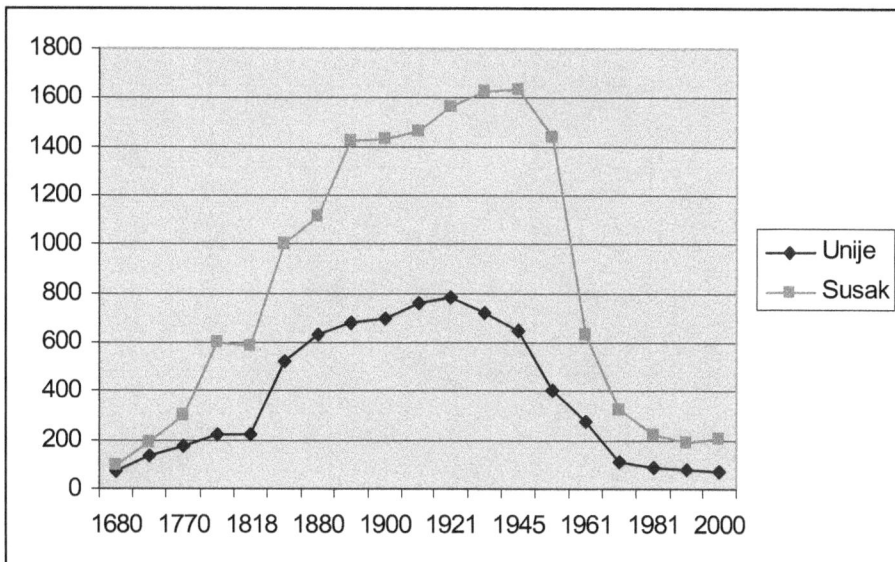

Populacijski grafikon za Unije i Susak 1680-2000

Na Unijama se je desilo isto, a kad se populacija Unija usporedi s onom na Susku, sličnosti i razlike postaju još očitije. Unije su započele s manjim brojem stanovnika 1600-ih godina koja je od tada sporije rasla. Populacija na Susku započela je s bržim rastom početkom 1800-ih, dok je porast na Unijama započeo sredinom 1800-ih. Bolji zdravstveni uvjeti i uz njih vezano produženje životnog vijeka potpomogli su populacijski prirast na oba otoka, jednako kao i dolazak novih obitelji na Unije - Cecco, Pilepic, Radoslovich (Matesinich) i Segota. Populacija na oba otoka smanjivala se je u prvoj polovini 1900-ih, iako je na Unijama taj pad započeo otprilike dva desetljeća ranije zbog iseljavanja u Ameriku.

Poljoprivredna proizvodnja na otoku oslabila je nakon 1965. zbog iseljavanja stanovništva. Da bi se poljoprivreda obnovila kompanija «Jadranka» iz Malog Lošinja je od 1984. do 1991. vratila u proizvodno stanje više od 125 ha zemlje na kojoj je započet uzgoj alfalfe, ječma, kukuruza i mahunarki. Dodatno, na otoku je uzgajano 1200 ovaca i 600 koza. «Jadranka» je prekinula s radom nakon raspada Jugoslavije. Lov na prepelice na Unijama započeo je s 2 000 fazana i 5 000 jarebica koje se godišnje puštaju na otok. Na otoku su se provodili različiti eksperimenti vezani uz uzgoj pčela. 1996. izgrađena je pista za male jednomotorne avione na ravnoj zaravni južno od grada kojom upravlja hrvatska vlada.

Iseljavanje

Prije iseljavanja u Sjevernu i Južnu Ameriku u kasnom 19. stoljeću, stanovnici Unija bili su ograničeni na putovanja i zapošljavanje na susjednim otocima i kvarnerskim gradovima, te ponekad nešto udaljenijim gradovima poput Venecije. U 18. stoljeću nekoliko pojedinaca bavilo se je prodajom drva za ogrjev koje se je otpremalo u Veneciju. Putovanja u Osor, Mali Lošinj, Ćunski i otok Cres omogućavala su nekim pojedincima da se nasele na tim lokacijama. U ovom djelu date su genealogije unijskih obitelji koje su se doselile u Mali Lošinj i Ćunski.

Priča o iseljavanju vezana je uz pomorsku povijest Lošinja. Od 17. stoljeća nadalje stanovnici Lošinja gravitirali su prema moru i mnogi su postali pomorci na Jadranu i u Mediteranu. Pomorci s Lošinja bili su među prvim Hrvatima koji su posjetili oba američka kontinenta. 1779. Peter Budinić iz Velog Lošinja plovio je na «Santo Domenicu» na Karibe. Drugi su nastavili pomorsku trgovinu s Amerikama; Gasparo Budinich iz Velog Lošinja umro 1792. na u Kingstonu na otoku Jamajka. 1834. Petar Jakov Leva, također iz Velog Lošinja, plovio je na «Ferdinandu V Re d'Ungheriji» oko rta Horn do Valparaisa u Čileu.[51] Jedan drugi lošinjski kapetan imenom Martinolich plovio je na «Amaliji Giuseppini» kako bi 1844 pokupio pamuk u teksaškoj luci Galveston. Hrvatska zajednica postojala je u New Orleansu već za vrijeme 1820-ih. Lošinjski kapetani počeli su uplovljavati u tu luku u prvoj polovini 19. stoljeća i kroz nju su mnogi lošinjski iseljenici stigli u Ameriku. Marko Ragusin iz Velog Lošinja stigao je u Ameriku preko New Orleansa do 1849. Ragusin je otišao u Sacramento, Kaliforniju i kasnije u San Jose. Drugi Lošinjani iselili su sredinom 19. stoljeća u Sjedinjene Države i Australiju. Fortunato Corsano, rođen u Malom Lošinju 1841. godine, iselio je u Australiju 1867. Većina iseljenika s Unija u Australiju je došla nakon Drugog svjetskog rata, s iznimkom Mattea Carcicha (1878-) koji je došao neposredno prije rata.

Većina iseljavanja s Lošinja u Ameriku odvijala se krajem 1870-ih i u ranim 1880-ima. Venanzio Martinolich (1848 – 1913) iz Malog Lošinja, ali s rodbinom na Unijama, doputovao je u Ameriku preko New Orleansa i 1888. neko vrijeme živio u Coloradu gdje je njegov brat Benjaminus (1849 -) doselio dvije godine ranije. 1891. Venanzio je s obitelji preselio u Port Guichon, vankuversko područje Britanske Kolumbije. Drugi poput John A. Martinolicha (1877 -) također su stigli u Britansku Kolumbiju 1893, ali do 1902. on je upravljao brodogradilištem u Docktonu, država Washington. Obje zajednice, ona u Vancouveru i ona u Docktonu postale su mali centri hrvatskog iseljeništva s određenim brojem obitelji s Lošinja i Unija. I druge obitelji iz Malog Lošinja nastavile su dalaziti u to područje: Giuseppe Nicolich (1864 – 1934) iz loze Muscardin, koji je imao daleke srodnike na Unijama te oženio Elviru Ivančić (1871 – 1942). Podigli su dva sina, Eugena i Josepha L. (1896 – 1973), u Vancouveru i Seattleu.

U drugoj polovini 19. stoljeća mnogi otočani s Unija putovali su na istočnu obalu, na zapadnu obalu i Colorado u Sjedinjenim Državama u potrazi za poslom. Antonio Carcich (1860 -) s Unija spominje se u New Yorku 1874. Poznato je da su i drugi pojedinci s Unija živjeli u New Yorku od 1885. nadalje. Popis tih pojedinaca koji su radili u New Yorku može se naći u dodatku. 1890-ih i u prvom desetljeću 1900-ih praktički svaka obitelj na Unijama imala je jednog ili više članova obitelji na radu u Americi.

Nekoliko unijskih obitelji došlo je u Britansku Kolumbiju i državu Washington. Tipični iseljenik s Unija bio je i Andrea Domenico Galosich (1866 – 1948). Andrew je došao je u Deltu, Britanska Kolumbija 1890, a 1900. doveo je i svoju ženu Thomasinu Nicolich (1869 -). Njegov brat Giovanni Galosich (1964–1918), pomorac, bio je u New Yorku 1888. preko kojeg je Andrea vjerojatno stigao na zapadnu obalu. Do Prvog svjetskog rata Andrea i Thomasina živjeli su na području Seattlea, a ranih 1920-ih preselili su u Kaliforniju. Za vrijeme Prvog svjetskog rata na području Seattlea živio je znatan broj ljudi s Unija. Benjamin Carcich (1864–1919) i Dominic Ferluga (1896–1993) živjeli su tamo do smrti. Matteo Nicolich (1888 –1959) i njegova žena Mary Simicich (1893–1978) živjeli su u Seattleu gdje su im rođeni i sinovi Mathew (1918 -) i Lawrence (1921 -). Obitelji Giuseppea Nicolicha (1879–1945) i Mattea Karcicha (1890–1963) živjele su u Seattleu, a tamo je rođen i njihov sin Joseph (1913–1990). Antonio Carcich (1876 -) stigao je i Sjedinjene Države 1905. da bi se dvije godine kasnije oženio i doveo svoju ženu Antoniju (1880-). Antonio i Antonia podigli su dvoje djece na području Seattlea - Stellu (1908-) i Matta (1910–1978).

Drugi su s Unija na područje Seattlea stigli pojedinačno. Domenico Simeone Carcich (1858–1925) radio je u toj regiji, a Giovanni Andrea Nicolich (1875–1961) bio je prijavljen za vojnu službu u Seattleu 1917. Rose Carcich (1915–1990) također je živjela na tom području. Theodore Carcich (1905–1988) rođen na Unijama kasnije je postao potpredsjednik Adventističke crkve sedmog dana te je doselio u Seattle 1942. Nedugo nakon 1942. njegova obitelj doselila je u Colton, Washington.

Već vrlo rano neki su pojedinci s Unija odlazili na rad u rudnike ugljena u jugoistočnom Coloradu. Nakon izgranje žaljeznice Santa Fe prema Trinidadu 1879. godine, u rudnicima ugljena iskorištavana je jeftina imigrantska radna snaga. Ovi ljudi radili su u rudnicima Forbesa i Tobasca, tada novoizgrađenih rudarskih zajednica. Dotok iseljenika iz Hrvatske donio je 500 radnika na područje Trinidada, Colorado. Do 1900. rudari su pristizali iz Ćunskog i Malog Lošinja i do kraja stoljeća najmanje trojica muškaraca u ovoj grupi bila su s Unija. Andro Karcich s Unija i njegova žena Suzanna Mihlik tu su živjeli i radili oko 1908. Također, negdje u to vrijeme Mat Karcich iz Ćunskog, čiji je otac bio s Unija, i njegova žena Anna Galecich živjeli su i ostali na ovom području do 1915. Andrea Carcich s Unija živio je u Trinidadu. Nekoliko drugih s Unija radili su ovdje jedno kratko vrijeme, vratili se u New York ili odselili negdje drugdje. Mnogi rudari napustili su ovo područje za vrijeme i nakon štrajka 1913–14 u kojem je došlo do velikog nasilja i nemira. 1914. godine Forbes gdje je radilo nekoliko muškaraca s Unija spaljen je do zemlje pri čemu je nekoliko čuvara i rudara poginulo. Najmanje jedna obitelj s Unija ostala je u Forbesu sljedećih godina. Danas ništa nije ostalo od tog grada, a slična sudbina zadesila je i susjedni Hastings, u kojem se je populacija smanjila 1920-ih i 1930-ih, te je napušten do 1952. U Hastingsu se je desila tragična eksplozija u rudniku 1917. u kojoj je 121 rudar izgubio život. Matt P. Carcich, projeklom iz Ćunskog, a kasnije iz Trinidada, Colorado, imenovan je upraviteljem imovine preživjelih iz rudarske eksplozije.

Potomci ovih obitelji iz Forbesa, Tabascoa i Trinidada, Colorado danas žive u Coloradu, Novom Meksiku, Kaliforniji i New Yorku. Neki su se na tom području zadržali malo duže, ali do 1920. većina ih je otišla u druga mjesta, neki u New York gdje su se već bile naselile neke unijske obitelji. Jedna obitelj Carcicha iz Ćunskog ostala je u Trinidadu, Colorado i njihovi potomci danas žive na zapadu Sjedinjenih Država. Nekoliko obitelji preselilo je u druge centre kao što je San Pedro (Los Angeles), Kalifornija.

Prije 1903. većina iseljenika morala je putovati u talijanske, nizozemske ili luke te u njemački Bremer ili Hamburg kako bi se ukrcali na putničke brodove za Ameriku. Neki od brodskih radnika s Unija prešli su Atlantik na brodovima kao što su «La Champagne», «La Touraine», «Aquitaine» i «Spartan Prince». Nakon 1902. bliža ruta otvorena je od Trsta do New Yorka na austrijsko-američkoj liniji (Cosulich) i liniji Cunard. New York je bio prva ulazna luka za većinu putnika s Unija. Neki su stigli preko njujorške luke i nastavili dalje prema zapadnoj obali. Od 1885. nadalje zabilježen je stalan dotok pojedinaca u Unija u Sjedinjene Države, dokumentiran u brodskim popisima putnika i federalnim popisima stanovništva. Većina je ostala u New Yorku.

Mnogi useljenici s Unija radili su na dokovima Manhattana. Odabrali su život u središnjem Manhattanu između 42. zapadne i 50. ulice, te između 9. i 12. avenije, regiju pod nazivom «Paklena kuhinja» [Hell's Kitchen]. Ovaj dio Manhattana graniči s rijekom Hudson i imao je mnogo dokova na kojima su novopridošlice radile. U 42. ulici bila je klaonica, jedna od mnogi koji su se protezale sve do 35. ulice. Na križanju rijeke i 42. ulice postojala je trajektna veza s New Jerseyem. Na rijeci na 54. ulici i 12. aveniji nalazilo se je gradsko odlagalište smeća. Teretni kolodvor na Manhattanu bio je smješten na križanju 60. i 11. avenije, a drugi je bio u 30. ulici. Željeznička pruga išla je niz 11. aveniju. «New York Central Railroad» bio je glavni poslodavac ljudi koji su pristigli u New York. Drugi poslodavac bio je lanac Schraftovih restorana gdje je radilo nekoliko žena s Unija.

Raniji stanovnici Hell's Kitchena od 1851. nadalje bili su Irci. Kasnije su se tamo doselili Talijani, a mala crnačka populacija proširila se je od 59. do 65. ulice. Novoprodošlice s

Unija bili su muškarci - samci i oženjeni. Obično su živjeli u grupama, s bratom, rođakom, ujakom ili prijateljem iz stare domovine, dijeleći troškove i obroke. Neke obitelji s Unija nastavile su živjeti u Hell's Kitchenu do 1950-ih. Iako ih relativno malo danas stanuje na Manhattanu, većina obitelji porijeklom s Unija preselila je u susjedne regije New Yorka i New Jerseya.

807 Greenwick Street, Manhattan, N.Y. 1935

Stanovnici s Unija koji su stanovali na Manhattanu običavali su odlaziti su u dvije trgovine. Jednu je vodila obitelj Angelich, a drugu obitelj Andree Vallicha s Unija koja se je do 1914. nalazila na križanju zapadne 544. i 45. ulice i koja je postala mjesto okupljanja za one koji su s Unija stigli prije Prvog svjetskog rata. Kasnije je Gaudentio Radoslovich s Unija upravljao taksi kompanijom na Manhattanu, a potom restoranom na adresi Greenwick Street 807 (od 1922. do 1950.). Bila je to lučka zgrada blizu teretnog kolodvora New York Central Railroad's St. James Park.

Prva hrvatska crkva na Manhattanu u koju su dolazili novi doseljenici s Unija bila je crkva Svetog Ćirila i Metoda na križanju 50. zapadne i 10. avenije. Više od dvanaestero djece i nekoliko odraslih iz unijskih obitelji kršteno je i vjenčano u ovoj crkvi. Crkva je na ovoj lokaciji bila od 1913. do 1970-tih kad je premještena na križanje 502. zapadne i 41. avenije. Nekoliko društava utemeljeno je kako kako bi se pomoglo i stanovnicima Unija i iseljenicima s Unija u Sjedinjenim Državama. Societa di Mutuo Soccorso Unione *(Società di Mutuo Soccorso)* osnovana je na Unijama 9. kolovoza 1897, a Istrian

74

Benevolent Association utemeljena je u New Yorku 28. prosinca 1922. Direktori Asocijacije bili su John Carcich sa broja 557 na 11. aveniji, Dominick Carcich sa broja 557 na 11. aveniji, Andrew Nicolich sa broja 636 na 45. ulici, Bortolo Rerecich sa broja 597 na 11. aveniji i Paul Rerecich sa broja 552 na zapadnoj strani 45. ulice, svi iz New Yorka.[52] Također osnovano radi pomoći Unijama bilo je društvo pod nazivom the Sveti Andrija Society iz New Yorka. I the Societa i the Association osnovani su kako bi se pomoglo onima kojima je potrebna novčana pomoć. Kasnije su to postali klubovi za društvena okupljanja. The Benevolent Association počela je s 32 članova, a prije no što je društvo prestalo s radom 1994. imalo je do 72 članova.[53]

LA STORIA DI UNIE :
compendio e genealogia di famiglie dell'isola di Unie, Croazia

Libro dei morti 1815, Unie

Annotazioni

Ringrazio mio padre per avermi trasmesso l'amore per la storia, raccontandomi le sue storie di guerra e di avventure. Desidero esprimere la mia gratitudine a coloro che fornirono informazioni genealogiche riguardanti le famiglie di Unie. Tra i primi a raccogliere dati che contribuirono alle genealogie di questo libro, ci sono Andrea Karcich da New York, Antonio Rerecich (1912-1996) e suo figlio Toni. Un ringraziamento particolare ad Andrea Depikolvane, per il suo sostegno a fornire dischi di chiesa di Unie a Veglia.

L'autore desidera ringraziare Fiorella Rivera ed Enzo Valencich per la traduzione del testo in italiano. L'autore ringrazia altresì Anton Angelich, Dorothy Buffington, Silvana Borrelli (Nicolich), Maria Carcich, Marina Carcich, Ted Carcich, Milka Fatović (Nikolić), Maria Gelinas, Vlatko Janeković, Dominic Karcic, Gary Loverich, Adrijano Nikolić, Irene Nicolich, Gaudent Radoslovich, Joanne Rasco, Fred Scopinich, Letizia Valic e Ron Weddle per il loro contributo fotografico. Le fotografie non segnalate sono dell'autore. Questo volume contiene parte della storia orale tramandata dai miei genitori, da altri parenti ed abitanti di Unie, verso i quali mi sento in obbligo.

Prefazione

Nell'ottobre del 2005, alcuni operai di Unie scoprirono dei documenti tra i calcinacci di una casa che stavano ristrutturando. Questi documenti erano dei resoconti della parrocchia di Unie a partire dal 19° secolo, scritti in italiano e in latino. Questi documenti comprendevano un registro dei decessi ed un censimento dell'isola, rosicchiati dai topi. Entrambi sono rimasti nascosti tra i muri di una cucina per circa cent'anni. I documenti mostravano importanti dati genealogici e mettevano in luce la storia di Unie dei secoli precedenti. Durante la transizione al governo italiano (1919-1921) i preti di Unie e delle isole vicine furono obbligati a partire (1) e, sebbene questo sia solamente un'opinione, i documenti nascosti potrebbero essere un effetto di questo passaggio. Come per i documenti suddetti, molta della storia di Unie rimase nascosta perchè nessuno vi aveva fatto delle ricerche. Unie, nel 18° secolo possedeva dei registri della parrocchia scritti in slavo antico (2), ma questi non esistono più. Questo volume cerca di rivelare parte della storia nascosta del passato di Unie.

I nomi e i cognomi forniti in questo testo provengono da varie fonti, scritti in una varietà di lingue, comprendendo il croato, l'italiano e il latino e pertanto gli stessi nomi appaiono in differenti forme. I dati usati per la compilazione di questa storia, nonché delle genealogie delle famiglie, provengono da varie fonti storiche, includendo registri parrocchiali (nascite, battesimi, matrimoni e decessi, documenti legali, censimenti, documenti navali e storie di famiglie).

Introduzione

Unije (pronunzia: uni-ye), in italiano Unie e in latino Nia, è un'isola croata situata nell'Adriatico settentrionale (14° 15' E, 44° 38' N). Corre da nord a sud per nove chilometri, mentre da est a ovest ha una larghezza massima di due chilometri e minima di cinquecento metri. Appartiene all'arcipelago del Quarnero e fa parte della Contea Primorsko-Goranska.

Ad eccezione di Brioni, lungo le coste istriane, Unie è l'isola più a ovest dell'insieme di isole croate. Pola rimane a trentasei chilometri a nord-ovest e Rimini, sulle coste orientali italiane, dista all'incirca cento chilometri. Più a nord troviamo gli importanti centri di Rijeka (Fiume) e di Trieste. Le isole più vicine a Unie, verso sud-est, sono Vele Srakane (Canidole Grande) e Male Srakane (Canidole Piccolo), mentre a nove chilometri verso sud c'è l'isola di Susak (Sànsego). Immediatamente a est si trova Losinj (Lussino) con i centri di Mali Losinj (Lussinpiccolo) e Veli Losinj (Lussingrande). A fianco dell'isola di Losinj, verso nord, sorge la città di Osor (Ossaro), la mitica *Apsoros*, illustre e splendida al tempo romano e capoluogo delle due isole sino alla fine del Medioevo.

La storia dell'isola, analizzata in una veduta generale, è stata preservata attraverso fondate documentazioni. Il primo periodo di arte ceramica preistorica, il primo periodo Liburniano, il periodo romano e quello successivo sono riportati in appendice, in riferimento alla parte archeologica dell'isola. (3) La presenza del periodo romano traspare nei nomi locali dell'isola ed in alcuni vocaboli usati nel dialetto parlato di Unie. Una varietà di antiche parole, prese a prestito dal latino è divenuta parte della lingua ed è stata utilizzata da comunità dalmate dell'Adriatico. Questo mare evidenzia l'esistenza di una popolazione precedente che occupò la regione prima della migrazione slava del settimo secolo.

La storia degli abitanti di Unie si rimonta per un lungo periodo al passato e illustra la lunga sequenza che collega il popolo di Unie alle isole vicine. Attraverso i secoli, le famiglie della vicina Lussino, contribuirono sostanzialmente alla composizione dei nuclei familiari di Unie. Altri abitanti da Cherso, da Veglia e dal continente, concorsero alla formazione della comunità isolana. La maggior parte delle famiglie che si sistemarono a Unie era di origine slava e la lenta migrazione delle famiglie verso Unie, durante parecchi secoli, è indicativa di come fossero composte molte delle isole dell'Adriatico.

Età Media: primi inizi

Dopo la fine del periodo romano, i vari popoli slavi emigrarono nella regione della Croazia costiera. Anche se le popolazioni slave entrarono nei Balcani nel sesto secolo, il loro insediamento nelle isole del Quarnero avvenne molto più tardi. Sebbene risultino elementi archeologici di un'occupazione a Unie, a Baia di Mirisce, tra il primo e il quarto secolo d.C., tale presenza non è segnalata durante il sesto e l'ottavo secolo, per la mancanza di nuclei abitativi permanenti nell'isola durante il primo periodo dell'Età Media. (4) Tra il sesto e l'undicesimo secolo le isole si spopolarono per una serie di motivi, tra i quali le malattie ed un governo bizantino debole. Quando nell'ottavo secolo la flotta saracena conquistò l'isola di Sansego, vicino ad Unie, non si seppe se quegli abitanti sopravvissero allora. Anche se Sansego fu occupata fino al 1071, Unie fu probabilmente presa dopo quella data. (5)

Unie rimase verosimilmente disabitata durante la maggior parte del tredicesimo secolo, essendo nuovamente occupata in anni indefiniti del secolo successivo, perchè nell'isola di Unie rimangono evidenti le tracce di muri che risalgono al 1477 (6), il che induce a pensare ad uno stanziamento permanente. La popolazione moderna delle isole del Quarnero, attorno a Lussino, comincia nel 1280 con l'insediamento di Obrado Harvovich (Harvojic) e di dodici famiglie provenienti dalla Dalmazia, nell'attuale Lussingrande. (7) (8)

Gradualmente le famiglie a Lussino crearono un secondo insediamento. Questi due ultimi sono stati denominati Velo Selo e Mali Selo e probabilmente si svilupparono nei centri Veli Losinj (Lussingrande) e Mali Losinj (Lussinpiccolo). Le isole vicine di Ilovik (Asinello) e di Unie furono probabilmente abitate posteriormente alla migrazione a Lussino. La famiglia Rerecich è stata una delle prime a stabilirsi a Lussino e, successivamente a Unie.

Presto si unirono altri gruppi e vennero a formarsi famiglie estese che si divisero i compiti di lavoro. A Unie i fratelli della famiglia Nicolich (Agatin) costruirono quattro case adiacenti che esistono ancor oggi. La tradizione orale racconta che queste case furono costruite con un provento di denaro celato in un nascondiglio segreto. Un altro gruppo di case fu eretto dalle famiglie Bravarof Carcich, utilizzando le collette per la chiesa.

Le persone di Lussinpiccolo possedevano i *polje* o campi pianeggianti a Unie, ai confini occidentali dell'isola, dove piantarono delle vigne, lavorate e custodite dalle loro donne. Gli abitanti di Unie si presero cura delle loro viti e seminarono i loro campi sull'altro lato dell'isola ove dovevano guidare i loro buoi attraverso le colline dell'isola, per raggiungere i piccoli appezzamenti di terra. Le terre di *polje* furono acquistate più tardi dai residenti di Unie, procedimento che è andato avanti fino agli inizi del ventesimo secolo, sebbene alcune famiglie di Lussino continuassero a possedere degli appezzamenti a Unie nel secolo scorso. Nel periodo medioevale famiglie slave vissero e lavorarono insieme in *zadrugas*, formando altre grandi famiglie, amministrate solitamente da fratelli.

Le *zadrugas* erano delle collettività nell'antica Croazia, Bosnia, Serbia e Montenegro e si basavano su un'antica struttura sociale, dal momento dell'arrivo dei primi slavi in Croazia. Nell'economia contadina, il denaro non era una componente importante e i contadini dipendevano soprattutto dai prodotti dei loro campi e dal loro bestiame. In questa società, la *zadruga* costituiva un vantaggio perché metteva in comune i prodotti agricoli e gli attrezzi per poterne usufruire in un'economia comune. Una *zadruga* era solitamente composta da un numero di fratelli o di zii imparentati tra loro. Le case, in una *zadruga*, erano abitate da fratelli sposati, in stanze separate con il loro camino individuale, però spesso sotto lo stesso tetto. La proprietà veniva ereditata in parti uguali tra fratelli e genitore.

Le *zadrugas* continuarono a esistere in Croazia fino al 19° secolo, quando persero di importanza a causa della comparsa della proprietà e della ricchezza privata. Unie, precedentemente, era costituita da famiglie che lavoravano nel tipo di economia della *zadruga*, mentre altre famiglie lavoravano come nucleo o come singole. Questo spiega perché Unie possedeva un numero notevole di famiglie che vivevano in certi casi fianco a fianco e altre vivevano in abitazioni singole. Qualsiasi influenza che avessero potuto avere le *zadrugas* in Unie, scomparve all'inizio del 20° secolo, sebbene tale influenza avesse cominciato a perdersi nel secolo precedente.

 I residenti di una zadruga riconoscevano un antenato comune e portavano lo stesso nome. Era conosciuto come stirpe (bratstvo). Questo lignaggio proveniva da un capostipite, usualmente maschio, però quando una vedova si sistemava in famiglia separata con i suoi figli, anch'essa poteva divenire una capostipite. Tali lignaggi avevano nomi di gruppo che finivano in –ić, -ović o -ičić. Altre discendenze prendevano un nome patronimico, basato sul cognome paterno e terminante in –ov, -ev, -ef o –in. Alcuni nomi di lignaggio facevano riferimento a questi patronimici. Tali lignaggi venivano aggiunti ai cognomi, in modo tale che le famiglie potevano avere sia il cognome che il nome di lignaggio. Ad Unie un terzo delle famiglie portava il cognome Carcich/Karcich, però un gran numero di lignaggi distingueva le diverse famiglie Carcich/Karcich. I lignaggi Carcich comprendono: Andricev, Baldic/Baldich, Bardar, Bravarof, Cicola (trovato in Cunski), Gevin/Jevin, Pasquic/Pasquich, Prussian, Rocov e Zburkin.

Secoli XVI e XVII

Unie risulta come *Nia* sulle mappe dei secoli XVI e XVII, mentre a partire dai documenti del XVIII secolo si aggiunge una vocale iniziale che risulta nelle varianti di *onia* e *unij*. Verso la fine del XVI secolo esisteva un piccolo insediamento nell'isola ed è probabile che esistessero anche altri nuclei temporanei in quell'epoca. Agricoltori e viticoltori si trovano a Unie a partire dal 1588 (9). Nel 1600 le isole di Lussino, Asinello, Sansego e Unie contavano circa mille anime, di cui da seicento a settecento residenti a Lussino e il resto a Unie, Sansego e Asinello (10). Se distribuiamo i trecento abitanti in queste isole e tenendo conto che Sansego aveva il doppio di abitanti rispetto a Unie, questo paese nel 1600 aveva dunque una popolazione tra i settantacinque e i cento abitanti.

L'inizio della storia moderna di Unie è stata turbolenta, dovuto agli spostamenti della popolazione, causati dalle incursioni turche sulla terraferma. Gli Uskoks che spesso depredavano le isole attorno a Unie, si rifugiavano nella piccola baia di Gnisca, a nord dell'isola. Gli Uskoks erano persone sradicate dalla Dalmazia e dall'interno dei Balcani, a seguito dell'occupazione turca. Si sistemarono lungo le coste adriatiche, avendo la loro base principale a Senj, a circa 57 km a nord-est di Unie. Essi inizialmente assalirono le zone turche della Dalmazia, ma più tardi cominciarono ad attaccare e a depredare la penisola istriana e le isole del Quarnero. Era in uso per gli Uskoks compiere razzie di bestiame e appropriarsi di beni. La tradizione locale racconta che sulle alture di Stiene si trovavano di guardia delle vedette per avvisare gli abitanti dell'avvicinarsi dei pirati. In certe occasioni gli Uskoks attaccavano in gran numero. Nel 1543 depredarono Cherso, Ossero e incendiarono Lussino. Le autorità veneziane costruirono una torre sull'isola di Canicole Grande nel 1573 per proteggere gli abitanti nell'area intorno a Unie. La popolazione locale fu tassata per la costruzione della torre e per altre misure difensive (11). Si ripeterono attacchi contro Ossero negli anni 1573, 1575, 1605 e 1614. Sansego venne attaccata nel 1579 e nel 1617. Lussingrande e Lussinpiccolo vennero nuovamente attaccati nel 1580 e nel 1614.

Nel mese di agosto del 1612, quattordici navi Uskoks usarono l'isola di Unie come base per assalire le navi in quell'area (12). Durante la guerra tra Venezia e l'Austria, dal 1614 al 1617, gli Uskoks non trovarono ostacoli per depredare l'Istria e il Quarnero, ma nel 1617 l'Austria che amministrava il quartier generale di Senj, firmò un trattato di pace con Venezia e accettò di risistemare gli Uskoks all'interno. Terminava così il lungo regno della pirateria Uskoks attorno a Unie e alle isole vicine.

Maračol, Mišnjak e isola di Lussino

Storie non confermate dicono che alcuni Uskoks si stabilirono a Unie (13). I furti di bestiame comunque non cessarono dopo che gli Uskoks furono dispersi, ma continuarono ad affliggere le isole nel diciottesimo secolo, attraverso incursioni sporadiche dei nuovi coloni in Istria e al nord-ovest di Unie.

Nel 1588 sono registrati i nomi degli agricoltori di Unie, in una transazione riguardante la vendita di vigneti tra Zorzem Pracin e Tomic Susnačić, figlio di Jakov. Questi cognomi non esistono più in nessuna di queste isole, ma Pracin può essere stato trasformato in Pagien (Pajcen), cognome trovato nella prima metà del XVII secolo in Lussinpiccolo. Nel 1591 altri vigneti, a Unie, furono coltivati da Mikula Dalgčić, Mikoli Posibelić, Mikula Skrivanić, Marka Dorčić, e Matic Digčić. I testamenti indicano altri coltivatori proprietari di terre a Unie. La famiglia Scrivanich prese in affitto delle terre nella vicina isola di Canicole Grande ed i loro vigneti a Unie furono a loro volta affittati. Nel 1608 Petar Gojaković vendette il suo vigneto a Martin Žižić e nel 1618, Antonic Skrivanić lasciò in testamento il suo vigneto a Unie ai "fratelli di Sant'Antonio" e due anni più tardi, il figlio Antonio di Antonio Raguzinić donò loro il suo vigneto (14). Componenti dei Ducich e Radoslovich (15) sono registrati come abitanti di Unie nel 1620 e nel 1630. Alcune di queste famiglie lavorarono come mezzadri, fornendo una parte dei loro prodotti, come decima ai proprietari.

I cognomi ritrovati a Unie nei secoli XVI e XVII provengono da tre aree diverse e si riferiscono alle rotte migratorie delle prime famiglie di Unie. Uno di questi gruppi comprendeva i cognomi Halić, Ragusinić, Rerecich, Skrivanić e Nicolich (Mikulić) e appare agli inizi del XVI secolo nei registri della chiesa di Lussinpiccolo e lo stesso avvenne a Lussino durante la colonizzazione di quell'isola da sud. Un altro gruppo comprende i cognomi Ducich, Zurich, e Zizic che provengono pure da sud, dalla regione della Dalmazia in particolare. Un altro gruppo consistente di cognomi proviene dalla regione a nord di Unie. Questo gruppo include Dorcich, Gojaković, Zuanich (Ivanić) e

Matiasich ritrovati in Istria, (Raguzin), Raguzinic sull'isola di Veglia, Dedich da Arbe e Radoslovich e Velcich dall'isola di Cherso. È interessante notare che molti dei cognomi menzionati nelle querele, come Radoslovich e Rerecich, sono presenti attualmente sull'isola oggi, mentre altri, come Matiasich e Dedich, non sono rimasti nell'isola.

Alcuni dei cognomi che vengono associati in seguito a Unie, appaiono presto nella regione. Una famiglia Radoslovich si trovava ad Unie nel 1624. Le famiglie Rerecich a Unie risultano originate da due fratelli: Jeric e Sime (Simon) da Lussingrande, da cui si svilupparono i due clan Rerecich più importanti di Unie: i lignaggi Jercich e Simef. I Rerecich arrivarono all'isola di Lussino durante il 13° secolo. Nel 1684 il cognome Karčić (Carcich) appare in relazione con Unie, per mezzo del cognome Nadalin, che si rimonta al 16° secolo a Lussinpiccolo, dove appare nella forma di Nadalinić. Un Luka Karčić si trova associato alla città di Vrbnik, a Veglia nel 1490 e nel 1497. (17)

Nel 15° e 16° secolo il cognome Karčić con le relative derivazioni di Kerčić e di Karsić, si trova nell'isola di Veglia. (17) e più tardi la versione Chercich, appare nella cittadina di Cherso. Un lignaggio Karčić (Carcich), i Bravarof, si rimonta agli inizi del 18° secolo e oltre. Il termine generico bravari è usato per guardiani e pastori. I dati genetici possono illustrare che le famiglie Carcich (Karčić) si sono insediate vicino a Unie per un periodo più lungo di quanto dicano i documenti. L'autore, che è un Carcich, porta il DNA paterno che si accorda strettamente con i cromosomi Y che si trovano spesso nella popolazione della contea di Primorko-Goranska (18) alla quale appartengono Unie e Lussino.

Il flusso migratorio di famiglie a Unie, come nelle altre isole vicine, segue un corso sia a settentrione che a meridione. Questo sistema continua nel tempo fino al XIX secolo. Solitamente le famiglie si spostano dalle isole vicine, ma col passar del tempo un maggior numero di famiglie arriva dal continente. Durante il periodo, fino al 1943, una parte di migrazione viene dall'Italia, a causa delle rotte commerciali tra questa regione e le isole di Cherso e Lussino. È solamente nel secolo scorso che le migrazioni tradizionali da nord e da sud, furono rimpiazzate da quelle della Iugoslavia e oggi dall'interno della Croazia, dalla Bosnia e dalla Macedonia.

Gli abitanti di Unie vissero con le risorse della terra, allevando pecore, capre, maiali e bovini e, allo stesso tempo, coltivando le viti, gli olivi e facendo diversi raccolti di grano. Anche se i coloni delle isole intorno a Unie, come Sansego e Lussino si dedicarono alla pesca e al commercio marittimo, i coltivatori di Unie erano predisposti a questo lavoro. L'economia di Unie si basava sul gran numero di pecore, con i relativi prodotti di latte, formaggio e carne che si ricavavano. La maggior parte delle famiglie si prese cura dei propri greggi, avendo ognuno un marchio che indicava la proprietà e che veniva impressa sulle orecchie delle pecore (19). Questi marchi furono quindi trasmessi da padre in figlio. Si fa menzione che nel 1631 i bovari che lavoravano per la parrocchia di Unije non tenessero sufficientemente bene il bestiame e "sull'isola di Unie nelle acque del Quarnero noi abbiamo 20 capi di bestiame bovino, 100 pecore e 5 vacche e inoltre un numero imprecisato di giovenche che ancora succhiano il latte" (20).

La Chiesa Cattolica Romana rivestì un ruolo importante nella comunità. Altri documenti del 1650 menzionano che gli abitanti di Unie pagarono 400 lire veneziane per decime alla chiesa. I registri delle cresima a Unie nel 1677 indicano un Martin Chercich, Antonia Radoslovich, Antonio Susovich, Antonia Picinich, Antonia Guslomanich e Maria Dedich (21). L'isola di Unie fu posseduta e amministrata dal Vescovo di Ossero. I contadini, nell'isola di Unie, rimanevano sottomessi alla chiesa. Nel settembre del 1679, i residenti locali cercarono di essere sollevati dal pagamento di un terzo della loro produzione al vescovo di Ossero e all'Abbazia di San Pietro. Nella causa del 13 giugno 1680 dell'Ufficio episcopale di Ossero e dell'Abbazia di San Pietro, i querelanti erano contro i bovari di Unie, o pastori, e gli individui seguenti: Kasper Zuanich, Luke Robcich, Zane Matiasich, Anton Velcich, Nickolas Dedich, Anton Radoslovich, Frane Zauncich, Nicholas Rerecich, Luke Rerecich, Anton Zurich. Le ragioni della questione erano il pagamento di una decima per la chiesa sul bestiame ed una tassa statale. Il testo completo del litigio appare nell'appendice di questo libro.

I residenti di Unie persero la loro causa contro la chiesa. Nella sentenza il giudice ordinò agli abitanti di Unie di:

> "prendersi preferibilmente cura dei loro vigneti e delle altre coltivazioni [e di provvedere] ogni anno a pagare la terza parte, libera di decima, di tutta la produzione di grano, di avena, di miglio, di segale, di legumi di tutti i generi e di erba medica che sarà raccolta sull'isola senza detrarre lo "zobure" e il "potkupje e il "mast", dei prodotti di vino e dei vini di ogni tipo presenti sull'isola... Un quinto completo della produzione di ogni vigneto sarà diviso tra l'Abbazia di San Pietro a Ossero e il Vescovado, così come la decima che i coloni pagheranno sui prodotti citati, e la quarta parte che sarà il terratico. Loro pagheranno la decima sui vitelli, come sugli agnelli nati ogni anno dalle pecore e capre di questi greggi che appartengono all'Abbazia e all'Ufficio vescovile. Questo riguarderà anche gli animali appena nati appartenenti ai pastori (22).

Tale accordo unilaterale si rinforzò attraverso diverse generazioni, poiché il litigio fa menzione che tutti gli abitanti "di Onie e i loro successori devono mantenerlo e osservarlo in maniera inviolabile, senza opporvisi, sotto nessun pretesto, tributi o fazioni immaginabili: così, da obbligare i due contendenti e i loro eredi nella forma più amplia possibile"(22). Così, gli abitanti dovevano pagare parte dei loro prodotti alla chiesa, in forma di reddito e di normale tributo e inoltre dovevano pagare le tasse allo stato, per la costruzione delle difese che i veneziani edificarono attorno a Unie. Questa situazione lasciò gli abitanti appena al di sopra della condizione di servi, legati alla terra e non in grado di sostenersi durante i periodi di carestia.

La chiesa in Unie

La chiesa di Sant'Andrea Apostolo, aperta di giorno, fu costruita nel 1680. Questa chiesa esiste ancora ed è ubicata nel cimitero. La chiesa cattolica romana a Unie era retta da un prete locale che ne dava conto al vescovo di Ossero. Un orcio di pietra trovato presso la famiglia Nicolich (Agatin) conteneva olio d'oliva, con un'iscrizione del prete, Matij Brnich, datata 1676. Nell'iscrizione, in Glagolitico croato si legge:

CHNE NA DAN IG MISECA IJULIJA JA MATIJ BRNIĆ UČINIH TU KAMENICU (23) (1676, il 24 luglio, io don Matteo Brnich feci questo bacino di pietra). Il testo è in croato, inciso nell'antico Glagolitico.

Gran parte della vita religiosa degli abitanti fu amministrata da preti glagolitici, come Matij Brnich di Veglia, come si legge in un orcio per l'olio, del 1676. Le messe furono celebrate in Slavonico e i registri di battesimi, matrimoni e decessi furono registrati nella scrittura Glagolitica. Queste usanze erano conosciute dalle comunità vicine di Cunski e di Lussinpiccolo e furono ugualmente mantenute a Unie.

L'uso del Glagolitic a Unie, indica che la parrocchia dell'isola aveva diritto ad avere i servizi della chiesa in croato e letti in Glagolitico antico. Solo alcune delle parrocchie sull'Adriatico, avevano diritto a celebrare messe, battesimi e funerali in croato. Questo era un diritto che si riportava ai primi croati che giunsero nelle isole intorno a Unie nel X secolo. Poiché questo diritto si estese prima della separazione tra la chiesa cattolica romana e la chiesa Greco-Ortodossa, la chiesa croata continuò ad operare in autonomia quando si cominciò ad usare il vernacolo natio. Nonostante le isole del Quarnero e parte dell'Istria e Dalmazia fossero sotto l'amministrazione della Chiesa Cattolica Romana, esse avevano diritto ad adoperare la lingua e la scrittura croata nei loro servizi. Molte chiese croate nelle comunità costiere, non usarono il latino nelle loro funzioni religiose, bensì usarono una forma arcaica di croato precedente all'uso del vernacolo nella chiesa protestante, da parecchie centinaia di anni.

1676 Giara per l'olio con l'iscrizione di Kamenica, Unie

Gli immigranti slavi che arrivarono nelle isole del Quarnero, portarono con loro una nuova lingua scritta in alfabeto slavo, il Glagolitico. L'alfabeto Glagolitico fu portato nelle isole dell'Adriatico settentrionale dagli immigranti slavi che penetrarono lentamente nell'area, dall'interno: deriva dalla scrittura originale creata dai santi missionari slavi Cirillo e Metodio, che convertirono le tribù slave della Moravia, della Slovenia e della Croazia nel nono secolo. Quando Metodio morì nel 884 d.C, la scrittura del Glagolitico fu mantenuta dal clero slavo in Istria e in altre parti della Croazia occidentale e continuò in uso nelle parrocchie cattoliche romane dove c'era una comunità slava. Gli scritti religiosi in Glagolitico produssero libri cattolici, come messali, inni di chiesa e breviari in slavo, lingua usata dalla Chiesa Slavo-Croata, una variante del vecchio croato. Più tardi i testi ufficiali furono scritti in Glagolitico, adoperando il dialetto locale Cakavian, come si parla nella Croazia litoranea.

La chiesa a Unie, nel diciassettesimo secolo, celebrava le funzioni religiose in Glagolitico, utilizzando i libri, sempre in Glagolitico, sin dal 1744 (24). In quell'anno la chiesa di Sant'Andrea a Unie è menzionata dal vescovo italiano come avente *Carte nuove in illirico* e un *Messale nuovo illirico (Nuovo Messale Glagolitico)*. Cent'anni prima, il prete a Unìe, nel 1647, era Don Marco Petrina. Il vescovo di Ossero assieme all'abate di San Pietro, pure di Ossero, amministrarono l'isola di Unie facendovi delle visite annuali, tradizione che perdura tutt'oggi. Durante le visite del vescovo nel 1670, nel 1671 e nel 1674, molti libri di chiesa sono menzionati in glagolitico: un Rituale Illirico, un Evangeliario, così come molti messali ed un messale latino. A questo punto il parroco è menzionato come Taddeo Vitcouich in italiano e Tadija Vitković, in croato. Nel giugno del 1785 un Messale Il lirico, elencato nella chiesa di Sant'Andrea, indica che il glagolitico era in uso a Unie alla fine del 18° secolo (24). La scarsità di libri di chiesa in glagolitico e la mancanza di preti capaci di leggerli, probabilmente contribuirono all'abbandono del croato nelle funzioni religiose. La lingua slava in Chiesa e la scrittura glagolitica furono sostituite dalla lingua italiana e dalla scrittura romana, così che intorno al 1803 il glagolitic non è più in uso a Unie.

La prima canonica, all'interno del paese, è stata costruita nel 1753, secondo l'iscrizione sull'architrave della porta: "1753 D.T.R." Si ritiene che questa casa sia la prima costruita a Unie con un tetto di tegole e con i muri in calcare tagliato e levigato. La torre campanaria della chiesa di Sant'Andrea fu costruita nel 1857 e la fontana pubblica, di fronte alla chiesa nel 1886. Le campane in uso durante il governo austriaco probabilmente sono state fuse durante la prima guerra mondiale. Queste furono sostituite da una coppia di campane nel 1918 e finalmente rimpiazzate con campane elettroniche nei primi anni del 1990. Sebbene iniziata nel tardo 18° secolo, la chiesa di Sant'Andrea fu ampliata più tardi, acquisendo la sua forma attuale nel 1911 ed alcuni ritocchi furono eseguiti nei primi anni del 1960, del 1980 e nuovamente nel 2006. Il dipinto di Nostra Signora del Carmelo, sopra l'altare maggiore e le colonne marmoree sono in stile barocco.

Madonna vicino lago

Capella

Secolo XVIII

Parecchi nuovi cognomi di famiglie appaiono in relazione ai registri dell'isola nel 18° secolo. Questi sono Bellanich, Haglich, Galosich, Giurich, Mancich, Nicolich, Ragusin e Valich. Gli archivi riscontrano un numero di famiglie Carcich che vivevano a Unie durante le prime decadi del 18° secolo. Nel 1715 si conferma il cognome Carcich con Cristoforo, figlio di Paolo, Biaso Carcich figlio di Piero e un Paolo Carcich (25).

Alcune delle più antiche famiglie di Unie possono trarre le loro origini direttamente da un ancestro nella prima parte del 18° secolo. Durante questo periodo i cognomi familiari fecero riferimento al lignaggio bratstvo. Nomi di lignaggio (conosciuto come nadimak in croato e soprannome in Italiano) si usano comunemente per distinguere le famiglie tra di loro. Spesso un cognome può contenere parecchi nomi di lignaggio. I nomi di lignaggio si basano su di un nome personale, una località o una professione e spesso traggono origine da un soprannome che più tardi viene formalmente adottato dalle future generazioni di una famiglia. I Carcich (Bravarof) sopra menzionati, si rifanno agli inizi del 18° secolo e parecchi rami della famiglia si svilupparono a Unie e a Cunski. I Radoslovich (Kalcic)si rimontano a Martin Radoslovich (1715-1750), sebbene non è chiaro quando sia stato adottato questo nome di lignaggio.

Dai registri di matrimonio di Lussinpiccolo tra il 1710 ed il 1740 (26) risulta un certo numero di famiglie residenti a Unie. Questi includono: Biaso Bellanich, Karstić Karcić, Matteo Karcich, Martin Karcic, Matteo Giurich, Matij Halic, Gasparo Nicolich, Martin Nicolich, Franić Radoslović, Gaspar Radoslovich, Karstić Radoslović Martin Radoslovich, Mattio Radoslovich Simun Radoslović, Augustin Rerecić, Martin Rerecić, Matij Rerecić, Mikula Rerecich e Jivan Valic.

I registri di Lussingrande mostrano che c'erano almeno 24 famiglie a Unie. Queste erano: Bellanich (1 famiglia), Carcich (5 famiglie), Galosich (1 famiglia), Giurich (1 famiglia), Haglich (1 famiglia), Mancich (1 famiglia), Nadalin (1 famiglia), Nicolich (2 famiglie), Radoslovich (5 famiglie), Ragusin (1 famiglia), Rerecich (3 famiglie), Valich (2 famiglie).

Basandosi sul numero esiguo di individui registrati a Unie tra il 1720 e il 1730, vi erano in quell'epoca almeno 68 individui ivi residenti. Poiché le persone registrate avevano inoltre i propri figli, per i quali non esistono dati, abbiamo un conteggio insufficiente e famiglie come Bellanich e Nicolich sono elencate a seguito, dove risulta chiaro che il conteggio qui riportato non è sufficiente per fornire un numero esatto di residenti a Unie. Più realisticamente tale numero potrebbe essere raddoppiato, così la popolazione di Unie salirebbe a 136 persone.

Nel primo periodo del 1700, sarebbe risultato quindi "un collo di bottiglia" in termini di partners di matrimoni praticabili. Si può presumere che questo rappresenti la prima generazione adulta pronta per contrarre matrimonio dopo l'arrivo di nuovi coloni nel tardo 17° o all'inizio del 18° secolo. Con una popolazione così esigua a Unie in quest'epoca, quelli che volevano sposarsi dovevano cercare moglie in altre comunità. Lussinpiccolo sarebbe stato il posto ideale per cercare spose, poiché si trovava vicino e aveva una popolazione molto superiore a quella di Unie.

Altri cognomi che non esistono più a Unie si trovano nei vari registri dal 1740 al 1783 ed includono Juric (Giurich), Marcic, Ivancich Ragusin Riezo e Sepcich. (27) (28) Mattio Giurich formò una famiglia a Unie dopo il 1740 e, sebbene i suoi discendenti fossero deceduti a Unie nel 19° secolo, la sua famiglia proviene da Lussino fin dal 17° secolo. La genealogia di questa famiglia Giurich si trova in questo volume. Similmente, una delle famiglie Nicolich di Unie discende dalle famiglie di Lussingrande nel 17° secolo. Qualche cognome può essersi estinto quando i loro discendenti si sposarono con altre famiglie di Unie. Qualche cognome non aumentò di numero. Per esempio la famiglia Valich restò a Unie con pochi membri. Jivan Valić di Antonio, si sposò nel 1722, e Maria Valić di Jivan si sposò nel 1726. Il numero esiguo delle attuali famiglie Valić di Unie, può attribuirsi al gran numero di femmine contro le nascite di maschi con questo cognome attraverso gli ultimi duecento anni. In seguito molte famiglie Carcich e Radoslovich di Unie si stabiliscono a Lussinpiccolo e a Cunski. Le famiglie Radoslovich da Lussingrande e le famiglie Carcich da Cunski si trovano nell'elenco genealogico di questo volume.

Alla fine del 1770, Alberto Fortis (1741-1803), un naturalista italiano, scrittore di viaggi e frate, visitò le isole di Cherso e Lussino e il racconto in inglese della sua visita fu inviato a John Strange, Vescovo di Londonderry. All'epoca in cui Alberto Fortis passò da Unie, l'isola aveva una popolazione stabile, forse di 150 o 200 individui. Comunque per il mondo esterno, gli abitanti di Unie avevano poca importanza, così che Fortis poté scrivere:

> *[Unie] ha pochi abitanti e questi eccessivamente poveri. Il prodotto principale è la legna da ardere poiché gran parte del territorio è boschivo. Probabilmente produce miele e cera in abbondanza e allevano bestiame bovino; ma la produzione è scarsa, per ragioni evidenti ai nostri giorni, specialmente per coloro che si applicano allo studio di economia pubblica. Nelle acque di Onie [Unie] la pesca è una risorsa importante; essa*

consiste principalmente in tonno, sgombro e sardelle; i poveri abitanti però non possono trarne profitto e gli estranei sottraggono loro tutto il guadagno sotto i loro occhi (29).

Pescando lungo la costa, sempre che ci fosse stato del pesce, si usavano amo e lenza come fu in uso più tardi, ma forniva solamente una quantità limitata di alimenti. La campagna e le greggi furono le forme principali di sostentamento sull'isola. Con la parte nord dell'isola coperta di boschi, Unie produceva legna da ardere per l'esportazione. Fortis menziona "la legna da ardere come un prodotto considerevole di commercio… Gli alberi usati comunemente per legna da ardere sono: quercia sempreverde, olmo argentato e inoltre viti selvatiche, *arbutus, pheleaea*, ginepro e altri" Due abitanti di Lussinpiccolo, i cui genitori erano di Unie trasportavano legna da ardere da Cherso e Lussinpiccolo a Venezia nel 18° secolo. Mattia Carcich figlio di Paolo e Cristoforo Radoslovich, figlio di Simone, entrambi viaggiavano da Lussino a Venezia regolarmente (30).

Dopo il ritiro degli Uskoks, la navigazione nel Quarnero ebbe la possibilità di riprendersi. Comunque ai loro danni si aggiunsero dei disastri naturali. Ci furono molti naufragi intorno a Unie. Nel maggio del 1757 a metà isola di Unie, una nave di Segna si trovò in difficoltà. Nel mese di novembre del 1764, tra l'isola di Unie e Canidole, la nave San Giuseppe, al comando di Andrea Sreglich, discendente dagli Scrapona, ebbe difficoltà a superare i banchi di sabbia. Il San Giuseppe aveva lasciato Venezia facendo rotta verso Corfu e Salonicco. Nell'ottobre del 1786, sulla piccola isola di Misgnac, lungo la costa est di Unie due piccole imbarcazioni si scontrarono e persero parte alcuno del loro carico di legname (31). Gli abitanti di Unie raramente si dedicarono al commercio marittimo o della pesca. Fu principalmente un secolo dopo che gli uomini di Unie emigrati negli Stati Uniti divennero stivatori. La pesca nelle acque circostanti fu lasciata ad altri delle vicine isole e nel 19° secolo ai pescatori dell'Italia, particolarmente di Chioggia. In seguito, altri lavori marittimi coinvolsero il trasporto di merci tra le isole e la terra ferma.

Fortis fornisce notizie sui lavori agricoli più conosciuti nelle isole del Quarnero. Egli scrive: "Ogni casa ha il suo piccolo giardino e le donne sono molto robuste e abituate a portare carichi molto pesanti sulla loro testa, sia andando in su che in giù dalle colline; i bambini delle famiglie povere sono abituati a lavorare sin dalla tenera età, sia coltivando la terra che pescando o accudendo al bestiame bovino…molti lavorano la rascia, che è un tipo di lana ruvida.

I buoi non sono sempre usati per arare la terra, però questo lavoro è

quasi sempre portato a termine dalle braccia robuste degli uomini, che generalmente sono ben pagati per il loro lavoro, in proporzione alla scarsità di mano d'opera. Questi lavoratori svolgono veramente una grande quantità di lavoro, più dei

> *nostri. Per prima cosa essi sono obbligati a ripulire la loro*
> *porzione di terreno dalle pietre e quello è un lavoro continuo.*
> *Queste pietre loro le adoperano per creare un muro di*
> *recinzione nel loro appezzamento. Generalmente questi campi*
> *hanno una figura circolare o ellittica e sono chiamati coronale*
> *dagli isolani". (32)*

Egli segnala che le coltivazioni erano prevalentemente di ulivi e di viti, e c'erano grandi greggi di pecore. Seppur la maggior parte delle osservazioni di Fortis furono fatte mentre si trovava a Cherso, queste si riferirebbero ugualmente a Unie e alle altre isole del Quarnero. C'erano quantità limitate di granturco e le patate erano sconosciute in queste isole. I fichi erano la frutta primaria, mentre pesche, pere ed albicocche erano scarse. Una certa radice della pianta Arus fu usata per fare il pane, sebbene Fortis la ritenne non nutritiva. "L'olio viene esportato dall'isola; ma quasi tutto il guadagno viene utilizzato per l'acquisto di mais, le cui coltivazioni sono sufficienti agli abitanti per mantenerli quattro mesi all'anno... Il vino non è di buona qualità in proporzione all'olio. Questo probabilmente si deve alla poca conoscenza che hanno sulla vendemmia, sulla pigiatura dell'uva e sulla fermentazione del vino". (33) Fortis descrive la diligenza con cui si prendono cura delle viti:

> *gli isolani usano stendere ogni anno un mucchietto di terra su*
> *ogni vite, che è tenuta molto bassa e quasi totalmente spoglia di*
> *tralci e questi cumuli mantengono le radici fresche nella*
> *stagione asciutta e d'inverno e durante la stagione ventosa della*
> *primavera servono per coprire completamente le viti. Essi*
> *piantano comunemente le viti, come noi facciamo con il mais*
> *indiano. (34)*

"Le pecore sono la specie più numerosa di quadrupedi sull'isola; buoi, animali da soma e porci non sono in gran numero... Ogni proprietario di greggi o molti di loro insieme, le affidano a un pastore e ogni pecora ha un taglio diverso nell'orecchia per distinguerne l'appartenenza". (35)

Il 18 secolo fu testimone di furti di bestiame sull'isola di Cherso. Fortis afferma che "i ladri morlacchi, e particolarmente quelli delle colonie dell'Istria: Castelnuovo, Carnizza, Medolino, e Altura molto spesso arrivano sull'isola e portano via tutti gli animali di ogni specie che riescono a mettere insieme e ciò avviene frequentemente sotto gli occhi dei custodi stessi che non sono in condizioni di opporsi a predoni armati (36) Ci è stato riferito che gli abitanti, a Unie, mentre facevano la guardia contro i ladri, dai gusci ritrovati, risulta evidente che hanno mangiato lumache mentre stavano di vedetta sulla collina".

Molte delle case Unie, in quest'epoca, erano piccole capanne di pietra con tetti ricoperti di paglia, senza finestre. Durante la sua visita all'isola di Sansego, Fortis (37) descrive queste case aventi " una sola apertura che serve come porta, finestra e sbocco per il fumo; non ci sono divisioni nell'interno; neppure un pavimento, eccetto quello in terra battuta che è più basso rispetto all'esterno". Queste condizioni di vita per famiglie numerose abitanti una piccola capanna, con poca ventilazione, non erano salubri. Nel periodo di Fortis, la popolazione di Lussinpiccolo, aveva sofferto un'epidemia di vaiolo e la dissenteria era presente nel paese di Cherso (38); la salute degli abitanti di Ossero era spesso minacciata dalla malaria, al punto che anche il vescovo di quel luogo stette via buona parte dell'anno da Cherso. Le vie di comunicazione con Unie passavano attraverso Ossero e Lussino per cui gli abitanti di Unie presero queste malattie venendo a contatto con gli abitanti di questi paesi.

Sebbene il dialetto croato locale fu usato dalle persone comuni, l'influenza dell'italiano era egualmente in crescita, dovuto probabilmente al contatto commerciale con le altre isole e con i mercanti del continente. Fortis (39) rileva che la lingua croata, o lo schiavone, come egli lo chiamò, su Cherso e Lussinpiccolo è "diffusa più estensivamente degli altri dialetti europei ed è usata comunemente dalle persone e dai contadini dell'isola." Riferendosi al discorso di S. Vito (Fiume), Fortis afferma che "la lingua del paese è il croato, ma tutte le persone colte di ambo i sessi parlano un buon italiano." Lo stesso vale per le lingue parlate nelle isole del Quarnero.

La Chiesa Cattolica Romana manteneva ancora una forte influenza nelle isole durante gli ultimi anni del 18°secolo. Fortis scrive:

> *Le decime dell'isola di Cherso e di Ossero sono distribuite in quattro parti. Una parte è assegnata ai poveri; la seconda è assegnata alla chiesa per riparazioni, ornamenti e altro; la terza appartiene ai Canonici di Cherso ed Ossero, Lubenice e Caisole; la quarta è assegnata al vescovo, per tutta la diocesi. Nei due Lussini, la parte del povero fu data tempo addietro al parroco e ai curati che non avevano fondi per la loro manutenzione (40).*

XIX secolo

L'inizio del 19° secolo annunziò un periodo nuovo con un'ascesa del nazionalismo e con una nuova amministrazione politica. Dopo le Guerre napoleoniche, Venezia non era più uno stato a sé e la sua supremazia sulle isole del Quarnero giunse alla fine. L'Austria assunse l'amministrazione civile e governò dal 1814 al 1918 e lo sviluppo della politica croata e italiana a Unie, probabilmente datano dal tempo di questo governo.

Il censimento del 1815 a Unie (41) registra 222 abitanti e 45 abitazioni sull'isola; il censimento del 1819 elenca 49 abitazioni dalle quali si deduce che quattro strutture nuove furono costruite in quattro anni, prima del 1819. Le popolazioni a Unie e a Sansego stavano aumentando rapidamente e questo spinse persone a cercare più terra coltivabile. Nel periodo di Fortis, la popolazione di Sansego contava approssimativamente 300 abitanti. Presto la sua popolazione aumentò rapidamente, come si nota dallo sviluppo del paese nel 1820, che si sviluppò verso la costa. A causa dell'incremento della popolazione e alla povertà del suolo per coltivare gli ulivi, alcuni abitanti di Sansego cominciarono a costruire ad Unie, sul lato orientale dell'isola. Questi abitanti di Sansego costruirono case e muri di contenimento. Tale insediamento fu abbandonato verso il 1850, dovuto alla resistenza degli altri abitanti di Unie che, a quel tempo, scacciarono questi nuovi venuti da Sansego.

La popolazione di Unie cominciò a svilupparsi nella prima metà del 19° Secolo e continuò a crescere nel secolo successivo con un massimo di 783 abitanti nel 1921. Ciò fu dovuto alla diminuzione della mortalità, come risultato di migliori risorse sanitarie. Lussingrande aveva un dottore nel 18° e nel 19° secolo e Unie ne trasse beneficio dalla vicinanza con la città.

Il registro dei decessi a Unie dal 1815 al 1880 mostra che gli isolani morirono a causa di una serie di fattori, tra cui la carestia, le febbri e le epidemie. L'aspettativa di vita alla nascita, basata su un campione di 243 defunti a Unie, durante il periodo dal 1815 al 1850, era di 35 anni di età. Ciò è simile ad altre comunità europee e a quelle trovate nello stesso periodo in Nord America. Tenendo come campione i decessi a Unie, fu compilata una tabella di rilevamento. Molti bambini morirono nei primi dieci anni di vita a causa delle varie malattie che contribuirono a tali morti. Se riuscivano a sopravvivere nei primi anni dell'infanzia, le persone avevano una buona possibilità di arrivare ai 50,

60, 70 o a 80 anni. Alcune famiglie a Unie hanno dei componenti vissuti fino ai 90 anni durante il tardo 19° secolo.

Parecchie famiglie di Unie hanno avuto un gran numero di componenti con il cancro, dovuto a cause genetiche. Il numero di malati di cancro nelle isole di Veglia, Cherso e Lussino risulta maggiore che nell'entroterra croato (42). Queste isole hanno una gran incidenza di cancro alla prostata, stomaco e pancreas nella popolazione maschile e cancro alle ovaie, petto, stomaco, intestino e cervello nelle femmine; l'incidenza si può paragonare alle cifre del continente. La migrazione storica tra le isole di Unie,Veglia Cherso e Lussino aiuta a spiegare perchè l'incidenza del cancro è superiore nelle isole.

Prospetto dei decessi 1815-1850		
Intervallo di anni	Numero dei decessi	Aspettativa
0-1	50	35.4
1-10	60	42.8
11-20	15	47.1
21-30	17	41.3
31-40	15	36.1
41-50	14	30.1
51-60	20	23.5
61-70	22	18.3
71-80	19	13.8
81-90	11	10.0

Il 19° secolo iniziò con nuove famiglie a Unie. Lovro Segota, originario di Jalanac, ebbe sei figli nati all'inizio del secolo. Le famiglie Cecco e Pillepich si stabilirono sull'isola durante la seconda metà del 19° secolo. Si dice che la famiglia Cecco provenisse da Ragusa, poiché ciò è basato sul lignaggio di famiglia; i primi archivi della famiglia Raguseo appaiono nei registri di Lussinpiccolo nella prima parte del 19° secolo, mentre i Pillepich sono arrivati da Fiume assieme ad altri Pillepich e si sono stabiliti a Lussinpiccolo nello stesso secolo. La famiglia di Giovanni (Ivan) Radoslovich del clan Mattesinich si era formata a Lussinpiccolo; più tardi egli si stabilì coi suoi genitori a Unie creando una grande famiglia, i cui discendenti sono ora sparsi in tutto il mondo. La famiglia Mattesinch di Lussinpiccolo ha il suo capostipite in Simone Radoslovich, originario di Unie, il quale morì prima del 1749.

Nonostante la famiglia Carcich (Bravarof) si rimonti al 18° secolo ed anche prima, qualche membro della famiglia Carcich deriva da questo lignaggio più antico. La famiglia di Antonio Carcich (Bravarof) e due altre (Bravarof) sono conosciute in questo periodo. Due di queste famiglie vivevano a Unìe. Un Bravarof, Martino, figlio di

Martino si sposò e formò una famiglia a Cunski, nell'isola di Lussino. Infatti molte famiglie Carcich, prima di questo periodo si stabilirono a Cunski. I Bravarof, Ciadic Cicuola, Pasquic e Vlasich, primi coloni, danno origine alle famiglie Carcich a Cunski.

Altre famiglie Carcich a Unie, tra il 1810 ed il 1820, furono i Jevin, Pasquich, Rocov, Andrijice, e Zburkin. La famiglia Zburkin inizia con Mikula Carcich che sposò una Stefanich, del nord di San Martino, nell'isola di Cherso e si sistemò a Unie con due figli, Mikula e Gaudenzio, nacquero nel 1786 e nel 1795 rispettivamente.

Giuseppe Rieger pubblicò nel 1845 delle scene panoramiche sulle coste dell'Istria e Dalmazia. L'immagine di Unie mostra il paese e parte dell'isola dal lato sud-ovest, sebbene alcune raffigurazioni non sono accurate. Ad esempio non ci sono vedute del "polje" o terra piatta che si protende sul mare ad ovest dell'isola. Altre immagini rappresentate da Rieger concordano con strutture tutt'oggi esistenti. L'immagine mostra molti sentieri o strade. Uno percorre il contorno di Kris, la collina sopra il paese e un altro dalla parte superiore di Kris si dirige verso i campi e i muri di contenimento che ancora sono visibili. Si distingue un certo numero di case.

Unie 1845, del Giuseppe Rieger

Durante la guerra tra l'Austria e lo stato italiano appena formato, nel 1866 Ivan Nicolich di Unie fu arruolato come coscritto di diciannove anni. Egli servì nella marina militare di Pola e neutralizzò l'azione sull'isola dalmata di Vis durante quella spedizione. In quest'azione, il 20 luglio 1866, la marina militare italiana attaccò le difese costiere di Vis per preparare uno sbarco anfibio. La marina militare italiana fu colta di sorpresa dalla marina militare austriaca che si diresse velocemente verso Vis e che affondò molte navi italiane durante l'attacco. Questa fu l'unica battaglia navale della Guerra austro-prussiana combattuta nell'Adriatico e fu anche l'ultima azione navale nella regione prima dell'inizio della prima Guerra mondiale. Uno stabilimento per inscatolare il pesce fu costruito vicino al porto, ma non era più in uso nel 1930, essendo già in rovina.

Nel 1885 gli abitanti chiesero al governo di istituire scuole italiane nell'isola (43). Probabilmente una scuola croata era già stata fondata prima, come fu per Sansego, che ebbe una scuola nel 1845.Un disegno di Giuseppe Rieger, nel 1845 mostra un edificio simile alla successiva scuola costruita vicino alla chiesa. Verso il 1888 esisteva una scuola sull'isola (44) e gli studenti imparavano il catechismo, la lettura, la scrittura e il far di conto da Padre Antonio Andrijčić. L'anno scolastico durava da ottobre a luglio, con esami due volte all'anno (45). L'insegnante, dal 1911-1912 fu Marija Fučić. L'anno successivo c'erano 39 studenti nella scuola croata. Lino Nicolich (Niccoli) (1894-1964) fondò una banca negli Stati Uniti e Andrea Karčić (1888-1972) divenne avvocato a Karlovac; ambedue iniziarono i loro studi nella scuola di Unie. Giovanni Radoslovich (1879-1973), di Unie, divenne maestro elementare nell'isola di Asinello, prima della Grande Guerra. In seguito Andrea Carcich (1921-2004), pure di Unie, divenne maestro elementare a Cunski, prima della seconda Guerra Mondiale.

Durante il 1893 e negli anni successivi, la *phyllossera,* un insetto che produce la peste dei vigneti, cominciò a distruggerli a Unie. Introdotta dall'America, la *phyllossera* (Daktulosphaira vitifoliae) decimò i vigneti dell'isola, fino a che una varietà di vitigno americano, innestato sulle viti locali, *(Vitis Vinifera)* si dimostrò resistente alla malattia. Le varietà di viti piantate ad Unie furono: *suscan, bielikuc, troviscia,plavac (zinfandel), jiakuc, belcina, boldun and muskat.* Le tre prime varietà erano le più produttive ad Unie.

20° secolo (XX secolo)

Il 20° secolo portò molti cambiamenti a Unie, sia con la guerra che con il cambio di lingua e con l'immigrazione. Il censimento del 1900 indica che a Unie ci sono 176 case e 696 abitanti. Il censimento divide i residenti tra quelli parlanti italiano e quelli croati, con 446 per i primi e 250 per gli altri. Queste divisioni linguistiche e culturali tra Italiani e Croati ebbero un ruolo importante nella formazione della comunità, specialmente a seguito della rottura con l'Impero Austriaco, dopo la prima Guerra Mondiale e l'insediamento dell'amministrazione italiana.

Furono create due cooperative a Unie basate sull'identità nazionale. Il risultato fu la costruzione di due frantoi, uno per gli italiani e uno per i croati. Dei due mulini sul porto, quello all'inizio del molo era italiano e l'altro, a sud del porto, era croato. Il frantoio croato fu iniziato nel '900 e quello italiano, circa nello stesso periodo. C'è un elenco dei membri del frantoio italiano nell'appendice. Uno stabilimento per sardine fu egualmente iniziato vicino alla parte sud del paese.

In questo periodo l'italiano diventò d'uso comune nell'isola. Parole prese dall'italiano appaiono nel dialetto di Unie prima del 1945. Qualche parola del dialetto quotidiano include: *liber* (gratuitamente) dal *libero* italiano; *mul* (bacino, *molo* in italiano), *libar* (*libro* in italiano); *fermat* (*fermare* in italiano), *funiestra* (*finestra* in italiano), *mestar* (insegnante, *maestro* in italiano), *iorda* (*giardino* in italiano) e *iornol* (*giornale* in italiano). Il dialetto di Unie contiene anche molte vecchie parole latine che sono entrate nella lingua locale attraverso un lungo periodo e si trovano anche nel croato comune e nei dialetti parlati sulla costa adriatica. Nel dialetto di Unie si trovano anche dei termini sloveni. C'è un numero ridotto di parole, usate nel dialetto di Unie, che sono più comuni in sloveno che in serbo-croato. Alberto Fortis rilevò che "delle parole in sloveno adoperate nell'isola di Veglia nel 1770, sono un gergo misto di schiavonico carnico, di latino e d'italiano."(46) Un'osservazione simile fu fatta all'inizio del 19° secolo dal linguista sloveno Oblak, pure a Veglia.

L'uso crescente dell'italiano, in questo periodo, può essere un fenomeno culturale recente, però il legame con lo sloveno può manifestarsi sia culturalmente che geneticamente, risalendo agli immigrati slavi, com'è evidente da una forte correlazione genetica tra la popolazione della Croazia occidentale e quella della Slovenia (47).

Durante la guerra morirono otto uomini di Unie, combattendo per l'esercito austriaco, specialmente sul fronte galiziano. Essi furono: Mate Nicolich (1894-1915), Zaccaria Nicolich (1875-1917), Andrea Nicolich, Ivan Carcich (morto 1917), Andrea Carcich, Antonio Carcich (1898-1917), Sime Nicolich (1885-1915) e Toni Radoslovich (morto nel 1915). Quando l'Italia partecipò alla prima Guerra mondiale, a fianco dell'Inghilterra e della Francia, il cacciatorpediniere austriaco *Viribus Unitis* si trovava lungo la costa italiana, vicino ad Ancona. Non appena l'Italia dichiarò guerra all'Austria, il cacciatorpediniere aprì il fuoco sulla ferrovia litoranea, provocando gravi danni. Sul sommergibile si trovava a quel tempo Toncich Segota di Unie, nato nel 1886. Un altro abitante di Unie, Luca Carcich, era invece sul cacciatorpediniere austriaco *Tegetthof*, quando abbatterono un aereo italiano.

Allorché l'Italia entrò in Guerra, alleata delle potenze Occidentali, Nazario Sauro, di Capodistria (Austria) si unì alle forze armate italiane. Mentre era al comando del sottomarino *Pullino*, il 1° agosto 1916, questo cominciò ad imbarcare acqua, nei pressi della piccola isola di Galiola, a otto chilometri a nord-ovest di Unie. Sauro portò il sottomarino alla fonda, di fronte a Galiola. L'equipaggio del sommergibile, sospettando di Nazario, sabotò il sottomarino e lo lasciò sull'isola, navigando subito dopo verso l'Italia, in un vascello catturato con la forza. Nazario, temendo le autorità austriache, riuscì a trovare una barca a remi e si diresse anch'egli verso l'Italia. Galiola, a quel tempo, aveva un faro e sull'isola vivevano quattro famiglie. Una di queste era la famiglia Nicolich, di Unie. Il capo di questa famiglia, Toni Nicolich ed un altro uomo, dopo che Nazario partì, si diressero verso Unie. Essi riuscirono a giungere al faro di Unie e poterono informare le autorità dell'incidente. Usando il telefono del faro, comunicarono l'accaduto agli austriaci di Pola, i quali inviarono una nave per recuperare l'equipaggio del sommergibile ed anche Nazario, prima che essi potessero raggiungere l'Italia. Nazario, temendo di essere riconosciuto dagli austriaci, tentò di sfregiarsi per modificare il suo aspetto. Le autorità, ciononostante, scoprirono la sua identità e chiamarono anche sua madre per identificarlo. Dopo un sommario processo, Nazario Sauro fu impiccato a Pola come traditore, il 10 agosto 1916. Più tardi furono erette statue in suo onore a Pola e a Galiola. Apparentemente il sottomarino fu rimorchiato nel canale di fronte a Pola e in seguito affondò in acque profonde, sebbene l'Italia asserisse di aver recuperato il sottomarino nel novembre del 1916. Durante la seconda Guerra mondiale un cavo telefonico fu posato accidentalmente da Galiola a Unie e i tedeschi distrussero il faro sull'isola durante la guerra. Il faro fu ricostruito in seguito.

Da 1919 a 1943 solamente la lingua italiana e la storia furono insegnate a scuola. L'asilo infantile fu aperto a Unie per i bambini di quattro anni. Venivano altresì svolte lezioni dalla prima alla quinta elementare, nonché alcune lezioni di scuola media. Oltre le materie insegnate nel periodo austriaco, si aggiunsero quelle di geografia, storia e fisica. (48). Nel 1929 si costruì una caserma militare a fianco della scuola.

Una stazione elettrica, funzionante con il generatore, operava dal 1932 fornendo parecchie ore di elettricità durante il giorno. Questa stazione dapprima fu utilizzata come luogo provvisorio d'inscatolamento del pesce. Un nuovo edificio per inscatolare il pesce sorse nella piccola baia di Maracol, gestita dalla società Arrigoni. La fabbrica assunse molte delle donne dell'isola come lavoratrici stagionali. Il tonno proveniva dal Mar Nero e le sardine dalla pesca locale. La fabbrica chiuse nel 1943, ma fu riaperta per un breve periodo dalle autorità iugoslave subito dopo la seconda Guerra mondiale.

Durante la seconda Guerra mondiale fu più difficile assumere personale, poiché molte famiglie erano emigrate negli Stati Uniti. Uomini delle famiglie di Unie combatterono pertanto negli eserciti italiani e degli Stati Uniti. Parecchi uomini lottarono per gli americani in Europa e nel Pacifico. John Nicolich, nato nel 1922 a Unie, fu paracadutato su Firenze, in Italia, durante la guerra degli americani, dove egli diventò una spia a favore di essi. Andric Nicolich (1921-1944), combattendo per le forze armate americane, morì in Europa lo stesso giorno di suo cugino, nato negli Stati Uniti da discendenti di Unie. Due componenti la famiglia di John Carcich combatterono nella guerra del Pacifico, come Andrew Karcich e Papà Joe Radoslovich. Un altro John Carcich morì a Saipan, alla fine della guerra.

St. Andrija Church 1930: Carabiniere, Andrea Radoslovich –Gartljic (1871-1947), Soldato, Jovanin Pillepich (1886-1948), Antonio Braiko (1922-), Nicolo Radoslovich (1921-1945), Giovanni Radoslovich (Kalcic), Soldato, Don Andrea Virla, Luigi Miceleti, Antonio or Marco Bellanich (Preruc) (1912-)? ,Francis Ferrara (1925-), Gasparo Carcich (1924-), Joseph Nicolich (1921-), Soldato, Osip Nicolich (Sancich) (1909-1993), Carabiniere.

Lino Nicolich (1894-1964), che aveva seguito i corsi presso l'Accademia Marittima di Lussino, comandò l'*Enrico Meigs*, una nave della compagnia *American Liberty* nel Pacifico. In precedenza Lino aveva combattuto nella Prima Guerra mondiale e fu insignito con la seconda onorificenza più alta nell'esercito austriaco, dall'Imperatore Francesco Giuseppe.

Andric Karcic (1888-1972) servì nell'amministrazione Ustash, come collegamento all'armata italiana in Croazia. Egli aveva un ufficio a Sansego ed altre persone di Unie svolgevano per lui il compito di guardie. Verso la fine della guerra, Andric lavorò nel Consolato Generale a Vienna e in seguito, dopo la guerra, visse negli Stati Uniti.

La maggior parte dei giovani di Unie entrò nelle forze armate italiane e servì nella marina militare. C'era pure Andrea Radoslovich (1913-1942), il quale morì dopo che la sua nave fu colpita e affondata tra l'Italia e Valona, in Albania. Rufino Niccoli (Nicolich), capitano di un sommergibile italiano, scomparve nei primi giorni dell'entrata in guerra dell'Italia. Andrea Valic lottò nell'Esercito italiano e perse la vita nel 1943, nel combattimento vicino al fiume Don, in Unione sovietica.

Quando l'Italia capitolò, nel settembre del 1943, i soldati di Chetnik occuparono l'arsenale a Lussinpiccolo e allo stesso tempo sbarcarono a Unie, ricacciando i nostri. Più tardi, quando i partigiani attaccarono questi stessi Chetniks a Lussino, essi fuggirono su due imbarcazioni. Una di esse sostò a Unie, per rifornimenti. Essi partirono in tutta fretta per l'Italia. L'occupazione partigiana di Lussinpiccolo non durò molto, poiché l'esercito tedesco sferrò un attacco, prendendo la città che tenne sotto controllo fino agli ultimi mesi della seconda Guerra mondiale. Luca Karcich (1889-1945) che si era imbarcato sul *Tegetthof* durante la prima Guerra mondiale ed era vissuto a Unie nel periodo bellico, lavorò negli Stati Uniti negli anni successivi. Quando i tedeschi occuparono il territorio, verso la fine della Guerra, cercarono persone come Luca che possedevano la cittadinanza americana. Egli fu arrestato e portato in Germania e non si ebbe più notizia di lui.

Non appena i Cetniks lasciarono Unie, i partigiani entrarono nell'isola. Essi vi rimasero nascosti, specialmente durante il periodo seguente all'occupazione tedesca. I partigiani giustiziavano gli italiani e i tedeschi simpatizzanti. Andrea Radoslovich (1898-1950), appartenente al ramo della famiglia Radoslovich di Unie, giunse all'isola quando l'Italia capitolò, nel settembre del 1943. Egli volle indagare sull'assassinio di cinque famiglie isolane sospettate di avere simpatie per l'Italia. Fu dissuaso dall'eseguire il suo piano da Mati Carcich (Jevin). Lo stesso Andrea soffriva di un cancro alla gola e morì poco dopo la fine della guerra.

Durante la notte del 14 gennaio 1945, tre imbarcazioni tedesche di perlustrazione, S33, S58 e S60 di 30 metri di lunghezza, arrivarono in secco vicino al faro di Unie. Le barche avevano lasciato Pola ed erano dirette a Lussino. I tedeschi immediatamente tentarono di rimettere le barche in mare, ma erano troppo in secca per riuscirci.. Essi si misero di pattuglia sul lato sud-occidentale dell'isola e mandarono pattuglie in paese. Al 15 gennaio tre navi inglesi apparvero in direzione delle barche tedesche e iniziarono a colpirle. Alcuni proiettili arrivarono nella baia e uno di loro cadde al numero 124. Il bombardamento fu breve e dopo circa cinque minuti le navi inglesi invertirono la rotta e si diressero verso l'Italia. Il giorno dopo i tedeschi abbandonarono le navi pattuglia e le incendiarono. Nel 1945 il comandante delle forze tedesche a Lussino, Platzcomandir Fischer, si arrese ai partigiani. Egli fu portato segretamente da Lussino a Unie. In seguito fu trasferito in Dalmazia e giustiziato dai partigiani vicino a Spalato.

Fabrica Arrigoni, Unie

Alla fine della seconda Guerra mondiale, i 639 residenti di Unie si registrarono come 421 croati e 216 italiani (49). Il numero di famiglie, a quei tempi era: Belanic 7, Busanic 1, Ceko 4, Citcovic 1, Delconte 1, Deroia 1, Galosic 1, Haljic 1, Karcic 59, Nadalin 5, Nicolic 43, Picinic 1, Pilepic 3, Poljanic 1, Radoslovic 18, Rerecic 15, Segota 6, Valic 2, Verbora 1, Vidulic 1.

L'avvento del regime comunista provocò nel dopoguerra la forzata stasi dell'emigrazione all'interno della Iugoslavia, dopo l'esodo iniziale di famiglie italiane e neo-italiane dalla regione del Quarnero. Lo spostamento fu controllato e ci sono stati casi di assassinio per intimidire persone e famiglie dal fuggire attraverso il mare Adriatico. I resti di John Carcich di Unie insieme con altri tre furono scoperti in una caverna vicino a Cunski nel 1996. Si seppe che John ed i suoi compagni progettavano di navigare attraverso l'Adriatico e li videro per l'ultima volta nel 1956. Da 1945 a 1960 sei famiglie ed un totale di 30 individui di Unie fecero la traversata clandestina dell'Adriatico.

La popolazione di Unie rimase stabile fino alla seconda Guerra Mondiale e, in seguito, cominciò a diminuire. Nel 1980 gli abitanti di 70 anni e oltre erano numerosi (50). Ai giorni nostri circa 70 persone abitano a Unie durante tutto l'anno, ma molti di più vi risiedono durante i mesi estivi. Soprattutto i vacanzieri croati dell'entroterra e altri dalla Slovenia, dall'Italia e da oltre mare, vi hanno le loro case o le prendono in affitto durante l'estate. Durante l'inverno arrivano all'isola i cacciatori di fagiani. Le famiglie che si sono insediate a Unie da oltre trecento anni vi si possono ancora trovare, però il loro numero è diminuito e la maggior parte di esse si sono sistemate nel Nord America, in Italia e in Australia. I nuovi arrivati a Unie, negli ultimi cinquant'anni, sono stati prevalentemente croati e pochi bosniaci dall'entroterra.

Popolazione per Unie 1600 - 2000

Anno	Popolazione	Anno	Popolazione
1600	75-100*	1921	783
1730	136*	1931	717
1770	150-200*	1945	649
1815	222	1948	457
1818	220	1953	402
1869	520	1961	273
1880	630	1971	113
1890	678	1981	85
1900	696	1990	82
1910	758	2000	70

*stima

Attraverso gli ultimi quattrocento anni molte delle isole minori in Dalmazia hanno subito un incremento graduale nella popolazione, seguito da una forte diminuzione nella metà del secolo scorso. Unie segue questo sistema e quando la sua popolazione è paragonata a quella di Sansego, le somiglianze e le differenze sono apparenti.

Unie cominciò con una popolazione inferiore nel 1600 e, in seguito, crebbe più lentamente. La popolazione di Sansego cominciò con una crescita più notevole all'inizio del 1800, mentre la crescita di Unie cominciò verso la metà del 1800. Le migliori condizioni di salute e la longevità aiutarono le popolazioni delle due isole, mentre i nuovi arrivi di famiglie a Unie, come i Cecco, Pilepic, Radoslovich (Matesinich) e Segota incrementarono il numero degli abitanti. Unie e Sansego ebbero un declino nella popolazione durante la prima metà del 1900, sebbene Unie cominci il suo declino circa due decadi prima, dovuto all'emigrazione in America.

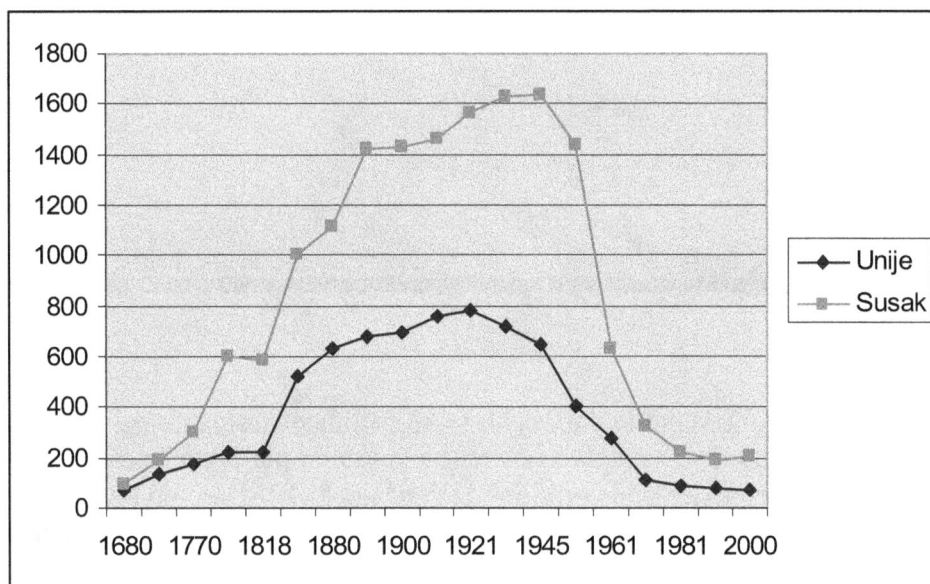

Popolazion per Unie e Susak (Sansego) 1680 to 2000

Dopo il 1965 l'agricoltura ad Unie ebbe un forte calo a causa della partenza di molti abitanti. Per incrementare nuovamente l'agricoltura, la compagnia Jadranka di Lussinpiccolo rese produttivi 125 ettari tra il 1984 ed il 1991, coltivandosi alfalfa, orzo, mais e legumi. Inoltre furono allevate nell' isola 1200 pecore e 600 capre. Jadranka cessò le sue operazioni dopo la rottura con la Jugoslavia. La caccia al fagiano era stata immessa ad Unie con 2.000 fagiani e 5.000 pernici, che venivano portati annualmente nell'isola. Vi sono stati creati diversi allevamenti di api a Unie. Nel 1996 si creò nella zona piana, a sud del paese, una pista di atterraggio per piccoli aerei monorotore, che attualmente viene utilizzata dal governo croato.

Emigrazione

Prima che l'emigrazione verso le Americhe fosse facilmente attuata negli ultimi anni del 19° secolo, gli abitanti di Unie erano costretti a spostarsi per lavoro nelle isole vicine e nei paesi del Quarnero e qualche volta fino a Venezia. Nel 18° secolo parecchi individui vendevano legna da ardere e probabilmente commerciavano con Venezia. Alcune famiglie di Unie si stabilirono ad Ossero, a Lussinpiccolo e a Cunski. Altre lavorarono per un certo periodo nelle città di Ossero e di Lussinpiccolo o andarono nell'isola di Cherso. La genealogia di queste famiglie si trova alla fine del presente volume.

La storia dell'emigrazione è legata alla storia marittima di Lussino. Dal 17° secolo in avanti, la gente di Lussino gravitava intorno al mare e molti divennero marinai lungo le coste adriatiche e mediterranee. I marinai di Lussino sono stati i primi croati ad arrivare in America. Nel 1779 Pietro Budinich di Lussingrande viaggiò sul *San Domenico* in Giamaica. Altri continuarono il commercio marittimo con le Americhe e Gasparo Budinich di Lussingrande morì a Kingston, Giamaica nel 1792. Nel 1834 Petar Jakov Leva, anch'egli di Lussingrande, navigò sul *Ferdinando V Re d'Ungheria* intorno al Capo Horn verso Valparaiso, Cile (51).

Un altro Capitano di Lussino, Martinolich, navigò sulla *Amalia Giuseppina* per caricare cotone nel porto di Galveston, Texas, nel 1844. Una comunità croata esisteva a New Orleans verso il 1820. I capitani di Lussino cominciarono a navigare verso questo porto nella prima metà del 19° secolo e molti emigranti di Lussino arrivarono in America attraverso questo porto. Marko Ragusin, di Lussingrande si crede sia entrato in America via New Orleans nel 1849. Ragusin andò a Sacramento, California, e più tardi a San Josè. Altre persone di Lussino emigrarono durante il 19° secolo negli Stati Uniti e in Australia. Fortunato Corsano, nato a Lussinpiccolo nel 1841 emigrò in Australia nel 1867 e si crede che uno dei suoi fratelli sia emigrato in Canada. La maggior parte degli emigranti di Unie in Australia arrivarono dopo la seconda guerra mondiale, ad eccezione di Matteo Carcich (1878 -) che vi giunse prima.

Durante la seconda metà del 19° secolo molti emigranti dall'Impero austriaco viaggiarono negli Stati Uniti per cercare lavoro. Quelli di Unie arrivarono nella costa est, nella costa ovest e nel Colorado. Un Antonio Radoslovich (Mulecich) è citato per essere stato il primo di Unie a giungere in America, ma nessuna documentazione è stata ancora trovata per dimostrarlo. Antonio Carcich (1860) di Unie è in un elenco di New York nel 1874. Si seppe che altre persone di Unie si trovavano a New York dal 1885 in poi. Si può trovare un elenco di queste persone di Unie che lavorarono a New York in appendice. Durante il 1890 e nella prima decade di questo secolo praticamente ogni famiglia di Unie aveva uno o più membri che lavoravano in America.

Il massimo dell'emigrazione da Lussino verso l'America avvenne alla fine del 1870 e ai primi anni del 1880. Venanzio Martinolich (1848-1913) di Lussinpiccolo arrivò attraverso New Orleans e visse per un periodo in Colorado dal 1888, dove suo fratello Benjaminus (1849) si era stabilito due anni prima. Nel 1891 Venanzio si trasferì con la sua famiglia a Port Guichon (Vancouver) nella Colombia britannica. Altri, come John A. Martinolich, arrivarono nella Colombia britannica nel 1893 e nel 1902 egli dirigeva un cantiere navale a Dockton, Washington. Entrambe le comunità di Vancouver e di Dockton divennero piccoli centri di emigranti croati con un certo numero di famiglie delle isole di Lussino e di Unie. Altre famiglie da Lussinpiccolo continuarono ad arrivare in quest'area, come quella di Giuseppe Nicolich (1864-1934) e di Elvira Ivancic (1871-1942) che si sposarono a Lussino nel 1892, ma poi esse si trasferirono a New York. Il loro ultimo figlio, Eugenio Nicolich, nacque a Vancouver nel 1910. Elvira e suo figlio Giuseppe Lewis (1896-1973) rimasero a Seattle.

Molte famiglie di Unie arrivarono nella Columbia britannica e nello Stato di Washington. Un immigrante tipico di Unie fu Andrea Domenico Galosich (1866-1948). Andrea giunse a Delta, nella Columbia britannica, nel 1890 e nel 1900 fece arrivare sua moglie Thomasina Nicolich (1869 -). Il fratello di Andrea, Giovanni Galosich (1864-1918), marinaio, giunse a New York nel 1888 ed Andrea probabilmente arrivò sulla costa ovest via New York. Durante la prima Guerra mondiale Andrea e Thomasina vissero nell'area di Seattle e nei primi anni del 1920 si trasferirono in California.

Durante la Prima Guerra Mondiale c'era un numero piuttosto grande di persone di Unie nell'area di Seattle. Beniamino Carcich (1864-1919) e Dominic Ferluga (1896-1993) vissero lì fino alla loro morte. Matteo Nicolich (1888-1959) e sua moglie Mary Simicich (1893-1978) vissero a Seattle ed i loro figli, Mathew (1918 -) e Lorenzo (1921 -) vi nacquero. La famiglia di Giuseppe Nicolich (1879-1945) e di Mattea Karcich (1890-1963) vissero a Seattle e il loro figlio Giuseppe (1913-1990) nacque là. Antonio Carcich (1876 -) arrivò negli Stati Uniti nel 1905 e due anni più tardi si sposò e vi portò sua moglie Antonia (1880-). Antonio ed Antonia allevarono due bambini nell'area di Seattle: Stella (1908 -) e Matt (1910-1978).

Altre persone di Unie vennero nella zona di Seattle separatamente. Domenico Simeone Carcich (1858-1925) lavorò nella regione e Giovanni Andrea Nicolich (1875-1961) risulta nei registri del servizio militare a Seattle nel 1917. Una Rosa Carcich (1915-1990) visse nell'area di Seattle. Teodoro Carcich (1905-1988), nato a Unie e più tardi diventato vicepresidente della chiesa Avventista del settimo giorno, si trasferì a Seattle subito dopo il 1942. La sua famiglia si stabilì a Colton, Washington.

Persone di Unie andarono a lavorare nelle miniere di carbone a sud-est del Colorado. Dopo la costruzione della ferrovia da Santa Fe a Trinidad, nel 1879, le miniere di carbone furono sfruttate con pochi costi di manodopera fornita dagli immigranti. Queste persone lavorarono nelle miniere di Forbes e di Tobasco, a quei tempi comunità di minatori appena costituite.

Un afflusso di immigranti dalla Croazia portò 500 lavoratori nell'area di Trinidad di Colorado, agli inizi del 1900. I minatori arrivarono da Cunski e da Lussinpiccolo e, all'inizio del secolo, c'erano almeno tre uomini di Unie in questo gruppo. Andro Karcich da Unie e sua moglie Suzanna Mihlik vissero e lavorarono qui nel 1908. In questo periodo anche Matt Karcich, di Cunski, il cui padre era di Unie e sua moglie Anna Galecich vissero qui fino al 1915. Andrea Carcich, di Unie visse qui per un certo tempo. Molti altri di Unie lavorarono qui per poco tempo e ritornarono a New York o si spostarono altrove. Molti minatori lasciarono la zona durante e dopo lo sciopero del 1913-14 che scatenò una violenza in grande scala e finì con lo scioglimento delle manifestazioni. Nel 1914, Forbes, dove lavoravano molti uomini di Unie fu rasa al suolo da un incendio e parecchie guardie e minatori vi morirono.

Almeno una famiglia di Unie rimase a Forbes negli anni successivi. Attualmente non rimane niente della città e probabilmente la stessa sorte toccò alla cittadina vicina di Hastings, che andò in declino negli anni venti e trenta e fu abbandonata nel 1952. Hastings ebbe una tragica esplosione nella miniera nel 1917, dove 121 minatori persero la loro vita. Matt P. Carcich, originario di Cunski, stabilitosi più tardi a Trinidad, Colorado, fu nominato amministratore degli appezzamenti di terra dei superstiti dell'esplosione della miniera.

I discendenti di queste famiglie di Forbes, di Tabasco e di Trinidad, Colorado, attualmente vivono in Colorado, Nuovo Messico, California e New York. Alcuni rimasero nella regione più a lungo, ma verso il 1920 la maggior parte si era trasferita in altri luoghi, qualcuno verso New York, dove ci sono attualmente molte famiglie di Unie. Una famiglia Carcich di Cunski si fermò a Trinidad, Colorado e i loro discendenti ora si trovano ad ovest degli Stati Uniti. Alcuni si spostarono verso San Pedro (Los Angeles), California.

Prima del 1903, molti emigranti dovevano recarsi nei porti dell'Italia, dell'Olanda, a Le Havre (Francia), a Brema o ad Amburgo (Germania) per trovare navi passeggeri dirette in America. Alcuni dei marittimi di Unie attraversavano il mare su queste navi: *La Champagne, La Touraine, L' Aquitaine* e il *Principe di Sparta*. Dopo il 1902, una rotta più vicina si aprì da Trieste a New York sulla Linea Austro-Americana (Cosulich) e sulla Linea *Cunard*. Il porto di New York fu il primo obiettivo per la maggior parte dei viaggiatori di Unie. Altri arrivarono al porto di New York, perdigrigersi verso la coasta ovest. Dal 1885 in poi un afflusso di persone arrivo dall 'isola negli Stati Uniti, cosi come e documentato nell'archivio delle navi passeggeri e dai censimenti federali. Molti rimasero e lavorarono a cittàdi New York.

Molti immigranti di Unie lavoravano sui moli della città. Parecchi decisero di vivere nel centro di Manhattan, tra la 42a e la 50a Strada Ovest e tra il nono e il dodicesimo Viale. A nord, questo stato è chiamato la *Cucina dell'Inferno*. Questa zona di Manhattan fiancheggiava il fiume Hudson ed aveva molti moli dove lavoravano i nuovi arrivati. Nella 42a Strada c'era un macello, uno dei tanti che si estendevano fino alla 35a Strada. Sul fiume, all'altezza della 42a Strada, c'era un traghetto che collegava con il New Jersey e tra la 54a e la 12a Strada, sul fiume, c'era una discarica di rifiuti urbani. Un deposito della ferrovia di Manhattan era situato tra la 60a e la 11a Strada ed un altro magazzino si trovava sulla 30a Strada. Un binario del treno funzionava sull'undicesima Strada. La Ferrovia Centrale di New York fu un grande impresario per gli uomini che arrivarono a New York. Altri datori di lavoro furono il ristorante Schraft's e Horn e Hardart, dove parecchie donne lavoravano alle loro dipendenze.

I primi residenti della *Cucina dell'Inferno,* dal 1851 in poi, furono irlandesi. Più tardi gli italiani vi si stabilirono ed un piccolo numero di popolazione Nera si estese dalla 59a alla 65a Strada. I primi arrivati da Unie erano uomini, sia celibi che sposati. Essi vissero in gruppi, con fratelli, cugini, zii o amici del vecchio paese, dividendo spese e pasti. Qualche famiglia di Unie continuò a vivere nella *Cucina dell'Inferno* fino agli anni cinquanta. Sebbene poche persone risiedano a tutt'oggi a Manhattan, la maggior parte delle famiglie di Unie si è trasferita nelle zone adiacenti di New York e di New Jersey.

C'erano due negozi di alimentari frequentati da gente di Unie che viveva a Manhattan. Uno era gestito dalla famiglia Angelich e l'altro da una famiglia di Unie, Andrea Vallich, al numero 544 West 45th Street, fino al 1914 e divenne un punto di riunione per le persone di Unie prima della Prima Guerra Mondiale. Più tardi, Gaudenzio Radoslovich di Unie, in un primo tempo possedetrte una compagnia di taxi a Manhattan e in seguito gestì un ristorante al numero 807 di Greenwick Street, dal 1922 al 1950. Era un edificio dinanzi al porto, vicino all'ufficio della Dogana di St. James Park, accanto alla stazione centrale.della Ferrovia di New York.

La chiesa croata originale a Manhattan, frequentata dai nuovi immigranti di Unie, era dedicata ai Santi Cirillo e Metodio e si trovava tra la 50a Strada Ovest e il 10° Viale. Più di dodici bambini e parecchi adulti delle famiglie di Unie furono battezzati e sposati in questa chiesa. La Chiesa dei Santi Cirillo e Metodio esistette in questo luogo dal 1913 al 1974, quando fu trasferita al 502 della 41a Strada Ovest.

807 Greenwick Street, Manhattan, N.Y. circa 1935

Molte società per aiutare gli emigranti furono fondate sia ad Unie che negli Stati Uniti. La *Società di Mutuo Soccorso* è stata fondata ad Unie il 9 agosto 1897 e l'*Associazione Istriana di Beneficenza* fu fondata il 28 dicembre 1922. I direttori dell'Associazione furono John Carcich e Dominick Carcich, dell'11a Strada, al numero 557, Andrea Nicolich della 45a Strada, al numero 636, Bortolo Rerecich, al numero 597 della11a Strada e Paolo Rerecich al numero 552 Ovest della 45a Strada, sempre a New York (52). L'*Associazione di Beneficenza* iniziò con 32 membri, e prima di sciogliersi nel 1994, era composta da 72 membri. (53) Anche la *Società Sveti Andrija* si era organizzata per l'assistenza nel paese di Unie.

Genealogije unijskih obitelji

Genealogije su navedene abecednim redom prema prezimenu, a naziv klana ili obiteljsko ime je u zagradama. Obiteljsko ime ili ime klana poznato je pod talijanskim nazivom *soprannome* i *nadimak* na hrvatskom jeziku. Nadimci se također javljaju i u zagradama. Obiteljska imena izvedena su iz patronima osnivača (bilo muškarca ili žene) po imenu, a završavaju na –ić, –ović, –ičić, -ov, –ev, –of ili –in.

Svaka generacija označena je brojem, a započinje se s najstarijom generacijom pod brojem 1. Sa sljedećim generacijama broj se povećava (generacija 2, itd.). Svaka generacija je uvučena u tekstu kako bi se odvojila od prethodnih ili sljedećih.

Za označavanje rođenja, vjenčanja i smrti korištene su skraćenice kako je prikazano u doljnjoj tabeli, skupa s kraticama za mjesece u godini.

Hrvatske kratice

b. = rođenje	m.= vjenčanje	d. = smrt
Jan = Siječanj	Feb = Veljača	Mar= Ožujak
Apr = Travanj	May= Svibanj	Jun = Lipanj
Jul =Srpanj	Aug= Kolovoz	Sep = Rujan
Oct=Listopad	Nov= Studeni	Dec= Prosinac

Zbog sažetosti, neka imena ispuštena su iz iz genealogija. Pokrajnji ogranci i nepotpuna obiteljska imena nisu navedeni. Ta ispuštena obiteljska imena spominju se u tekstu.

Prepostavlja se da se mjesto rođenja, vjenčanja ili smrti nalazi na Unijama, osim ako nije navedeno drugačije. Neki od genealoških podataka su iz Malog Lošinja, Ćunskog i Osora, a taj podatak zabilježen je u popratnom tekstu za tu obiteljsku liniju. U izradi genealogija korišteni su i originalni zapisi te kopije tih zapisa na mikrofilmu. Glavne arhivske kolekcije potiču iz Nacioalnog arhiva u Zagrebu, Regionalnog povijesnog arhiva u Rijeci i Arhiva Rimokatoličke crkve iz krčke nadbiskupije. Drugi izvor genealoških podataka su nedavno pronađeni zapisi s Unija koji pokrivaju period prije godine 1881. Izvori ovih arhivskih zapisa navedeni su u bibliografiji.

Imena u genealogijama općenito su zapisana su kao što je zapisano u arhivskim izvorima.

Premda je velika pozornost posvećena točnosti podataka, postoji mogućnost pogrešaka zbog grešaka u transkripciji, lošeg prijevoda ili nečeg drugog. Za svaku takvu potencijalnu grešku isključivo je odgovoran autor.

U ovom djelu predstavljene su sljedeće obiteljske genealogije:

Prezime:	**Porijeklo:**
Bellanich, Belanić	(Tomov)
Carcich, Karcich, Karčić	(Andricev), (Baldich), (Bravarof of Unije & Cunski), (Cicola of Cunski), (Gevin), (Pasquich), (Rocov), (Zburkin)
Cecco, Ceko	
Cosulich, Kozulić	(Belon)
Gallosich, Galošić	
Giurich, Jurić	
Haglich, Halić, Haljić	
Martinolich, Martinolić	(Colonich)
Nadalin	
Nicolich, Nikolić	(Agatin), (Kambera), (Marketa), (Muscardin), (Sancich), (Tomicev)
Pillepich, Pilepić	
Radoslovich, Radoslović	(Calcich), (Matesinch), (Popich), (Rosso), (Sesturin)
Rerecich, Rerecić	(Jercich), (Simef)
Segotta, Segota	
Vallich, Valić	

Le genealogie delle famiglie di Unie

Le genealogie sono elencate alfabeticamente per cognome e anche per clan o nome di lignaggio e indicate tra parentesi quadrate. Il lignaggio o i nomi dei clan sono conosciuti come soprannome in italiano e nadimak in croato. I nomignoli appaiono anche tra parentesi I nomi di lignaggio derivano dal patronimico del fondatore, sia egli maschio o femmina, con i suffissi di -ić, -ović, -ičić, -ov, -ev, -of o -in.

Ogni generazione è numerata, iniziando con la più antica con il numero 1 e le successive sono in numero progressivo, in tal modo la seconda generazione è numerata con il 2 e così di seguito. Ogni nuova generazione tende a separarsi dalla precedente e dalle successive.

Le abbreviazioni sono adoperate per le nascite, i matrimoni e i decessi e sono elencate nella seguente tavola, unitamente con le abbreviazioni dei mesi dell'anno.

Abbreviazioni italiane

b. = nascita	m.= matrimonio	d. = morte
Jan = gennaio	Feb = febbraio	Mar= marzo
Apr = aprile	May= maggio	Jun = giugno
Jul = luglio	Aug= agosto	Sep = settembre
Oct= ottobre	Nov= novembre	Dec= dicembre

Ai fini dell'abbreviazione sono stati omessi dei nomi dalle seguenti genealogie. I rami secondari e i lignaggi incompleti sono stati tolti, sebbene nel testo sia stata fatta menzione a questi lignaggi mancanti.

Il luogo degli avvenimenti di nascite, matrimoni o decessi si presume si trovi a Unie, a meno che sia indicato diversamente. Alcuni dati genealogici provengono da Lussinpiccolo, Cunski e Ossero. Tale informazione è registrata nel testo allegato al lignaggio di famiglia. Ambedue i registri originali e le loro copie microfilmate furono consultati nella sistemazione di queste genealogie. La prima serie di archivi provenne dall'Archivio Nazionale di Zagabria, dall'Archivio Storico Regionale di Fiume e dall'Archivio della Chiesa Cattolica Romana dell'arcidiocesi di Veglia, Croazia. Un'ulteriore fonte di dati genealogici provenne dai registri recentemente scoperti a Unie che comprende il periodo precedente al 1881. Le fonti degli archivi sono elencate nella bibliografia.

L'analisi dei nomi menzionati nelle genealogie è generalmente attinta alle fonti di archivio.

Sebbene si fosse messa grande cura nello studio delle genealogie, possono esserci stati degli errori attraverso le trascrizioni o altre cause. Qualsiasi errore è da attribuirsi alla sola responsabilità dell'autore.

Le seguenti genealogie delle famiglie sono presenti in questo volume:

Cognome:	**Lignaggio:**
Bellanich, Belanić	(Tomov)
Carcich, Karcich,Karčić	(Andricev), (Baldich), (Bravarof of Unije & Cunski), (Cicola of Cunski), (Gevin), (Pasquich), (Rocov), (Zburkin)
Cecco, Ceko	
Cosulich, Kozulić	(Belon)
Gallosich, Galošić	
Giurich, Jurić	
Haglich, Halić, Haljić	
Martinolich, Martinolić	(Colonich)
Nadalin	
Nicolich, Nikolić	(Agatin), (Kambera), (Marketa), (Muscardin), (Sancich), (Tomicev)
Pillepich, Pilepić	
Radoslovich, Radoslović	(Calcich), (Matesinch), (Popich), (Rosso), (Sesturin)
Rerecich, Rerecić	(Jercich), (Simef)
Segotta, Segota	
Vallich, Valić	

Genealogies for the Families of Unije

The genealogies are listed alphabetically by surname and then by clan or lineage name in brackets. Lineage names are known as *soprannome* in Italian and *nadimak* in Croatian. Nicknames also appear in brackets. The lineage names are derived from the patronym of a founder, either male or female by name, with the endings of -ić, -ović, -ičić, ov, -ev, –of, or –in.

Each generation is numbered, starting with the oldest generation which is numbered as 1, and subsequent generations are increasing in number, so that the second generation following 1 is numbered 2, and so forth. Each generation is indented to separate from the previous and any following generations. Family, lineage, or nicknames often appear in round brackets next to the full name of individuals.

Abbreviations are used for birth, marriage and death and are listed in the following table, along with the abbreviations for the months of the year.

English Abbreviations

b. = birth	m.=marriage	d. = death
Jan = January	Feb = February	Mar= March
Apr = April	May= May	Jun = June
Jul =July	Aug= August	Sep = September
Oct=October	Nov= November	Dec= December

Where the genealogies warranted it, spouses are included and are displayed by the + sign. For the sake of brevity some names have been omitted from the following genealogies. Side branches and incomplete lineages have been omitted, though mention may be made to these missing lineages in the text.

The place where the birth, marriage, or death took place is assumed to be in Unije, unless otherwise stated. Some of the genealogical dates are from the town of Mali Losinj, Cunski, or other localities and that information is recorded in the accompanying text for that family lineage.

Both original records and microfilmed copies of these records were consulted in the construction of these genealogies. The primary archival collections came from the National Archive in Zagreb, the Regional Historical Archive in Rijeka, and the Roman Catholic Church archive at the archdioceses of Krk, Croatia. Still another source of genealogical data came from the recently discovered records for Unije covering the period prior to 1881. The specific sources of these archival records are listed in the notes. A list of some of these sources appears on the following page under the term vital statistics sources, which include baptismal (and birth), marriage, and death records.

Although great care was taken to ensure that genealogies are accurate, errors may have occurred through transcription faults, improper translation, or other causes. Any such potential errors are the sole responsibility of the author.

The following family genealogies are presented in this volume:

Surname:	Lineage:
Bellanich, Belanić	(Tomov)
Carcich, Karcich, Karčić	(Andricev), (Baldich), (Bravarof of Unije & Cunski), (Cicola of Cunski), (Gevin), (Pasquich), (Rocov), (Zburkin)
Cecco, Ceko	
Cosulich, Kozulić	(Belon)
Gallosich, Galošić	
Giurich, Jurić	
Haglich, Halić, Haljić	
Martinolich, Martinolić	(Colonich)
Nadalin	
Nicolich, Nikolić	(Agatin), (Kambera), (Marketa), (Muscardin), (Sancich), (Tomicev)
Pillepich, Pilepić	
Radoslovich, Radoslović	(Calcich), (Matesinch), (Popich), (Rosso), (Sesturin)
Rerecich, Rerecić	(Jercich), (Simef)
Segotta, Segota	
Vallich, Valić	

SOURCES OF VITAL STATISTICS

Unije:

• Death Register 1815-1880, Saint Andrew's Roman Catholic Church, Unije, Croatia

• Church census 1881, Saint Andrew's Roman Catholic Church, Unije, Croatia

• Births and Marriages, 1835-1900, Saint Andrew's Roman Catholic Church, Unije, Croatia, located in the Krk Archdiocese Archives, Krk, Croatia

Cunski:

• Marriage Register 1749-1824, Saint Nicolaus' Roman Catholic Church, Cunski, Croatia, microfilm no. 1738842-item 1, Family History Library, Salt Lake City, Utah and the Croatian National Archives, Zagreb, Croatia

• Marriage Register 1816-1859, Saint Nicolaus' Roman Catholic Church, Cunski, Croatia, microfilm no. 2084744-item 3, Family History Library, Salt Lake City, Utah

Mali Losinj:

• Marriage Register 1670-1704, Saint Maria's Roman Catholic Church, Mali Losinj, Croatia, microfilm no. 1738832-item 5, Family History Library, Salt Lake City, Utah

• Marriage Register 1704-1745, Saint Maria's Roman Catholic Church, Mali Losinj, Croatia, microfilm no. 1738833-item 1, Family History Library, Salt Lake City, Utah

• Marriage Register 1746-1821, Saint Maria's Roman Catholic Church, Mali Losinj, Croatia, microfilm no. 2084820-item 2, Family History Library, Salt Lake City, Utah

• Baptismal Register, 1749-1814, Roman Catholic Church, Mali Losinj, Croatia, microfilm no. 2084817-itme 1-4, Family History Library, Salt Lake City, Utah

Osor:

• Marriage Register 1611-1816, Roman Catholic Church, Osor, Croatia, microfilm no. 2099982-itme 2-5, Family History Library, Salt Lake City, Utah

Photograph Credits (contributors in brackets)

Unije School Group 1911/12; Unije circa 1900; Arrigoni Factory (Adrijano Nikolić); Cosulich Family at No. 66, Saint Cyril and Methodius church, Radoslovich Calcich Family, Catarina Segota b. 1852 (Anton Angelich); Unije School children 1927-1931, Karubin Carcich 1872-1930, Domenico Valich 1882-1943 (Letizia Valic); 807 Green Street Restaurant, Manhattan (Gaudent Radoslovich); Matteo Belanich 1898-1970, Lydia and Antonio Rerecich Simef 1867-1954 (Tony Rerecich); Maria Carcich Andricev (Ron Weddle); Domenico Carcich 1858-1925 (Marina Carcich); Agnes Gonxha Bojaxhiu, Carcich Jevin family (Ted Carcich); Benjamino Carcich 1864-1919 (Maria Carcich); "Captain" John Carcich 1867-1943, Carcich Restaurant and Shipyard (Fred Scopinich); Anton Carcich 1854-1918, Karcic Family Cicuola, Slovenia, John Karcich 1892-1973 (Dorothy Buffington); Theodore Carcich 1905-1988 (Joanne Rasco); Carcich family No. 109, Luca Cecco, Domenica Nicolich b. 1878, Carmen Carrozza and Matteo Radoslovich (Dominic Karcic); Andrea Karcic 1866-1951, Ivan Radoslovich 1829-1903, Ivan Radoslovich 1867-1957, Paul Rerecich Family (Andrew Karcich); Cosulich Family (Irene Nicolich); Antonia Carcich Pasquich 1862-1936, Maria Galosich b. 1875 (Milka Fatović Nikolić); Haglich Family (Maria Gelinas); Tacoma Washington group (Gary Loverich); Nicolich Muscardin Family, Valentino Nicolich 1907/08-1991 (Silvana Borrelli Nicolich); Antonio Nicolich 1879-1965, Osip Zidor Niccoli 1871-1949 (Vlakto Janeković)

BELLANICH, BELANIĆ

Small concentrations of Bellanich families are found in Unije, Veli Losinj and on the Istrian peninsula. However, the largest concentration of families with this surname in Croatia (14 families) in modern times is found on the island of Ilovik, sometimes referred to as Sveti Petar or San Pietro di Nembi, suggesting that the oldest established families and origin of this surname is on this island. Petar Šimunović in *Hrvatska Prezimena* claims Belanići is a patronym originating in Istria.[54]

The surname appears in a 1586 deed from Veli Losinj for a Matia Belanić. Several marriages of the Bellanich family from Unije are recorded in 1753, 1764, and 1787 and are listed in the Appendix. The family lineage for Unije reproduced here is named Tomov and begins with Martin Bellanich son of Jseppo (Joseph) who married Antonia Scrivanich in 1753. The Belcich branch of the Bellanich family dates to Toma Bellanich

Maria Bellanich (1867-1916)

born about 1790 and may be related to the family of Martin Bellanich though it is not listed on the accompanying genealogy. The Tomov lineage is probably derived from the name for Thomas (Toma), though whether it is from Toma born in 1790 is unknown. The patronym origins of the Belcich lineage is unknown.

Antonio Lorenzo Bellanich (1865-) of the Belcich lineage was in the United States in 1888 while Matthew Bellanich (1919-1993) was a police lieutenant in New York City.

Matteo Belanich (1898-1970)

Belanich, Belanić Family Home No. 140 Unije

Belanich, Belanić Family Home No. 147 Unije

Bellanich, Belanić — Unije, Croatia

Jseppo Belanich

Martin Belanich
+ Anta. Scrivanich m. 18 Jun 1753
    Martin Bellanich
    + Thomasina Rerecich b. 1765, d. 26 Apr 1840
        Tomaso Bellanich (Chiora) b. 1787, d. 23 Apr 1851
        + Joanna Rerecich b. 1784, d. 23 Aug 1832
            Martino (Toncic) Bellanich b. 26 Feb 1815
            + Maria Helena Carcich b. 1819, d. 4 Aug 1841
                Tomarello (Toma) Bellanich
                + Maria Karcich
                        Martin (Tome) Bellanich b. 1887, d. 10 Jan 1962
                        + Ana Karcic b. 1898, m. 1913, d. 22 Nov 1981
                                Marija Bellanich b. 1914
                                Matthew Bellanich b. 20 Oct 1919, d. 12 Nov 1993
                                Anna Bellanich b. 1921, d. 1986
                        Vittorio Bellanich b. 4 Aug 1896, d. 25 Nov 1955
                        + Anna Ricci (Rizzi) b. 13 May 1900, m. 3 Jan 1930, d. 3 Nov 1994
                                Mary Bellanich b. 1 Dec 1930
                        Matteo Bellanich b. 10 Jul 1898, d. 27 Aug 1970
                        + Domenica (Skilje) Nicolich b. 25 Dec 1892, d. 14 Mar 1982
                                Mary Bellanich b. 24 Mar 1920, d. 2 Apr 2003
                                Tommy Bellanich b. 10 Jun 1923, d. 4 Nov 1999
            + Antonia Nicolich b. 9 Sep 1829
                Martino Domenico(Toma) Bellanich b. 7 Feb 1854, d. 1932
                + Cattarina Vidulich b. 20 Oct 1851
                      Martino Stefano Bellanich b. 26 Dec 1879, d. 29 Dec 1879
                Anton Dinko Bellanich b. 22 Dec 1860
                + Marija Andrijana Karcic
                    Marco Bellanich b. 1912
                    + Marija Bellanich b. 1914
                        Norma Bellanich
                        Livia Bellanich
                        Anna Bellanich
        Matteo Bellanich b. 25 Jan 1829, d. 6 Dec 1916
        + Agata (Agatin) Nicolich b. 19 Oct 1833, d. 10 Feb 1904
            Matteo Tomaso Belanich b. 11 Jul 1859, d. 3 Aug 1906
            + Antonia Domenica Vallich b. 8 Jun 1861, d. 22 Aug 1923
                Ivan Bellanich b. 31 Aug 1890, d. 1 Mar 1962
                + Maria Carcich b. Sep 1890
                Agata Bellanich b. 1892, d. 1962
                Antonia Bellanich b. 1896, d. 1988
                Maria Bellanich b. 1904, d. 1989
            Maria Domenica Bellanich b. 19 Feb 1867, d. 17 Dec 1916

1   2   3   4   5   6   7   8

CARCICH, KARCICH, KARČIĆ (Andricev)

The Andricev lineage name is derived from the patronym for Andrea (Andrew). The genealogy listed here traces the descendents of Andrea Carcich (1784-1859) son of Andrea.

Several recent members of this family have distinguished themselves in the field of education. Andrea Carcich (1931-) was a school teacher in Cunski before the WWII and he later went on to study at Padua, Italy where he obtained a Doctorate in Engineering.

Andrić Karčić (1888-1972) graduated from secondary school in 1906 at Senj. Then he studied theology, and later in 1908 law in Zagreb and completed his law studies at Prague and Zagreb in 1914. He settled in Karlovac and opened a law office in Slunj from 1926 to 1941. He was appointed envoy to the Ministry of Foreign Affairs, and then consulate general for the NDH in Vienna. His two sons, Milivoj

Luca Carcich (1889-1944) served on the Austrian battleship *Tegetthof* in the Adriatic during WW I. He told of an encounter with an Italian Zepplin, which was shot down. After living in the United States he returned to Unije where he was arrested and died in German captivity during WWII.

Andric Karcic (1888-1972)   Luca Carcich (1889-1944)

Andrew Joseph Karcich (1950-) son of Joseph Karcich (1910-1966) obtained his Law Degree from Rutgers University in 1976. Andrew. Karcich was admitted to Bars of New Jersey and Pennsylvania and the United States Supreme Court. He operates the law firm of Lynch & Karcich in Voorhees, New Jersey.

Maria Carcich, Maria Nicolich (1859-),
Andrea Carcich 1883-1946)

Hrvoje Karčić (1921-2001) became a professor of history and taught in Erie, Pennsylvania, and Berislav (1926-2007) received his Ph.D. at Columbia, 1966 and taught at Iona College in New York.

Carcich, Karcich, Karčić (Andricev)
Family Home No. 46 Unije

Carcich, Karcich, Karčić (Andricev) — Unije, Croatia

Andrea Carcich
- Andrea Carcich (Senior) b. 1784, d. 29 Aug 1859 Unije
  - Andrea Carcich b. 27 Jan 1811
    - Andrea Carcich b. 24 Sep 1846
      - Ivan Carcich b. 1 Mar 1880, d. 30 Mar 1950 Unije
        - Maria Carcich b. 21 Feb 1911, d. 4 Jan 1934
        - Caterina(Katica) Carcich b. 14 Nov 1922 Unije
        - Iva Carcich b. 19 Nov 1929, d. Unije
      - Andrew Karcich b. 1879/80, d. 1959
        - Andrew Karcich b. 1902/09, d. 1915 Colorado
        - Mary Karcich b. 2 Jun 1904, d. 1970
        - Joseph Francis Karcich b. 2 Apr 1910, d. Jan 1966 New York
        - Frances John Karcich b. 1914 Lyons Mt.,New York, d. 1978
        - John Peter Karcich b. 30 Nov 1915 Trinidad, Colorado, d. Aug 1977 New Jersey
        - Peter Stephen Karcich b. 10 Jun 1917 Forbes, Colorado, d. Aug 1978
    - Domenico Michael Carcich b. 29 Sep 1851 Mali Losinj, d. 1 May 1917 Unije
      - Ambroggio Carcich b. 8 Sep 1885, d. 1946
        - Maria Carcich b. 1908
        - Domenica Carcich b. Aug 1912 Unije
        - Ambrogio (Gino) Carcich b. 1921
        - Gasparo Carcich b. Jan 1924
    - Antonio Valentinus Carcich b. 14 Feb 1853, d. 10 Mar 1925 Unije
      - Andrea Domenico Carcich b. 7 May 1883, d. 16 Oct 1946 Prescott,Arizona
        - Christina Maria Karcich b. 22 Sep 1908 Tabasco,Colorado, d. Mar 2002 Arizona
        - Tony Karcic b. 24 Apr 1915 Gallop,New Mexico d. 6 Nov 1975 Prescott, Arizona
        - Andrew Karcie b. 3 Oct 1916 Prescott,Arizona, d. 19 Oct 1980 Prescott
    - Luca Vinceslao Carcich b. 16 Oct 1860, d. 1934 Unije
      - Luca Carcich b. 31 Oct 1889, d. 19 Jun 1944 ,Germany
        - Felicita Carcich b. 12 Aug 1919, d. 16 Apr 1977
        - Andrea Carcich b. 21 Feb 1921 Unije
      - Maria (Babica) Carcich b. 1894, d. 30 Dec 1976
        - Lucy (Lucia) Carcich b. 1913, d. West New York
        - Gaudencije (Gemsi) (James) Carcich b. 16 Feb 1917 New York d. 2 Jul 1997 Fort Lee, New Jersey
        - Andrew Carcich b. Jul 1919 New York
      - Andrea Carcich b. 1899, d. Astoria, New York
        - Felicita (Phyllis) Carcich
      - Antonio Carcich b. 13 Jun 1902 Unije, d. 12 Jun 1983 Pascoe/Hillsboro,Florida
        - John Carcich b. 12 Jul 1925
        - Phyllis Carcich d. 1943
      - Giuseppe Carcich b. 28 Mar 1908, d. 24 Jan 1963 Unije
        - Ivan Carcich b. 1935
        - Luca Carcich b. 1946
        - Giuseppina (Pina) Carcich
    - Ivan Carlo Carcich b. 6 Nov 1863, d. 1915 Unije
      - Andric Karcic b. 19 Jul 1888, d. 18 Jun 1972 Schwabach,Germany
        - Milivoj Hrvoje Karcic b. 11 Mar 1921 Karlovac, d. 22 Feb 2001 Arlington,Virginia
        - Berislav Karcic b. 1926 Karlovac, d. 6 Apr 2007
      - Dragotin Carcich b. 1905
        - Ljerka Karcic

1   2   3   4   5   6

CARCICH, KARCICH, KARČIĆ   (Baldich, Baldić)

Chyrstophorus (Christopher) Carcich (1750-1834) was designated *Balde* on the death register for Unije and gave the lineage name of Baldich to this Carcich family branch. The derivation of *Balde* is unknown.

Gaudenzio Carcich (1851-1922) married in Unije in 1874 and raised a family on the island. His son Andrea, born in 1886, brought his family to New York City during WWI. Andrea's son, Gaudencije Carcich-Baldich (1917-1997) (also know as Gemsi or James) was a ships captain for the American Export Line after WWII and also served in the mercantile marine during the American war in Vietnam. Gaudencije's son James Carcich (1941-) was president and director of ConProp Inc. of Pacific Palisades, California.

Emilia Carcich (1891-1980), Ivan Karcich (1924-), Margarita Carcich (1912-)

122

Carcich, Karcich, Karčić (Baldich) — Unije, Croatia

Paolo Carcich

Cristoforo Carcich (Balde) b. 1750, d. 23 Dec 1834
+ Anna Nicolich m. 6 Jul 1779
   Antonius Carcich b. 1786, d. 20 Jan 1830
   + Ana Radoslovich
      Andreus Carcich b. 1811
      + Mariae Carcich b. 8 Jan 1819
         Gaudenzio Antonius (Saldotovice) Carcich b. 4 Dec 1851, bu. 5 Oct 1922
         + Lucia Giovanna Carcich (Pasquich) b. 11 Dec 1851, m. 9 Feb 1874, d. 25
           Dec 1924
            Maria Giovanna Carcich b. 20 Jan 1875
            + Giovanni Antonio (Jovanin) Carcich (Bravarof) b. 11 Oct 1869, d. 1954
            Giovana Adrianna Carcich b. 19 Oct 1877, d. 1917
            + Dominic Lupic b. 25 Feb 1870, m. 31 Jul 1895
               Maria Elisabetta Lupic b. 19 Nov 1896, d. 26 Feb 1899
               Franciscus Antonius Lupic b. 2 Oct 1897, d. 6 Oct 1897
               Antonius Tomislav Lupic b. 1 Mar 1899, d. 16 Jan 1959
               Aurora Rosa Lupic b. 5 Jan 1901
            Lucia Carcich b. 9 Sep 1883, d. 13 May 1958
            + Ivon Carcich b. 1881, d. 1917
              Giacomina Carcich b. 30 Aug 1912, d. 10 Sep 1994
              Louis (Luigi) Carcich b. 4 Nov 1913, d. 7 May 1997
              John (Giani) Carcich b. 23 Mar 1915
            Andrea Carcich b. 22 Aug 1886
            + Maria (Babica) Carcich b. 1894, d. 30 Dec 1976
              Lucy (Lucia) Carcich b. 1913
              Gaudencije Julius (James) Carcich b. 16 Feb 1917, d. 2
               Jul 1997
              Andrew Carcich b. Jul 1919
            Josephina (Bepa) Carcich
            + Andrea (Simef) Rerecich
              Paulina Rerecich d. 6 Jan 1986
            + Domenico Rerecich b. 1886, m. 1911
              Dominic Rerecich b. 18 Aug 1911, d. 15 Aug 1975
              Andrew Rerecich b. 23 Dec 1921,
               d. 10 Oct 1994
              Lucija Rerecich b. 30 May 1923, d. 5 Mar 1996
              Joseph (Juzepe) Rerecich b. 31 Dec 1924, d. 15 Aug 1995
            Emilia Carcich b. 12 Sep 1891, d. 18 Mar 1980
            + John Carcich b. 25 Mar 1886, m. 23 Nov 1910, d. 12 Nov 1964
              Margarita Carcich b. 5 Jul 1912
              Ivan Victor Karcich b. 8 May 1924
            Guidita Carcich b. 30 Jun 1893
            + Luca Carcich b. 31 Oct 1889, d. 19 Jun 1944
              Felicita Carcich b. 12 Aug 1919, d. 16 Apr 1977
              Andrea Carcich b. 21 Feb 1921
            Alessandro Carcich b. 28 Sep 1897, d. 23 Jun 1972
            + Giacomina Carcich b. 1897
              Alessandro Carcich b. 1929
         Anna Carcich b. 11 Sep 1857

1   2   3   4   5   6   7

CARCICH, KARCICH, KARČIĆ (Bravarof)

May be one of the oldest Carcich family lineages attested to by its occurence in 18th Century church records for Mali Losinj and Cunski. The name Bravarof likely is derived from *bravar* or lock-keeper. The name was used to describe the shepherds of Unije in records dating from 1631 and 1679.

One family of Bravarof dates back to Pavl Karčić from Unije whose son's Karstić, Mate, Paolo, and Martin raised several future Bravarof families in the early part of the 18th Century. Some members of this family established new families in Cunski on the island of Losinj. The Cunski families with origins in Unije are listed in the following family genealogies.

Antonio Giovanni Carcich (1860-) known as *Moli Toni* was one of the first people from Unije to go the United States arrived in New York in 1874.

Domenico Carcich (1858-1925)
and Francesca Nadalin (1859-1937)

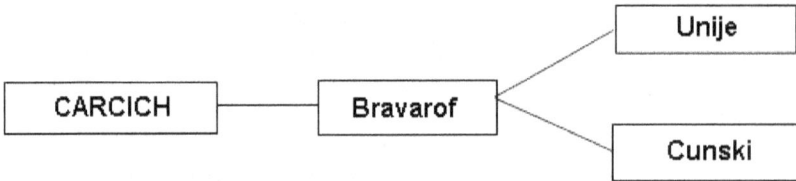

Carcich, Karcich, Karčić (Bravarof)
Family HomeNo. 24 Unije

Carcich, Karcich, Karčić (Bravarof)
Home No. 42 Unije

Carcich, Karcich, Karčić (Bravarof) — Unije, Croatia

Martin Carcich (Stari Bravar)
Andreas Carcich b. 1759, d. 8 Sep 1842
Dominicus Carcich b. 26 Apr 1801, d. 13 Aug 1871
Maria Carcich b. 1824, d. 1850
Maria Catharina Carcich b. 15 Oct 1829, d. 19 Oct 1829
Giovanni (Zaneto) Carcich b. 16 Apr 1831
Domenico Giobe Carcich (Carjeni) b. 21 May 1857, d. 28 Jan 1918
Giovanni Andrea (Zaneto) Carcich b. 29 Apr 1881
Domenico Carcich b. 1911, d. 12 Dec 1918
Domenico Carcich b. 19 Jan 1882, d. 31 Jan 1908
Giovanni Rafaele Carcich b. 24 Oct 1861
Benjamino Eduardo Carcich b. 12 Oct 1864, d. 30 Jun 1919
Ivan Carcich b. 23 May 1902, d. 24 Oct 1923
Maria Carcich b. 1908, d. 31 Dec 2000
Veneranda Carcich b. 1930
Maria Carcich b. 24 Jan 1934
Nerina Carcich b. 3 Jan 1938
Beniamina Carcich
Giana Carcich
Nicoletta Carcich b. 22 Jun 1909, d. 5 Nov 1988
Marco Domenico Carcich b. 10 Mar 1866
Iani (Kakao) Carcich b. 1897, d. 25 Aug 1958
Maria Carcich b. 14 May 1921
Berta Carcich b. 12 Mar 1925
Lina Carcich b. 1929
Ines Carcich b. 23 Jul 1935
Zaneto Carcich
Dorotea Gaudenzia Carcich b. 1 Jun 1875, d. 6 Jun 1875
Antonio Gasparo Carcich b. 14 May 1876, d. 1948
Anthony Carcich b. 4 Nov 1909, d. 30 Nov 1994
Anthony Carcich
Jean Carcich
Emily Carcich
Giacomina Carcich b. 1904
Maria Domenica Carcich b. 5 Jun 1878, d. 1961
Ana Carcich
Giacomina Carcich b. 1897
Alessandro Carcich b. 1929
Maria Carcich b. 28 May 1908, d. 19 Jan 1961
Urbano Segota b. 24 May 1928
Maria (Marica) Segota b. 19 Nov 1929
Concetta Carcich b. 8 Dec 1912, d. 24 Jan 1993
Bruna Radoslovich
Joseph Radoslovich
Giovanna (Zburkin) Carcich b. 1916
Iani Carcich b. 19 Jul 1919, d. Aug 1981
Giovanni Carcich
Maria Carcich b. 31 Oct 1944
Rosa Carcich
Dario Carcich b. 2 Jul 1946, d. 24 Mar 1948
Giovanna Dorotea Carcich b. 12 Jul 1880

1   2   3   4   5   6   7

Carcich, Karcich, Karčić (Bravarof) — Unije, Croatia

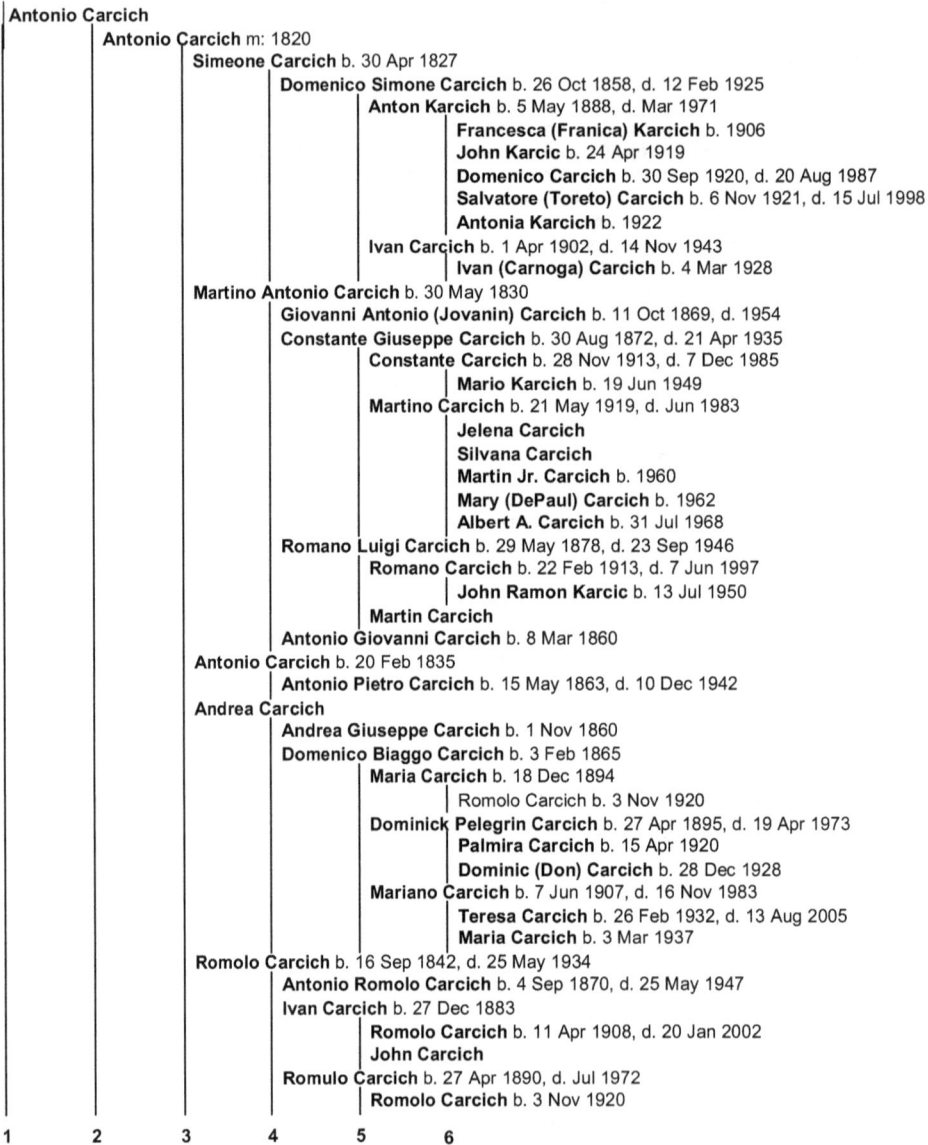

Antonio Carcich
  Antonio Carcich m: 1820
    Simeone Carcich b. 30 Apr 1827
      Domenico Simone Carcich b. 26 Oct 1858, d. 12 Feb 1925
        Anton Karcich b. 5 May 1888, d. Mar 1971
          Francesca (Franica) Karcich b. 1906
          John Karcic b. 24 Apr 1919
          Domenico Carcich b. 30 Sep 1920, d. 20 Aug 1987
          Salvatore (Toreto) Carcich b. 6 Nov 1921, d. 15 Jul 1998
          Antonia Karcich b. 1922
        Ivan Carcich b. 1 Apr 1902, d. 14 Nov 1943
          Ivan (Carnoga) Carcich b. 4 Mar 1928
    Martino Antonio Carcich b. 30 May 1830
      Giovanni Antonio (Jovanin) Carcich b. 11 Oct 1869, d. 1954
      Constante Giuseppe Carcich b. 30 Aug 1872, d. 21 Apr 1935
        Constante Carcich b. 28 Nov 1913, d. 7 Dec 1985
          Mario Karcich b. 19 Jun 1949
        Martino Carcich b. 21 May 1919, d. Jun 1983
          Jelena Carcich
          Silvana Carcich
          Martin Jr. Carcich b. 1960
          Mary (DePaul) Carcich b. 1962
          Albert A. Carcich b. 31 Jul 1968
      Romano Luigi Carcich b. 29 May 1878, d. 23 Sep 1946
        Romano Carcich b. 22 Feb 1913, d. 7 Jun 1997
          John Ramon Karcic b. 13 Jul 1950
        Martin Carcich
      Antonio Giovanni Carcich b. 8 Mar 1860
    Antonio Carcich b. 20 Feb 1835
      Antonio Pietro Carcich b. 15 May 1863, d. 10 Dec 1942
    Andrea Carcich
      Andrea Giuseppe Carcich b. 1 Nov 1860
      Domenico Biaggo Carcich b. 3 Feb 1865
        Maria Carcich b. 18 Dec 1894
          Romolo Carcich b. 3 Nov 1920
        Dominick Pelegrin Carcich b. 27 Apr 1895, d. 19 Apr 1973
          Palmira Carcich b. 15 Apr 1920
          Dominic (Don) Carcich b. 28 Dec 1928
        Mariano Carcich b. 7 Jun 1907, d. 16 Nov 1983
          Teresa Carcich b. 26 Feb 1932, d. 13 Aug 2005
          Maria Carcich b. 3 Mar 1937
    Romolo Carcich b. 16 Sep 1842, d. 25 May 1934
      Antonio Romolo Carcich b. 4 Sep 1870, d. 25 May 1947
      Ivan Carcich b. 27 Dec 1883
        Romolo Carcich b. 11 Apr 1908, d. 20 Jan 2002
        John Carcich
      Romulo Carcich b. 27 Apr 1890, d. Jul 1972
        Romolo Carcich b. 3 Nov 1920

1   2   3   4   5   6

Agnes Gonxha Bojaxhiu (Mother Teresa)
(1910-1997) and Ted Carcich (1929-2003)

Benjamino Carcich
(Bravarof) (1864-1919)

Domenica Carcich
(Pasquich) (1856-1918)

Carcich (Jevin) Family, Washington State 1997

CARCICH, KARCICH, KARČIĆ (Bravarof) Cunski

The Carcich families that settled in Cunski did so in the 18th Century and arrived there from Unije. Zuanne Carcich (1746-1819), son of Cristoforo was born in Unije and married Margarita Knezich in Cunski in 1774. His family gave rise to the Bravarof branch in Cunski of which there are several branches.

Giovanni Carcich (1867-1943) owned a restaurant in Freeport, Long Island, which he sold to the Hroncich family. He was known as Captain John and began working as a fish buyer who resold fish at Fulton's Fish Market in Manhattan. Giovanni also owned a shipyard in partnership with the Scopinich brothers to who he sold his share for $25,000 in 1929. The shipyard was afterwards known as the Scopinich Ship Yard and is still operated by the Scopinich family as the Hamptons Shipyards, Inc. in East Quoque, New York.

"Captain" John Carcich (1867-1943), Insp. Ford
Freeport, N.Y., 1925.

Carcich Restaurant and Shipyard, Freeport, N.Y.

Marriage record, November 13, 1774 Cunski for Zuanne Carcich (1746-1819) of Unije

Carcich, Karcich, Karčić (Bravarof) — Cunski, Croatia

Zuanne Carcich b. 1746 Unije, m. 13 Nov 1774 Cunski, d. 1 Oct 1819 Cunski
    Mattio Carcich b. 19 Feb 1780 Cunski
        Iuanne Carcich b. 28 Sep 1815 Cunski
            Dominicus Stephanus Carcich b. 30 Aug 1855 Cunski, d. 23 Mar 1927
                Giuseppe Carcich b. 1883, d. 13 Sep 1936 Buenos Aires,Argentina
                Giovanni Felice Carcich b. 28 Feb 1881 Austria, d. 1965
                    Corina Carcich b. 20 Aug 1910
                    Anita Carcich b. 23 Nov 1911, d. 2 Nov 1995 Cliffside Park,New Jersey
                    Renato Carcich b. 15 Dec 1914, d. 20 Aug 2001
                    John Carcich b. 19 Dec 1919, d. 18 Jul 2000 Cliffside Park, New Jersey

        Antonio Carcich b. 24 Jan 1819 Cunski
            Ioannes Ioachim Carcich b. 21 Aug 1859 Cunski, d. 2 Jan 1945 Cunski
                Giovanni Carcich b. 31 Dec 1898 Cunski, d. 1934
                    John Carcich b. 1923
                    Anthony Carcich b. 1925
                    Mario Carcich b. 1934
                    Venanzio J. (Joe) Carcich b. 1924
                    Anna Carcich b. 1927
              Toni Carcich
                    Maria Carcich b. 1913
                    Antonietta (Eda) Carcich b. 1915
                    Guido J. Carcich b. 1920
    Antonio Carcich b. 15 Apr 1785 Cunski, d. 3 Apr 1868
        Pietro Ludovico Carcich b. 25 Aug 1834 Cunski,Austria, d. 5 Nov 1908
            Giovanni Carcich b. 10 Dec 1866, d. 2 May 1941
                Anthony Simon Carcich b. 28 Oct 1907, d. 10 Nov 1973 Fairview, New Jersey
                Romeo (Peter) Carcich b. 1915
            Nicolo (Pasquich) Carcich b. 18 Feb 1882 Cunski, d. Jul 1964
                Nicolo Carcich b. 12 Aug 1914 Cunski, d. 22 Nov 1989 Keyport,New Jersey
                Antonio Carcich b. 29 Dec 1919 Cunski, d. 27 Jan 1998 Lovell,Maine
        Franciscus Rajmundo Carcich b. 2 Sep 1827 Cunski
            Antonio Carcich b. 1848, d. 6 Oct 1930 ,Colorado
                John Carcich b. 1874, d. 18 Jul 1906 Colorado
                    John Carcich b. 12 Dec 1900 Cunski
                    d. Mar 1985 Hasbrouck Height, New Jersey
                    Antonio Carcich b. 9 Feb 1905 Cunski, d. 14 Dec 1978
                Francesco Carcich b. 1886, d. 13 Jan 1936 ,Colorado
            Alexius Carcich b. 2 Nov 1853 Cunski, d. 29 Jun 1920
                Francesco Carcich b. 1882, d. Feb 1924
                  Frank Carcich b. 30 Jan 1915, d. Sep 1986 New York
                    Maria Carcich
                    Anna Carcich b. 24 Jul 1923, d. Jan 1988,New York
                    Milena Carcich
        Francesco Joannes Karcich b. 2 Jan 1860 Cunski
            Francesco Carcich b. Nov 1872, d. 1961 Cunski
                Mary Carcich b. 30 Jul 1906, d. 12 Sep 1982
                Domenica (Dinka \ Minnie) Carcich b. 6 Nov 1907
                Francesco (Frank) Carcich b. 12 Oct 1909, d. 15 Feb 1995
                Louis (Ljuborko) Carcich b. 12 Dec 1911, d. 20 Mar 1995 ,California
                Matteo Carcich b. 24 Feb 1915
            Matt P. Karcich b. 22 Feb 1876 Cunski, d. 29 Dec 1956 Trinidad,Colorado
                Antonia Karcich b. 1903
                Domenica Veronica (Minnie) Karcich b. 1913 Trinidad,Colorado
                Matthew F. Karcich b. 27 May 1915 Colorado Springs,Colorado
                Frank Karcich b. 6 Sep 1917, d. 3 Jul 2001 Colorado Springs,Colorado
                Dominic Karcich b. 1919, d. 17 Aug 1943
            Domenico Carcich b. 18 Jan 1880 Cunski, d. 4 Mar 1924 South America
                Federico Miro Carcich b. 1910, d. 1994 New Jersey

1   2   3   4   5   6

CARCICH, KARCICH, KARČIĆ (Cicuola-Cunski)

The origins of the Cicuola lineage name for this family is unknown.

The Cicuola Carcich family came late to Cunski from Unije. Mattio Karcich was born in Unije and married in Cunski in 1789 followed by his brother Martin in 1800. This family has many descendents in Cunski.

The family of Anton Bonaventura Carcich (1854-1918) had sons who moved away from Cunski. Son Bonaventura Carcich (1885-1962) saw service in the Austrian military during WWI and later settled and raised a family in Slovenia. His brother Vladimiro (Walter) Carcich (1890-1973) settled in Trinidad, Colorado. Walter's descendents are now found in Colorado, California, and Arizona.

Anton Bonaventura Carcich (1854-1918)

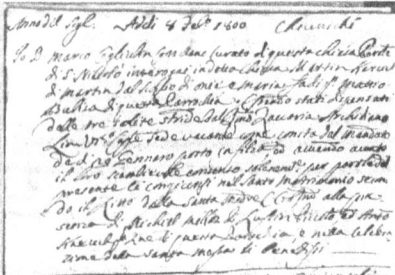

Marriage record Martin Carcich of Unije & Maria Bubiza February 8, 1800, Cunski

Karčić Family, Slovenia 1932: Bono (1925-1997), Ana Tomazić (1894-1973), Janko (1928-), Bonaventura (1885-1962), Niko (1927-)

Carcich, Karcich, Karčić (Cicuola) — Cunski, Croatia

Martin Karcich b. 1749, d. 7 Oct 1829 Cunski

    Martin Karcich b. Unije
    + Maria Bubiza b. 1780, m. 8 Feb 1800 Cunski, d. 6 Sep 1815 Cunski
        Matio Karcich b. 30 Jul 1802 Cunski
        + Anna Tarabochia b. 1808, m. 31 Jan 1827 Cunski
            Dominic Carcich b. 12 Sep 1841 Cunski
            + Dominica Belic b. 1842 Cunski, m. 5 Oct 1871 Cunski
                Matteo Carcich b. 1875
                + Giovanna b. 1874
                    Emma Carcich b. 1900, d. 1996
                    Matthew Carcich b. 13 Apr 1903, d. Apr 1970 New Jersey
                Giovanni Maria Carcich b. 20 Jun 1876 Cunski, d. 26 Jul 1970 USA
                + Maria Dominica Giuseppina Martinolich b. 7 May 1882 Mali Losinj, m. 21 Feb 1906
                Mali Losinj
                    Dominick Carcich b. 7 May 1907, d. 1947
                    Maria Antonia Carcich b. 24 Oct 1909
                    Giovanni Carcich b. 29 Jun 1912
                    Edward (Hector) Carcich b. 28 Dec 1913,
                  d. 31 Jul 2000 Atlantic Highlands,New Jersey
                    Giuseppe Carcich b. 8 Aug 1923 New York, d. 8 Sep 1989 ,New Jersey
                Nicholas Carcich
        Martin Karcich b. 1805 Cunski, d. 15 Nov 1871
        + Giovanna Carlich b. 1812, m. 17 Jul 1833 Cunski
        Ioanni (Joannes) Karcich b. Sep 1812 Cunski
        + Maria Carcich b. 13 Oct 1816 Cunski, m. 20 Oct 1836 Cunski
            Ivan (John) Karcich b. Dec 1844 Cunski, d. 24 Oct 1930
            + Ana Cattarina Karlic b. Nerezine
                Dominic Karcich b. 26 Jun 1886, d. Aug 1965
                + Maria Bussanich
                    Dinka Karcich b. 21 Dec 1914
                    John Karcich b. 1919
                    Anna Karcich b. 1920
                    Anthony E. Karcich b. 1923
                    Mario Karcich b. 1933
                John Karcich b. 1877
                + Marija Vogdanovic b. 1887, m. 7 Oct 1903 Cunski
                Anton Karcich b. 21 Apr 1879 Cunski
                + Mary Karcich b. 1882 Cunski, m. 28 Apr 1921
            Anton Bonaventura Carcich b. 14 Jul 1854 Cunski, d. 27 Jun 1918
            + Mika Karoline Vidulich b. 6 Dec 1862, d. 4 Jan 1951
                Bonaventura Karcich b. 26 Aug 1885, d. 23 Aug 1962
                + **Ana Tomazic** b. 20 Jul 1894, d. 24 May 1973
                    Bono Karcic b. 18 May 1925 Maribor
                  d. 12 Feb 1997 Zalec,Slovenia
                    Janko (Ivan) Karcic b. 28 Jan 1928 Maribor
                    Niko Karcic b. 8 Mar 1927 Maribor, d. 25 Apr 1997 Zalec,Slovenia
                Walter (Vladimiro) Karcich b. 20 Jul 1890
                d. 20 Jun 1973 Salinas,California
                + Edna Liley b. 1 Apr 1898, m. 23 Jan 1915, d. 15 Aug 1981
                    Walter Joseph Karcich b. 15 Mar 1918 Berwind,Colorado
                    Elmer George Karcich b. 22 Dec 1919 Alfalfa,Colorado, d. 12 Jan 1988 San
                  Bruno,California
                    Minerva Karcich b. 5 Mar 1922, d. 20 Jan 1923
                    Edward Bonaventura Karcich b. 18 Jun 1923 Sequndo,California, d. 22 Apr
                  1990 Bridgetown,Barbados
                    Dorothy Dean Karcich b. 22 Aug 1927

1   2   3   4   5   6

CARCICH, KARCICH, KARČIĆ   (Jevin/Gevin)

The origin of this lineage family name is derived from John or Ivan, written either as Jevin or Gevin. The earliest origins of this name is uncertain, but the Jevin branch may be descendent from the Bravarof clan during the first half of the 1700's.

Olivia Carcich (1888-1974)

Isadore (Theodore) Carcich-Jevin (1905-1988) was a coppersmith between 1925 and 1926 in Camden, N. J. Pennsylvania Railroad. He became a Seventh-day Adventist (SDA) in 1926. He received his high school education at the Greater New York Academy in New York between 1927 and 1930 and his post-secondary education at Atlantic Union College between 1931 and 1934 in South Lancaster, MA. He was Associate Pastor between July 1934 and 1935 in Glens Falls, New York, pastor in Binghamton, New York in 1936, Rochester, NY in 1937, and Syracuse, NY between 1938 and 1940. He was a pastor in Boston, MA between 1940 and 1942. He was President of Southern New England Conf. of SDA between 1942 and 1946 in South Lancaster, MA. He was president, of the SDA Illinois Conference between 1946 and 1950, the SDA Mid , Washington Conference between 1950 and 1957, the Mid American Union Conference

from 1957 to 1962. He was General Vice President of the SDA General Conference between 1962 and 1974 in Washington, D.C. He retired in July 1974 in Colton, Washington. Theodore Carcich had many descendents, which today are spread throughout the western United States.

Theodore Carcich (1905-1988)

Carcich, Karcich, Karčić Family Home No.109; Hakija Mujovic, Mate Karcic (1904-1996), Matthew Karcic, Martin Nikolic (1874-), in 1952

Carcich, Karcich, Karčić (Jevin) — Unije, Croatia

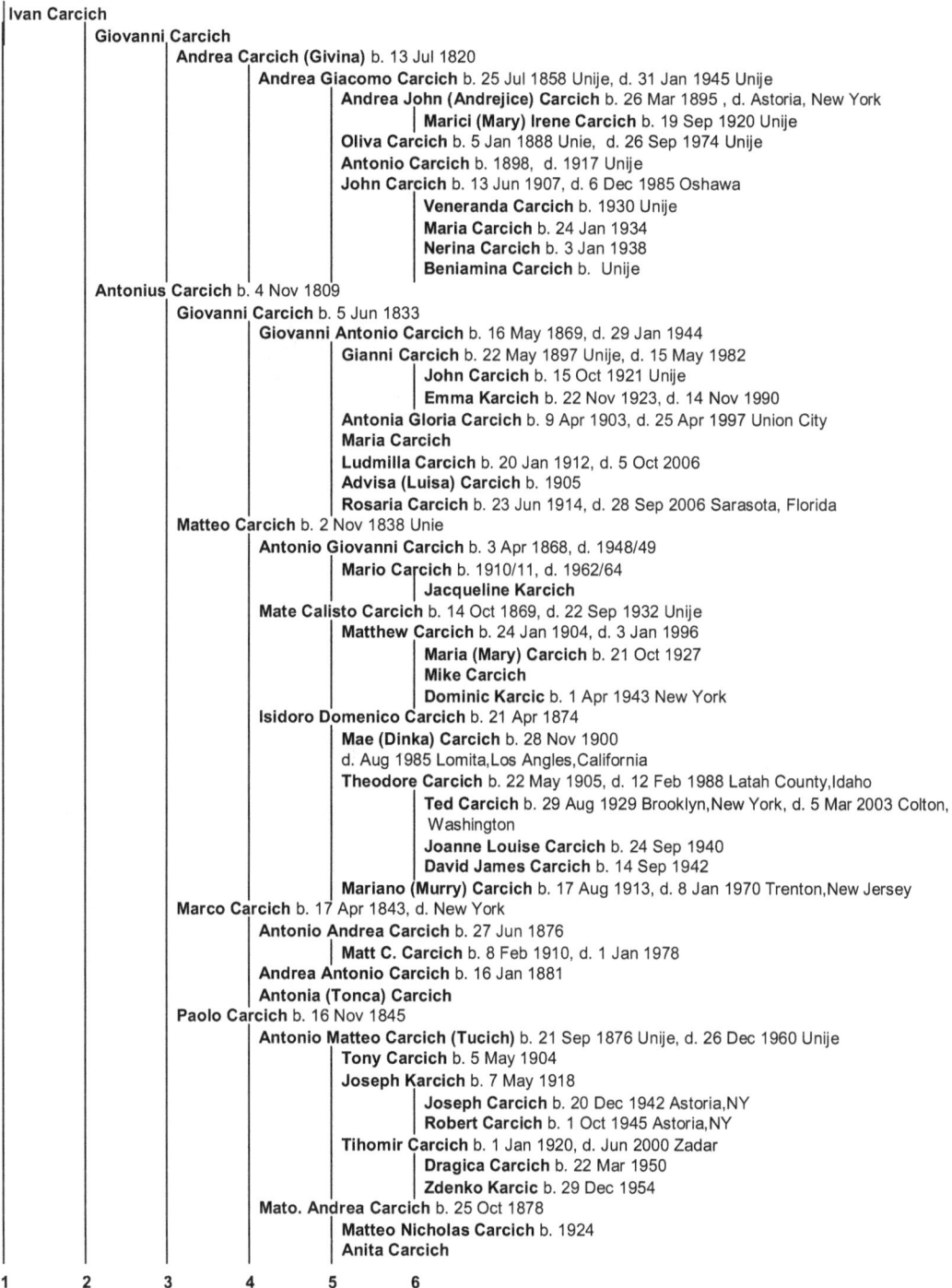

Ivan Carcich
- Giovanni Carcich
  - Andrea Carcich (Givina) b. 13 Jul 1820
    - Andrea Giacomo Carcich b. 25 Jul 1858 Unije, d. 31 Jan 1945 Unije
      - Andrea John (Andrejice) Carcich b. 26 Mar 1895 , d. Astoria, New York
        - Marici (Mary) Irene Carcich b. 19 Sep 1920 Unije
      - Oliva Carcich b. 5 Jan 1888 Unie, d. 26 Sep 1974 Unije
      - Antonio Carcich b. 1898, d. 1917 Unije
      - John Carcich b. 13 Jun 1907, d. 6 Dec 1985 Oshawa
        - Veneranda Carcich b. 1930 Unije
        - Maria Carcich b. 24 Jan 1934
        - Nerina Carcich b. 3 Jan 1938
        - Beniamina Carcich b. Unije
- Antonius Carcich b. 4 Nov 1809
  - Giovanni Carcich b. 5 Jun 1833
    - Giovanni Antonio Carcich b. 16 May 1869, d. 29 Jan 1944
      - Gianni Carcich b. 22 May 1897 Unije, d. 15 May 1982
        - John Carcich b. 15 Oct 1921 Unije
        - Emma Karcich b. 22 Nov 1923, d. 14 Nov 1990
      - Antonia Gloria Carcich b. 9 Apr 1903, d. 25 Apr 1997 Union City
      - Maria Carcich
      - Ludmilla Carcich b. 20 Jan 1912, d. 5 Oct 2006
      - Advisa (Luisa) Carcich b. 1905
      - Rosaria Carcich b. 23 Jun 1914, d. 28 Sep 2006 Sarasota, Florida
  - Matteo Carcich b. 2 Nov 1838 Unie
    - Antonio Giovanni Carcich b. 3 Apr 1868, d. 1948/49
      - Mario Carcich b. 1910/11, d. 1962/64
        - Jacqueline Karcich
    - Mate Calisto Carcich b. 14 Oct 1869, d. 22 Sep 1932 Unije
      - Matthew Carcich b. 24 Jan 1904, d. 3 Jan 1996
        - Maria (Mary) Carcich b. 21 Oct 1927
        - Mike Carcich
        - Dominic Karcic b. 1 Apr 1943 New York
    - Isidoro Domenico Carcich b. 21 Apr 1874
      - Mae (Dinka) Carcich b. 28 Nov 1900
        d. Aug 1985 Lomita,Los Angles,California
      - Theodore Carcich b. 22 May 1905, d. 12 Feb 1988 Latah County,Idaho
        - Ted Carcich b. 29 Aug 1929 Brooklyn,New York, d. 5 Mar 2003 Colton, Washington
        - Joanne Louise Carcich b. 24 Sep 1940
        - David James Carcich b. 14 Sep 1942
      - Mariano (Murry) Carcich b. 17 Aug 1913, d. 8 Jan 1970 Trenton,New Jersey
  - Marco Carcich b. 17 Apr 1843, d. New York
    - Antonio Andrea Carcich b. 27 Jun 1876
      - Matt C. Carcich b. 8 Feb 1910, d. 1 Jan 1978
    - Andrea Antonio Carcich b. 16 Jan 1881
    - Antonia (Tonca) Carcich
  - Paolo Carcich b. 16 Nov 1845
    - Antonio Matteo Carcich (Tucich) b. 21 Sep 1876 Unije, d. 26 Dec 1960 Unije
      - Tony Carcich b. 5 May 1904
      - Joseph Karcich b. 7 May 1918
        - Joseph Carcich b. 20 Dec 1942 Astoria,NY
        - Robert Carcich b. 1 Oct 1945 Astoria,NY
      - Tihomir Carcich b. 1 Jan 1920, d. Jun 2000 Zadar
        - Dragica Carcich b. 22 Mar 1950
        - Zdenko Karcic b. 29 Dec 1954
    - Mato. Andrea Carcich b. 25 Oct 1878
      - Matteo Nicholas Carcich b. 1924
      - Anita Carcich

1   2   3   4   5   6

CARCICH, KARCICH, KARČIĆ   (Pasquich)

Antonio Dominicus Carcich of Zne from Unije. (father John) married Pasqua Moricich in 1772. Pasqua was born in 1736 and may have given her name to the lineage name for this family, the Pasquich's.

John Gabriel Karcich, born in 1892 left Unije for the United States in 1910 and served in the U.S. military in 1917. He settled with his family in Price, Utah, where some of his descendents remain.

John Gabriel Karcich (1892-1973)

Andrea Karcich (1911-1970) was a draughtsman. His son Andrew A. Karcich (1942-) became the school principal of Central High School, Bridgeport, Connecticut. Emil S. Karcich (1916-1961) became a fireman on Long Island, while his son Emily John Karcich (1945-) became an attorney, and his second son, Kenneth James (1950-) became an engineer at the University of Rochester.

Antonia Carcich (1862-1936)

Carcich, Karcich, Karčić (Pasquich) Family Home, No. 139 Unije

Carcich, Karcich, Karčić (Pasquich) — Unije, Croatia

Zuane Carcich
  Paolo Carcich
  Anto. Dominicus Carcich b. Unie
      Andrija Carcich b. 1780, d. 26 Oct 1836 Unije, Austria
          Dominicus Carcich b. 1804, d. 3 May 1829 Unie
          Andrea Carcich b. 12 Oct 1806
              Maria Karcich b. 23 May 1844 Unije, d. 3 Dec 1939 Cunski
              Antonio Giuliano Carcich b. 1856 Unije, d. 10 Dec 1936 Unije
                  Emilia Antonia Carcich b. 9 Apr 1880
                  Andrea Karcich b. 22 Aug 1882, d. 25 Mar 1952
                      Anton Karcich b. 7 Nov 1906, d. 13 Jun 1978
                      Andrew Karcich b. 1 Aug 1911,
                      d. 9 Jun 1970 New Haven,Connecticut
                      John Karcich b. 21 Apr 1913 New York
                      Emil S. Karcich b. 18 Apr 1916, d. 25 Jul 1961
                      Mary Milka Karcich b. 1 Jun 1922 New York
                  Anthony Carcich b. 22 Sep 1903, d. 30 Dec 2000 Pennsylvania
                      Emilia Carcich b. 21 Mar 1927 Unije
          Matteo Carcich b. 20 Sep 1813
              Giovanni Filomeno Karcich b. 13 Jan 1856 Unije
                  Mate Karcich b. 1881 Cunski, d. 1951/52 Colorado
                      George John Karcich b. 22 Feb 1911 Trindad,Colorado
                      Catarina Mattea Karcich b. 20 Apr 1912 Colorado
                      Matt Giuseppe Karcich b. 2 Mar 1915 Trinidad,Colorado, d. 11 Apr
                        1999 Arvada, Colorado
                      Mary Anna Karcich b. 3 Oct 1916 Latuda,Utah
                  Mary Karcich
                  John Gabriel Karcich b. 17 Mar 1892
                  d. 26 Jul 1973 Price, Utah
                      Victor John Karcich b. 3 Oct 1921 Price, Utah, d. 6 Apr 1977
                        Price, Utah
                      William Sr. Karcich b. 10 Feb 1920 Mutual,Utah, d. 2 May 2000
                        Spring Glen,Utah
                      Lois Karcich d. Dec 1994
                      Leona Karcich b. 1923
                  Antonio Karcich
                      Claudio Karcich
              Maria Domenica Carcich b. 20 Jan 1861
              Filomena Carcich (Calebinca)
                  Mato. Andrea Carcich b. 25 Oct 1878
                      Matteo Nicholas Carcich b. 1924
                      Anita Carcich
              Antonia Anna Carcich b. 5 Jul 1875
              Maria Silvestra Carcich b. 26 Sep 1870
          Antonius Carcich b. 1819, d. 11 Apr 1838 Unije
          Giuseppe Carcich b. 12 Oct 1823
              Andrea Carcich b. 26 Aug 1849, d. 7 Aug 1921 Unije
                  Andrea Karcich b. 1 Sep 1911 New York, d. 20 Dec 1993 Port
                    Charlotte,Florida
              Antonia Carcich b.1862, d. 1936

1   2   3   4   5   6   7

CARCICH, KARCICH, KARČIĆ   (Rocov)

The Rocov lineage name is derived from the patronym for Rochus (Roco). The earliest known ancestor is Rochus Carcich (1761-1854) son of Nicolaus, who may have given this lineage name to the family.

Since the lineage name Rocovica appears to be the diminutive of Rocov, this family may very likely be a branch of the older Rocov lineage dating back to Rochus Carcich (1761-1854) son of Nicolaus. The Rocovica lineage can only be extended back to Antonio Gendarmo Carcich who was married some time prior to 1836.

Carcich, Karcich, Karčić (Rocov)
Home No. 113 Unije

Antonia Carcich (1869-1957)
and Andrea Karcic (1866-1951)

Carcich, Karcich, Karčić (Rocov) HomeNo.65 Unije

Carcich, Karcich, Karčić (Rocov) — Unije, Croatia

Nicolaus Carcich
    Rochus Carcich b. 1761, d. 29 Nov 1854 Unije
        Rocco Carcich b. 1792, d. 24 May 1866
        Gaudencio Karcich b. 1798 Unie, d. 24 Mar 1858 Unije
            Roco Carcich b. 23 Jan 1823
                Giovanni Gaudenzio Carcich b. 18 Aug 1865 Mali Losinj
            Gaudentius (Gavde) Karcich b. 7 Apr 1827 Unije
                Gaudenzio Andrea Carcich b. 15 Oct 1861
                    Domenico Carcich b. 14 Apr 1893, d. 6 Oct 1963 New York,New York
                        Julie Carcich b. 25 Jan 1920 Unije
                        Jolanda (Racof) Carcich b. 1921
                Giacomina Karcich b. 25 Jul 1863
                Andrea Nicolaus Karcich b. 1 Sep 1866, d. 11 Feb 1951 Unije
                    Andrea Karcich b. 7 Oct 1890, d. 15 May 1966 Astoria,New York
                        Andrew Karcich b. 2 Sep 1920
                        Antoinette Mary Karcich b. 30 Mar 1922 Mali Losinj
                        Ivo Karcich b. 26 Aug 1928
                        Osip (Joseph) Karcich b. 22 Oct 1933
                    Joseph Karcich b. 20 Oct 1898, d. 6 Mar 1970 Astoria,Queens,New York
                        Anna Maria Karcich b. 26 Mar 1941
                        Josephine Karcich b. 9 Jun 1942
                        Antoinette Karcich b. 1943
                        Joseph Karcich b. 1947 New York
                        Martin John Karcich b. 22 Mar 1956, d. 26 Jul 1968
                        Teresa Marie Karcich b. 17 Dec 1957
                        Johnny Karcich b. 1959
                    Vladimir Karcich b. 26 Jun 1905, d. 27 Dec 1957 Unije
                        Maria Karcich
                        Vladimira Karcich
                    Radovan Karcic b. 10 Aug 1911, d. 25 Aug 1987 College Point, New York
                        Andrea Karcic b. 1938, d. 1939
                        Antoniette Karcic b. 20 May 1940
                        Ivan Karcic b. 1942, d. 1949
                        Milka Karcic b. 25 Oct 1948
                        Franco (Frank) Karcic b. 28 Apr 1953
             Martin Carcich
                Andrea Carcich
                    Meniga Carcich
                    Maria Carcich b. 3 Apr 1908
                      Louis Ciceran
                    Andrea (Rocof) Carcich b. 21 Jul 1909, d. Jan 1980 Havasu City, Arizona
                    Marco Carcich
                    Matteo Carcich
                    Tonic Carcich

1   2   3   4   5   6   7

CARCICH, KARCICH, KARČIĆ   (Zburkin)

This family traces its genealogy to Mikula (Nicolaus) Carcich who had two sons Gaudenzio, born 1795, and Mikula, born 1786. This lineage name is derived from Zburka, a region on the island of Cres north east of the village of Martinscica. Mikula (Nicolaus) Carcich is said to have worked in that area for a man by the name of Stefanich. When Stefanich died, Mikula married his widow and raised his two sons, Mikula and Gaudenzio, in Unije. Gaudenzio's family kept the Zburkin lineage name, while Mikula's family took on the lineage name of Sburcich.

Carcich, Karcich, Karčić (Zburkin) Family Home No. 173 Unije

Karubin Carcich (1872-1930) worked in the United States as early as 1897, where he was joined by several of his brothers.

Carcich, Karcich, Karčić (Zburkin) Family Home, No.222 Unije

Karubin Carcich (1872-1930)

Giuseppe Carcich (1880-1955) and Domenica Carcich (1882-1955)

Carcich, Karcich, Karčić-(Sburcich) — Unije, Croatia

Mikula Carcich
    Mikula (Nicolas) Carcich) b. 1786, d. 1860 Unije
        Joannes Carcich b. 1813, d. 28 Jan 1856 Unije
            Joannes Dominicus (Kosmic) Carcich b. 16 Feb 1850, d. 9 Jan 1932
                Giovanni Domenico Carcich b. 18 Jan 1877
                Giacomo Carcich b. 1 May 1881
                John Carcich b. 25 Mar 1886, d. 12 Nov 1964 Unije
                    Margarita Carcich b. 5 Jul 1912
                    John Victor Karcich b. 8 May 1924 Mali Losinj
            Dominic Nicolo Carcich b. 7 Aug 1852, d. 1934
                Andrea Giovanni Carcich b. 20 Oct 1879, d. 1914/18 Galicia,Austria
                    Ana Carcich b. 1906, d. Veli Losinj
                    Andrew Carcich b. 1913
                    Maria (Sburcich) Carcich b. 1915
                Joseph (Osip) Carcich b. 19 Apr 1899, d. 31 Mar 1984
                    Anna (Sburcich) Carcich b. 12 Aug 1923
                    Josip Carcich b. 24 Dec 1924
                Luca Carcich b. 18 Oct 1900, d. Jul 1968 New Jersey
                    Andric Carcich b. 10 May 1924 Unije
        Nicolo Carcich b. 1815, d. 19 Mar 1861 Unije
            Nicolo (Castro) (Calebincin) Carcich b. 27 Oct 1846
                Nick (Mikula) Carcich b. 27 Oct 1879
                Andrea (Calebincich) Karcich b. 1886, d. 1965 Unije
                    Maria Carcich b. 1908
                    Mikula Karcich b. 1912
                    Thea Carcich b. 1917/19, d. 1994/95
                    Andrea Karcic b. 1923
                Maria (Topacina) Carcich b. 31 Aug 1891, d. 1 Dec 1982 ,New Jersey
                    Andrea Nicolich b. 1918
                    Marija Nicolich
        Andrea (Podesta) Carcich b. 1 Jan 1821, d. 14 Jun 1880 Unije
            Andrianna Carcich b. 7 Mar 1863
        Giancdomenico (Pretur) Carcich b. 20 Sep 1829
            Nicolo Andrea (Mikula) Carcich b. 26 Nov 1875
                Vitorina Carcich
                    Vincent Millin
                    Victoria Millin
                John Carcich
            Andrea Giuseppe (Pretur) Carcich b. 17 Feb 1878
                Maria Carcich d. Jan 1995 Mali Losinj
                    Avelina Nicolich
                    Dolores Nicolich
                Tonka Carcich
                    Eleanora Maria (Norina) Radoslovich b. 6 Nov 1929/30
                    Andrea Radoslovich
                    Antonio Radoslovich b. 1940
            Antonia Paolina Carcich b. 17 Sep 1863
            Domenico Enrico Carcich b. 13 Feb 1865
                Ivon Carcich b. 1903, d. 1964 Unije
                    Giuseppe Carcich b. 9 Dec 1928, d. 5 Sep 2007
                Diodoro Carcich b. 1 Dec 1904, d. 7 Jan 1987 Guttenberg,New Jersey
                    Catherina Carcich
                Menigo Carcich d. 1944
                    Mary Carcich b. 19 Jul 1922 New York, d. Dec 1983
                    John P. Carcich
                Dragotin Carcich
                Tonica Carcich

1   2   3   4   5   6

Carcich, Karcich, Karčić (Zburkin) — Unije,Croatia

Mikula (Zburkin) Carcich
    Gaudentus Carcich b. 5 Dec 1795, d. 19 Nov 1877
        Nicolo (Micula) Carcich b. 18 Sep 1821
            Andrea Felice Karcich b. 19 Nov 1854
                Ivon Carcich b. 1881 Unije, d. 1917 Galicia,Austria
                Andrea Karcich b. 29 Dec 1883, d. 30 Nov 1941 New Jersey
                Roko Karcich b. 9 Mar 1887, d. 12 Feb 1957
                Joseph Vincent Karcich b. 1894
                Martinello (Martin) Karcich
                Romano Karcich b. 1909/10
                Pasqua Karcich
            Antonio Proto Carcich b. 12 Jan 1857
            Giovanni N. Carcich b. 8 May 1866
            Gaudenzio Nicolo Carcich b. 7 Jun 1869
                Nikola (Mikula) Karcic b. 5 Jun 1901, d. 9 May 1985
                Antonio Karcich b. 9 Aug 1907, d. Feb 1976 Queens,New York
            Nicolo Gaudenzio Carcich b. 8 May 1872
        Giovanni Carcich b. 23 Oct 1829
            Giovanni Gaudenzio Carcich b. 11 Nov 1868
            Gaudenzio Andrea Carcich b. 3 May 1872, d. 5 May 1951
        Dominic Matheus Carcich b. 17 Feb 1835, d. 10 Feb 1917 Unije
            Cherubino Domenico Carcich b. 28 Jan 1872, d. 28 Dec 1930
                Elvera Carcich
                Anna Carcich b. 1914 Manhattan,New York
                Cerebino (Phil) Carcich b. 1918
                Vitorio (Victor) Carcich b. 28 Dec 1919 Manhattan,New York, d. 20 Sep 1982
                Mary Carcich
                Charles (Celestino) Carcich b. 1922, d. 2003
            Giovanni Gaudenzio (Ivancina) Carcich b. 10 Sep 1875, d. 1956 Unije
                Giacomina Carcich b. 1897
                Maria Carcich b. 28 May 1908, d. 19 Jan 1961 Unije
                Concetta Carcich b. 8 Dec 1912, d. 24 Jan 1993 New Jersey
                Giovanna Carcich b. 1916
                Iani Carcich b. 19 Jul 1919, d. Aug 1981 Caldwell,New Jersey
            Giuseppe (Bepo) Carcich b. 21 Apr 1880, d. 10 May 1955 Unije
                Dominick (Meme) Carcich b. 2 Jun 1912, d. 27 Aug 2000 Queens,NY
                Anita Carcich b. 13 Aug 1914, d. 21 Dec 1996 Udine,Italy
                Letizia Grazia Carcich b. 6 Mar 1921
                Piter (Peter) Carcich b. 1923
                Josephine Domenica (Pina) Karcich b. 2 Jan 1927, d. 5 Mar 2005 Oshawa, Canada
        Marco Carcich b. 25 Aug 1837
            Domenico Gaudenzio Carcich b. 30 Jul 1875, d. 1905
                Marco Carcich
                Dinko Carcich b. 3 Dec 1900, d. 14 Feb 1981 Unije
                Josip Sr. Carcich b. 24 Feb 1905, d. 17 Jul 1975

1   2   3   4   5

CARCICH, KARCICH, KARČIĆ - Early History

The earliest known recorded references for Karčić is at Vrbnik on the island of Krk in 1490 where the name of Luka Karčić appears in the statutes of that town. The surname Karčić and its variants Kerčić, Karšić, Keršić, Chersich, Karsich are found in Vrbnik from the 15th to the 16th Centuries. The surname did not survive on Krk into the 20th Century, but as late as the middle of the 18th Century the surname is found in association with the island of Krk. The variant, Charsich and Carsich are found in the records for Osor during the 17th Century. The migration pattern for the upper Adriatic islands radiates from Krk to the islands to the south, and it is highly likely that the Karčić / Carcich of Unije are a part of this migration. As late as the early 18th Century, one Chersich/Carsich family moved from Krk to Mali Losinj. Though the evidence is circumstantial, the lack of this surname in the records of the 16th century for the island of Unije suggests it originated elsewhere.

The church records for Osor from 1618 to 1690 show the name Carsich and Carcich. Since church records in Osor also covered the communities at the southern end of the island of Cres and the northern part of the island of Losinj, it is not known where these Carcich families made their home. It may have been on the island of Cres for the Zburkin lineage got its name from a location in the region north of Martinscica on the island of Cres.

Exactly when, the Karcic / Carcich surname comes to Unije, is not known. An early mention of the name Carcich occurs in connection with an Osor marriage in June of 1684 for Antonio Nadalin of Unije, whose marriage was witnessed by a Christoforo Carcich. A 1680 Osor petition launched by a number of inhabitants from Unije against the bishop of Osor mentions that some of the petitioners were known as *bravari* or shepherds. It is possible that these *bravari* are the Carcich clan name of Bravarof which lived in Unije and Cunski by the middle of the 18th Century. Such indirect evidence suggests the Carcich's were in Unije in the 1680's.

A large number of Carcich families are associated with Unije. Lineage names are used to distinguish the families from one another. The following lineage names are known: Andricev, Baldich, Bardar, Bravarof, Cicuola, Jevin (Gevin), Mariancich, Pasquich, Prusian (Prussianich), Rocovi, Rocovica, Zburkin. All these family genealogies, except for Bardar, Mariancich, Prusian, and Rocovica are included in this volume.

After the establishment of the Carcich surname in Unije, several individuals with the Carcich surname married and raised families in Cunski. The Carcich families in Cunski can be traced to these men from Unije who in the 18th Century moved to Cunski. The only other concentration of the surname Karčić, found anywhere in the former Yugoslavia occurs in the Visegrad region of Bosnia where up to the 1990's several ancient clans had lived. No known connection to the Karčić families in Croatia has been found.

In 1985 comet 8262 in our solar system was named "Carcich" by Brian Carcich (1956-) from Cornell University.

CECCO, CEKO

Also written as Čeko the surname is found in other parts of Croatia, particularly in the Šibenik, Knin and Sinj areas.

The genealogy for this family in Unije can be traced to Vincenzo Secco (Cecco) (1793-1837) son of Luca. Vincenzo was from Unije with the clan or lineage name 'Raguseo' while his father, Luca is listed as 'Epidauri'. Ragusa is modern day Dubrovnik, but it is uncertain if 'Raguseo' is derived from Dubrovnik in this case. Vincenzo married Anna Martinolich in Mali Losinj in 1825. Ana's family is an old Losinj family which dates back to Franic Martinolić born in 1647 and whose family genealogy appears in a separate family listing.

Antonio Cecco (1871-1958) from Unije had been in New York City by 1898.

Cecco, Ceko Home No. 36 Unije

Luca Cecco (1902-)

Cecco, Ceko Family Home No. 167 Unije

Cecco, Ceko — Unije, Croatia

Luca Cecco

    Vincenzo Cecco (Raguseo) b. 1793, d. 28 Aug 1837
    + Antonia Carcich b. 1800, d. 6 Jul 1841
        Lucas Cecco b. 1833, d. 5 Mar 1860
        Andreas Cecco b. 1833, d. 2 Jan 1834
        Andrea Cecco b. 29 Nov 1834
        + Giacomina Nicolich b. 4 May 1841
            Antonio Domenico Cecco b. 9 Nov 1866

                Andrea Cecco b. 1892
                Marija (Mary) Cecco b. 1901, d. 28 Mar 1922
                + Ivan (John) (Marketa) Nicolich b. 31 Jan 1897, d. 5 Oct 1977
                    Marica (Mary) Nicolich b. 28 Mar 1922
                Matthew (Mike) Cecco b. 1903, d. 1976
                + Mary Humphries b. 1913, d. 1998
                    Matthew Cecco b. 1933
            Domenico Giovanni (Menigo) Cecco b. 6 Apr 1869
            + Neria Domenica Radoslovich b. 23 Mar 1871, d. 1957
                Ana Cecco b. 15 Jun 1906, d. 1993

                    Dinko Ceko b. 20 Aug 1939
                    Luigi Ceko b. 20 Aug 1939, d. 16 Oct 1960
                Dinko Cecco b. 1908, d. Apr 1939
            Andrea Vincenzo Cecco b. 31 Oct 1872, d. 10 Mar 1958
            + Margherita Girolama Carcich b. 30 Sep 1877, d. 1969
                Luca Cecco b. 1902
                + Maria (Palijermica) Nicolich
                    Roza Cecco b. 5 Oct 1953
                Frane Cecco b. 4 Oct 1907, d. 10 Feb 1992
                + Maria (Andrica) (Martinica) Nicolich b. 28 Sep 1910, d. 6 Jan 1988
                    Marica Cecco b. 3 Mar 1932, d. 28 Nov 1991
                    Ferdinando Cecco
            Antonia Giacoma(Tonka) Cecco b. 20 Apr 1878
            + Atanazio Radoslovich b. 1886
            Giacoma Maria Cecco b. 21 Apr 1880
         + Maria Vallich b. 1833, d. Nov 1861
        Elena Cecco b. 2 Dec 1835
        Antonio Cecco b. 28 Nov 1837
        + Giovanna Radoslovich b. 13 Oct 1840
            Antonio Cecco b. 20 Sep 1871, d. 1958
            + Felicita Innocenta Carcich b. 28 Dec 1876, m. 1897
                Giovanna (Jovana Ninella) Cecco b. 21 Oct 1898, d. 6 Feb 1996
                + Jani Carcich b. 22 May 1897, m. 29 Jan 1921, d. 15 May 1982
                    John Carcich b. 15 Oct 1921
                    Emma Karcich b. 22 Nov 1923, d. 14 Nov 1990
                Anthony (Toni) Cecco b. 1903, d. 7 May 1976
                + Ernesta Radoslovich b. 13 Oct 1907, d. 2 Nov 1994
                    Anthony Cecco b. 24 Jan 1927
                    Josephine Cecco
                Vitorino Cecco b. 16 Oct 1909, d. 17 May 1964
                + Ludmilla (Mila) (Jevin) Carcich b. 1912
                    Vitorina (Vicky) Cecco b. 1935
                    Richard Cecco
                Felice Cecco b. 1911, d. 1947
                + Antonia (Bepina) Nicolich b. 1919, d. 19 Jul 2001
                    Guerina Cecco
                    Laura Donna Cecco

1   2   3   4   5   6

COSULICH, KOZULIĆ (Belon)

Šimunić claims Kozulić is a nickname dealing with animals (životinjski nazivi).[55] The largest number of families with this surname is found in Mali Losinj followed by other concentrations on the island of Ist and the cities of Rijeka and Varaždin.

In the Kvarner region the surname Kozulić dates back, at least to the 16th Century in Mali Losinj. The surname appears in deeds from Veli Losinj for the period 1589-90 and 1601. Several lineages carry this surname including the Grubessa, Miculich, and Sucich families.

The early Kozulić/Cosulich family from the Belon lineage carries the lineage name of Sucich. The Belon name begins with Domenico Kozulić born 1728 and married in Mali Losinj in 1752. Other Cosulich families from Mali Losinj carry the lineage names of Grubessa and Miculich.

The Cosulich family in Unije begins with Dominicus Cosulich (1836-1912) who intermarried with the Martinolich family from Mali Losinj. Details on Martinolich genealogy appear in a separate family listing. Dominicus Cosulich carried the clan name, Belon, while his father and grandfather are listed as Sucich.

Cosulich Family: Matteo Nikolich (1888-); Matieta Cosulich (1864-), Domenico (Belon) Cosulich (1836-1912), Sime Nikolich (1883-1915), Ita Nikolich (1882-1963)

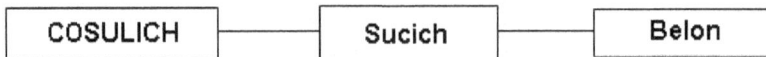

COSULICH	Sucich	Belon

Cosulich, Kozulić (Belon) — Mali Losinj & Unije, Croatia

Antic Kozulic

Mikula Kozulić (Sucich)
+ Boza (Natalia) Peracin m. 23 Feb 1694
   Tomic Kozulić (Sucich) b. 15 Feb 1700
   + Giulia Starcic b. 21 Jan 1700, m. 20 Jan 1722
      Domenico Kozulić (Belon) b. 10 Nov 1728
      + Augustina Radossich m. 15 Feb 1752
         Domenico Cosulich
         + Antonia Vidulich m. 10 Jan 1776
            Stephanus Cosulich b. 9 Nov 1780
            + Antonia Giadrosich m. 14 Nov 1807
               Dominicus Cosulich b. 1813
               + Margarita Haracich b. 1813, m. 8 Jan 1838
                  Anna Maria Teresa Cosulich b. 1843
                  + Giacomo Predonzan m. 1869
         Tomaso Cosulich b. 18 May 1758
         + Maria Scargotich m. 31 Jan 1785
            Hieronymus (Joannes) Cosulich b. 2 Jan 1799
            + Antonia Radoslovich b. 1801, m. 1 Feb 1826
               Marcus Antonius Cosulich b. 16 Jul 1840
               + Maria Barbalich b. 1843 Bueca, m. 20 Mar 1871
                  Marco Antonio Girolamo Cosulich b. 29 Oct 1878, d. 27
                  Nov 1964 Mali Losinj
               Dominicus Aloysius (Belon) Cosulich b. 28 Mar 1836
               Mali Losinj, d. 30 Jan 1912 Unie, Austria
               + Margarita Martinolich b. 28 Oct 1838, m. 10 Jul 1861
               Mali Losinj
                  Giovanni Girolamo Francesco Cosulich b. 9 Mar 1862
                  Matieta Cosulich b. 6 Jan 1864
                  + Andrea Calisto Nicolich b. 14 Oct 1856
                     Margarita Nicolich b. 13 Oct 1882, d. 1963
                     + Sime Nicolich b. 4 Feb 1883, d. 1915
                       Antonia Nicolich b. 1909, d. 2000
                     Mattea Nicolich b. 16 Dec 1914
                    Matteo Nicolich b. 1 Dec 1888, d. 13 Aug 1959
                  + Mary Simicich b. 1893, d. 1978
                     Matthew Nicolich b. 8 May 1918
                     Seattle, Washington
                     Laurence Vincent Nicolich b. 31 May
                     1921 Seattle, Washington
                  Irene Gabriela Giuseppa Cosulich b. 16 Mar 1874
                  Mali Losinj, d. 11 Sep 1942
                  + Giovanni Ferluga b. 3 May 1871, d. 14 Aug 1921
                     Olga Ferluga b. 21 Jan 1895, d. 17 Mar 1952
                     + Giuseppe Ulcigrai b. 16 Dec 1891, d. 1964/65
                     Dominic Ferluga b. 7 Nov 1896, d. 17 Jan 1993
                     Seattle, Washington
                     Maria Anna Ferluga b. 26 Apr 1898, d. 2 May
                     1980 New York
                     + Andrea Carcich b. 26 Mar 1895
                       Mary Irene Carcich b. 19 Sep 1920
                     Josephina Ferluga b. 12 Jul 1900, d. Jan 1996
                     + Antun Nicolich b. 17 Apr 1882, d. 15 Jun 1975
                       Maria Nicolich b. 28 Feb 1923
                       Elsa Nicolich b. 13 Apr 1924
                     Giusto Ferluga b. 7 Apr 1902, d. 19 Sep 1939
                     Erene Ferluga b. 5 Oct 1908, d. 5 Dec 1995

1   2   3   4   5   6   7   8   9   10

GALLOSICH, GALOSICH, GALOŠIĆ

The Gallosich family only dates back to the late 18th Century in Unije. The surname is not common in Croatia. In 1945 there was one family each in Unije, Mali Losinj, and Pula. The origin of this surname is unknown and may be derived from either Gallo or Gelussich. The surname Gallo(us) appears throughout Italy and also on the Istrian peninsula. Petar Šimunić states the origin of Galušic is not from Gallus but from Galeše[56] with the surname only found in the Zadar area.

Gelussich, later also spelled Galussich, appear in Mali Losinj in 1806 with the marriage of Antonio Gelussich from Rijeka.

Giovanni Galosich (1809-) son of Antonio carries the lineage name of 'Catania'. Andrea Galosich (1866-) son of Antonio was one of the first from Unije to migrate to western Canada in 1890 part of the movement of Losinj islanders to Seattle and Vancouver areas.

Maria Galosich (1875-) and daughter Maria (1892-)

Ivo Galosic (1910-1989)

Gallosich, Galosich, Galosić — Unije, Croatia

Antonius Galosich
+ Anna (---) b. 1783, d. Sep 1861
    Giovanni Galosich (Catania) b. 8 Sep 1809
    + Anna Bellanich b. 1810, d. 3 Oct 1848
        Antonio Galosich b. 8 Nov 1834
        + Maria Carcich b. 15 Jan 1832
            Giovanni Antonio (Zane) Galosich b. 7 Mar 1864, d. 14 Nov 1918
            + Marianna Nicolina Carcich b. 25 Mar 1863
                Andrea Galosich b. abt 1890
                + Maria Carcich b. 23 Apr 1890, d. 31 Jul 1985
                    Ivo Galosich b. 30 Jun 1910, d. 23 Jan 1989
                    + Maria (Jivana Jercich) Rerecich b. 1912, d. 1947
                        Andrea Galosich b. 15 Feb 1938
                        Milena Galosich b. 1940
                        Olga Galosich b. 1946
                    + Antonia (Bepina) Nicolich b. 1919, m. Feb, d. 19 Jul 2001
                Jakov Galosich
                + Maria Segotta
                    Maria (Jakova) Galosich b. 16 Aug 1911, d. 26 Apr 1973
                    + Pasquale Pinezic b. 1909, d. 30 Jan 1961
                        John Pinezic b. 1941, d. 18 Mar 1989
                        Peter Pinezic b. 1 Aug 1942, d. 11 Aug 1983
                Zane Galosich b. 25 Oct 1893, d. 2 Feb 1986
                + Maria Carcich b. 9 Apr 1899, d. 20 Apr 1977
                    Iani (John) Galosich b. abt 1920
                        Debra Galosich b. 1963
                        Steve Galosich b. 1970
                Marijana Galosich
                Bepa Galosich
             Andrea Domenico Galosich b. 5 Jul 1866
            + **Tomasina Maria Nicolich** b. 8 Oct 1869
                Alfred Galosich
                Mark Galosich
                Andrew Galosich
                Mary Galosich
             Antonio Domenico Galosich b. 22 May 1870
            Martino Domenico Galosich b. 25 May 1872
        Giovanni Gallosich b. 26 Jan 1837
        + **Maria Caterina Carcich** b. 25 Nov 1853
            Giacomo Giovanni Gallosich b. 25 Jul 1879
    + **Maria Carcich** b. 1 Sep 1841, d. 24 Jan 1876

1   2   3   4   5   6   7

GIURICH, JURICH, JURIĆ

The surname Jurich and Jurić are found in the Pula and Rijeka areas in modern times. The derivation for the surname likely comes from the name Jure, or George, a common Slavic given name. The surname Jurić is often found together with the surname Juricić (Juricich, Giuricich) and these two surnames could share a common origin.

The Giurich family in Unije is descendent from Matija Jurić of Mali Losinj who married in 1646. Mattio Giurich raised a family in Unije after 1740 and though his descendents died out in Unije in the 19th Century, his family comes from a 17th Century Losinj family. The family also has branches in Mali Losinj. In Unije the Giurich family married into the families of Carcich (Jevin), Nicolich, and Radoslovich (Mattesinich). The following genealogy indicates which individuals were associated with Unije.

Mali Losinj

Forze Divine
(Unie)

Postcard of Unije pre-1929

Giurich, Jurich, Jurić — Mali Losinj & Unije, Croatia

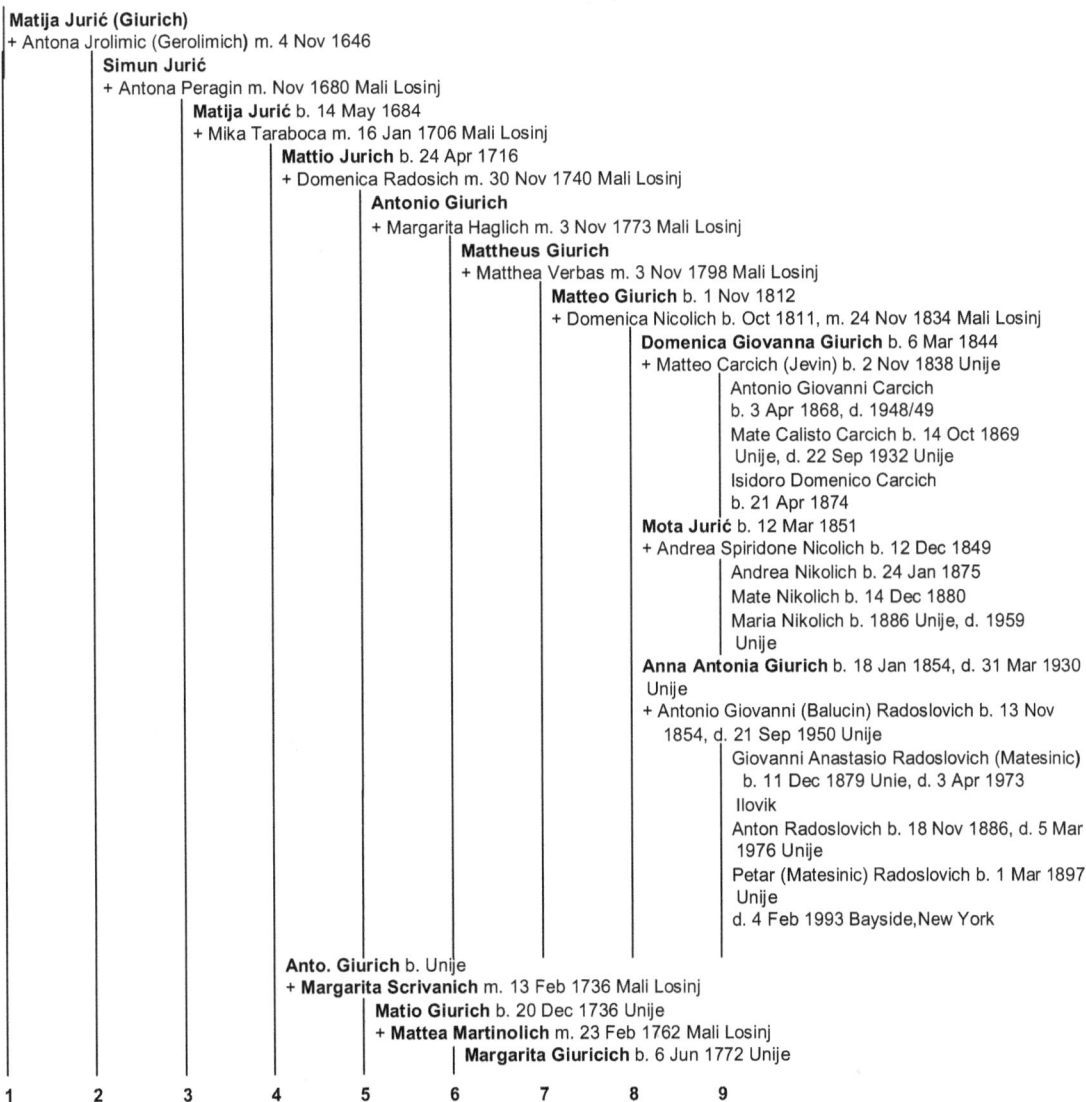

Matija Jurić (Giurich)
+ Antona Jrolimic (Gerolimich) m. 4 Nov 1646
    Simun Jurić
    + Antona Peragin m. Nov 1680 Mali Losinj
        Matija Jurić b. 14 May 1684
        + Mika Taraboca m. 16 Jan 1706 Mali Losinj
            Mattio Jurich b. 24 Apr 1716
            + Domenica Radosich m. 30 Nov 1740 Mali Losinj
                Antonio Giurich
                + Margarita Haglich m. 3 Nov 1773 Mali Losinj
                    Mattheus Giurich
                    + Matthea Verbas m. 3 Nov 1798 Mali Losinj
                        Matteo Giurich b. 1 Nov 1812
                        + Domenica Nicolich b. Oct 1811, m. 24 Nov 1834 Mali Losinj
                            Domenica Giovanna Giurich b. 6 Mar 1844
                            + Matteo Carcich (Jevin) b. 2 Nov 1838 Unije
                                Antonio Giovanni Carcich
                                b. 3 Apr 1868, d. 1948/49
                                Mate Calisto Carcich b. 14 Oct 1869
                                  Unije, d. 22 Sep 1932 Unije
                                Isidoro Domenico Carcich
                                b. 21 Apr 1874
                          Mota Jurić b. 12 Mar 1851
                        + Andrea Spiridone Nicolich b. 12 Dec 1849
                            Andrea Nikolich b. 24 Jan 1875
                            Mate Nikolich b. 14 Dec 1880
                            Maria Nikolich b. 1886 Unije, d. 1959
                            Unije
                        Anna Antonia Giurich b. 18 Jan 1854, d. 31 Mar 1930
                        Unije
                        + Antonio Giovanni (Balucin) Radoslovich b. 13 Nov
                          1854, d. 21 Sep 1950 Unije
                            Giovanni Anastasio Radoslovich (Matesinic)
                              b. 11 Dec 1879 Unie, d. 3 Apr 1973
                            Ilovik
                            Anton Radoslovich b. 18 Nov 1886, d. 5 Mar
                            1976 Unije
                          Petar (Matesinic) Radoslovich b. 1 Mar 1897
                            Unije
                            d. 4 Feb 1993 Bayside,New York

            Anto. Giurich b. Unije
            + **Margarita Scrivanich** m. 13 Feb 1736 Mali Losinj
                Matio Giurich b. 20 Dec 1736 Unije
                + **Mattea Martinolich** m. 23 Feb 1762 Mali Losinj
                    Margarita Giuricich b. 6 Jun 1772 Unije

1   2   3   4   5   6   7   8   9

HAGLICH, HALIĆ, HALJIĆ

This family name occurs as Halić in the records of Mali Losinj from the 16th and 17th Century.

The surname appears in deeds from Veli Losinj for the period 1586-88, 1591, 1593, 1603, 1605-06. Another early mention of this family in connection with Unije occurs in the Mali Losinj marriage record of May 5, 1718 where Matij Halic (Matteo Haglich) of Unije is listed as a witness. The family carried the lineage name of Lovrich, but its origins is unknown.

The family had property on the western part of Unije, north of the town. Several of the houses in Unije were constructed with the help of the Haglich family.

There are two genealogies which both date back to the early 1700's and both with a Lorenzo Haglich as the oldest ancestor. Though not certain, these two lineages could be from the same ancestor.

The family has a long tradition associated with the construction and building trades. Several generations worked in the trade including Nicolo Haglich (1786-), Antonio Haglich (1813-), and Domenico Haglich (1888-1951). With their long association with Mali Losinj, the Haglich family was also involved in the maritime business. Lonenzo Haglich (1756-) had the ship, the *Prudenza* constructed in Venice. The *Prudenza* became one of the early Losinj ships to make the voyage to America, when it was skippered by Antonio Premuda in 1795.

Haglich, Halić, Haljić Family Home No. 26 Unije

Haglich family- front row: Ann (1921-), Niko Haglich (1920-1987); Milan, Pierin, Gabriele; back row: Domenico, Agata (nee Radoslovich) (1888-1951), Domenico (1888-1951), Marica, Anton (1912-1982)

Haglich, Halić, Haljić — Mali Losinj & Unije, Croatia

Lorenzo Haglich

Lorenzo Haglich
+ Matta. Morin b. 1722, m. 23 Feb 1751, d. Feb 1808
    Zuane Haglich b. 23 Sep 1754
    + Cattarina Picinich m. 3 Feb 1781
        Nicolo Haglich b. 23 May 1786
        + Catharina Scopinich m. 31 Jan 1808
            Antonio Haglich b. 1813
            + Francesca Carcich b. 1814
                Giovanni Nicolo Haglich b. 1841
                + Maria Anna Scopinich b. 1843, m. 11 Nov 1867 Mali Losinj
            + Francesca Tarabochia b. 1821
                Niccolo Haglich (Lovrich) b. 30 Dec 1861, d. 10 Mar 1927
                + Antonia Barichievich b. Veli Losinj, m. 27 Nov 1884 Mali Losinj
                    Dinko Haglich b. 12 Jul 1888, d. 28 Feb
                    1951
                    + Agata (Tonova Matesinic) Radoslovich b. 19 Mar 1890 Unije,
                      d. 21 Apr 1971 Unije
                        Anton Haglich b. 14 Sep 1912,
                        d. 17 Nov 1982 Astoria,New York
                        Marica Haglich d. 1995/96 Mali Losinj
                        Dinko Haglich d. 1995 Trieste, Italy
                        Nick Stan (Niko) (Lovrich) Haglich b. 23 Sep 1920 Unije,
                        d. 16 Mar 1987 Bethpage,New York
                        Ann Haglich b. 1921
                        Milan Haglich
                        Pierin (Peter) Haglich b. 1924 Mali Losinj
                        Gabriele Haglich b. 28 Feb 1932/34
                  Antonio Haglich d. 1931
                  + Maria Radoslovich d. 1936
                        Nico Halglich b. 1912, d. 2002
                        Maria Halglich b. 3 Aug 1926
                Francis (Franica) Haglich
                Maria Haglich
                Mikulica Haglich
    Lorenzo Haglich b. 28 Oct 1756 Mali Losinj
    + Margarita Scopinich m. 19 Jan 1784
        Jacoba Haglich b. 24 Jul 1799
        + Andrea Carcich b. Unije, m. 15 May 1826
        Marcus Haglich b. 1804
        + Nicola Tarabochia b. 1810, m. 6 Nov 1826
            Marco Haglich b. 1834
            + Maria Vidulich m. 1862
                Marcus Haglich b. 1872
                + Natalina Vidulich b. 1875, m. 2 Jun 1897 Mali Losinj
            Antonio Eustachio Haglich b. 19 Sep 1846
            + Maria Luigia Giovanna Ragusin b. 1847, m. 17 Jan 1872

1   2   3   4   5   6   7   8

MARTINOLICH, MARTINOLIĆ

This family name occurs as Martinolić in the records for Losinj from the 16th Century. The surname appears in deeds from Veli Losinj for the period 1587, 1590, and 1601.

This family owned property in Unije. The main branch of the family lived in Mali Losinj and dates back to Ivan Martinolić married there in 1642. Those connected with Unije are indicated in the following genealogy. The family of Antonio Martinolich (Guardasusa) born in 1762 intermarried into several families in Unije. Daughter Maria married Cristoforo Carcich and lived in Unije. Antonio's son Giovanni Antonio Martinolich, born 1798

had two sons, Benjaminus (1849-) who immigrated to Colorado, United States in 1886 and Venatius (1849-1913) who immigrated to British Columbia, Canada in 1891 by way of Colorado. Venatius was married to Carolina Haracich descendent from a Unije family. Also Francesco Martinolich (1829-1912) and his son Matteo '(1860-1934) who began a shipbuilding company after arriving in Mississippi in 1883 are part of this Martinolich family, as is John A. (Giovanni Augustinus) Martinolich (1877-) who started a shipbuilding company in Tacoma, Washington.

The lineage name of Guardasusa does not have the common endings as found in the standard lineage or clan names and may be derived from a nickname for the founder of this lineage.

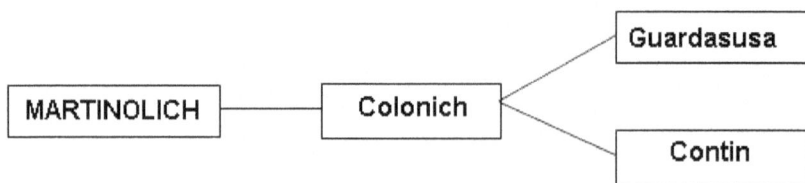

```
MARTINOLICH ──── Colonich ──┬── Guardasusa
                            │
                            └── Contin
```

Tacoma, Washington: First three standing: are unidentified, 4th standing Antonio Cosulich (1851-), 5th John Cosulich, 6th Anna Martinolich (1884-1960), 1st Sitting: Joannes Augustinus Martinolich(1877-)

Martinolich, Martinolić (Colonich) — Mali Losinj & Unije, Croatia

Francesco (Franić) Martinolich b. 27 Feb 1647
  Mihovil (Michele) Martinolić c. 11 May 1683
    Domenico Martinolich b. 19 Mar 1724 Mali Losinj
      Matteo (Povero) (Colonich) Martinolich b. 21 Sep 1747 Mali Losinj
        Matteo Martinolich b. 9 Jun 1783 Mali Losinj
          Antonio Pio. (Antonius Pius) Martinolich b. 1815
      Michels (Contin) Martinolich b. 28 May 1752 Mali Losinj
        Michael Martinolich c. 3 May 1801 Mali Losinj
          Matteo Giuseppe Martinolich c. 25 Sep 1835 Mali Losinj
      Domenico Martinolich b. 7 Dec 1756
        Franciscus Martinolich
          Nicolaus Martinolich b. 1804
          Matheus Martinolich b. 1806
          Joannes Martinolich b. 1818
      Antonio (Guardasusa) Martinolich b. 15 Jul 1762 Mali Losinj
        Maria (Margarita) Martinolich b. 22 Dec 1792 + Cristoforo Carcich m. 1812
        Giuseppe Martinolich b. 6 Aug 1796
          Antonio Martinolich b. 27 Mar 1824
          Giovanni Martinolich b. 11 Feb 1827
          Antonia Ioanna Martinolich b. 1830
          Giuseppe Anciento Martinolich b. 16 Apr 1834
        Gio. Antonio Martinolich b. 17 Nov 1798
          Giovanni (Angelo) Martinolich b. 18 Aug 1834
          Antonio Joseph Martinolich b. 7 Nov 1836
          Margarita Martinolich b. 28 Oct 1838
          Marcus (Marco) Joseph Martinolich b. 18 Jan 1844
          Venatius (Venanzio) Nicolaus Martinolich b. 10 Jan 1848 Mali Losinj,
            d. 22 Oct 1913 Ladner, British Columbia
          Benjaminus Martinus Martinolich b. 12 Nov 1849
        Anna Martinolich b. 12 Jul 1803
        Andrea Martinolich b. 24 Jun 1806
          Cashimiro Aloysius Martinolich c. 28 Oct 1848 Mali Losinj, d. 1907
  Jivan (Colonich) Martinolić b. 7 Jan 1674
    Franic Martinolić b. 11 Sep 1699 Mali Losinj
      Giovanni Martinolich b. 17 May 1722 Mali Losinj
      Giovanni Martinolich b. 21 Jan 1723 Mali Losinj
      Luca Martinolich (Colonich) b. 5 Feb 1724 Mali Losinj
        Margarita Martinolich b. 1753
        Sabrena Martinolich b. 1756
        Antonia Martinolich b. 1759
        Biasio Martinolich b. 3 Feb 1760
        Margarita Martinolich b. 30 Jun 1762
      Franic Martinolic b. 19 Sep 1730
      Giovanna Martinolich b. 28 Apr 1728 Mali Losinj
      Giovanna Martinolich b. 27 Feb 1738 Mali Losinj
      Marco Martinolich b. 25 Dec 1733 Mali Losinj
    Marco (Colonich) Martinolić b. 11 Nov 1701 Mali Losinj
      Katarina Martinolić b. 11 May 1727
      Jivan Martinolić b. 11 Apr 1730
        Mattio (Matheus) Martinolich b. 22 Feb 1777
          Joannes (Gio. Maria Rocco) Martinolich b. 15 Aug 1802
      Luca Martinolich b. 18 Feb 1733
      Marco Martinolich b. 6 May 1735
      Giovanna Martinolich b. 6 Jul 1738
      Luca Martinolich b. 24 Feb 1744

1   2   3   4   5   6

NADALIN

In modern times this surname occurs in the Grubišno Polje area of Croatia and in Unije.

However, the Unije families with this surname likely derive from Losinj, where this surname is found in the 17th Century written as Nadalinić. Šimunić suggests the orgin of Nadalini is from the Latin for birth (*natalis*) [57].

An early mention of this family in connection with Unije occurs with the marriage in Osor of Antonio Nadalin of Unije on June 22, 1684. There is also a marriage record in Mali Losinj for Matteo Nadalinich of Unije from November 28, 1748. The genealogy for this family begins with Matteo Nadalin (1743-1817) of Matteus.

In Unije a sub-branch of this surname is known by the lineage name, Delidich, possibly derived from Adelaide Comandich, born in 1825.

Francesco Nadalin (1854-) is believed to have lived in Philadelphia, Pennsylvania, and his brother Giovanni Nadalin (1856-) settled in San Francisco. A third brother, Matei Pietro Nadalin (1862-1936) also worked in the United States. His son Matteo (1903-1993) worked on the Italian oceanliner the *Saturnia* before WWII.

In more recent times, Matteo's son, Bruno Nadalin (1930-) became a ship's engineer in Yugoslavia and later worked in the United. States. His sister, Magda Nadalin (1940-) studied as a medical doctor in Rijeka specializing in bone treatment. Magda's mother, Iva Juzepine Carcich (1908-1996), studied in Trieste as a mid-wife before WWII.

Matteo Nadalin (1903-1993)

Nadalin Family Home, No. 144 Unije

Nadalin — Unije, Croatia

Matteus Nadalin

Matteus Nadalin b. 1743, d. 17 Jan 1817 Unije
+ Helena Pizzulich b. 1746, m. 24 Jun 1782 Mali Losinj, d. 23 Sep 1816 Unije
    Matteo Vlassich Nadalin b. 1789, d. 3 Apr 1872 Unije
    + Francesca Nicolich b. 1794, d. 23 Apr 1865 Unije
        Franciscus Nadalin b. 27 Jun 1819
        + Adelaide Domenica Francisca Martinolich (Comandich) b. 25 Jan 1823, m. 1 Apr 1852
        Mali Losinj
            Francesco Nadalin b. 13 Jun 1854
            Giovanni Nadalin b. 15 Dec 1856
            Giuseppe (Bepica) Nadalin b. 5 Apr 1861
            + Giacomina Segota
                Andrea Nadalin b. 1902 Unije, d. 1938 Spain
                Frane Nadalin
            + Paolina Valich
                Giuseppe Nadalin d. 1936
                Caterina (Katina) Nadalin b. 1902
            + Maria Giovanna Carcich b. 8 Dec 1866
                Adelaide (Adelina) Nadalin b. 1908, d. 1932
                Anica Nadalin d. 1993 Como,Italy
            Matei Pietro (Delaidic) Nadalin b. 2 Dec 1862 Unije, d. 1936
            + Maria Bellanich b. 19 Feb 1867, d. 17 Dec 1916 Unije
                Andrew (Delajdic) Nadalin b. 7 Jun 1893 Unije, d. 22 Sep 1967 Los
                  Angeles,California
                Margherita Nadalin b. 1901/02, d. 1929/30
                Matteo Nadalin b. 8 Jan 1903, d. 26 Oct 1993 Unije
                Giuseppe Nadalin (Delajdic) b. 19 Aug 1905 Unije, d. 14 Dec 1984
                  Jackson Heights, New York
                Adelaide (Delida) Nadalin b. 1907, d. 1984
                Maria (Mikulice) Nadalin b. 7 May 1909, d. 21 Jul 1999 Unije
                Giovanni Nadalin b. 1911, d. 1987 New York
            + Maria Cecilia Segotta b. 22 Nov 1876
                Frane (Frank) John Nadalin b. 20 Jan 1919 New York,
                  d. 8 Apr 1984 San Francisco,California
    Andrea Nadalin (Vlassich) b. 10 Jan 1833
    + Tomazina Rerecich b. 10 Jan 1825, m. 13 Feb 1858 Unije
        Giovanni Andrea Nadalin b. 27 Aug 1862
        Mattio (Matej) Pasquale Nadalin b. 16 May 1865 Unije, d. 5 Mar 1942 Unie
        + Caterina Antonia (Kata) Carcich b. 30 Dec 1864 Unije, m. 6 Feb 1888 Unije, d. 9
        Apr 1943 Unije
            Maria (Vlasic) Nadalin b. 15 Sep 1890 Unije
            d. 26 Dec 1963 Unije
            Mattea Nadalin b. 10 Aug 1897 Unije
            d. 9 May 1974 Astoria,New York
            Katarina (Katica) Nadalin b. 27 Nov 1902 Unie
            d. 15 Oct 1963 Unije
            Marco Nadalin b. 1905, d. 15 Feb 1992 Zagreb
            Mate Nadalin b. 25 Apr 1907 Unie, d. 7 Feb 1927 Unije
            Antonia Nadalin
    Pietro (Petar) Nadalin b. 24 Jun 1835
    + Elena (Jelena) (Eliza) Carcich b. 3 Nov 1832, m. 19 Feb 1859 Unije
        Gaudenzio Natale Nadalin b. 24 Dec 1862
        + Maria Carolina Carcich b. 2 Nov 1866
            Ivan Nadalin b. 30 Sep 1893, d. 1 Mar 1966 Goshen, New York
            Jelica Nadalin b. 1898, d. 1971
            Peter Nadalin b. 1903
            Marco Nadalin b. 1907

1   2   3   4   5   6

NICOLICH, NIKOLIĆ   (Agatin)

The Agatin branch of the Nicolich family in Unije can lay claim to Martin Nicolich and may be descendent of an older Mali Losinj family. There were many Martin Nicolich's in the Losinj records from the 18th Century and so it is difficult to determine its ancestry. Two different Nicolich families, either the Salata or the Muscardin branches are the likely ancestors to Unije's Agatin family both dating back to the 17th Century.

In Unije this family was known by the name Agatin, possibly derived from Agata Baldin(i) who married Martin Nicolich and whose descendents settled on the island.

Antun Nicolich (1882-1975) between WWI and WWII, had a fleet of taxis in New York City, which he later sold to a partner from the island of Olib. His family came to New York at the outbreak of WWII. He may have also worked as a longshore foreman.

Lino Dominic Niccoli (Nicolich) (1894-1964) studied at the Maritime Academy in Lussin Piccolo, graduating in 1914. During World War I while in the Austrian army he was awarded the second highest citation in the Austrian army by Franz Joseph. During 1919 to 1923 he served in the Italian merchant navy and the American merchant navy during World War II in Pacific where he skippered the Liberty ship *Henry Meigs*.

Domenica Nicolich (1878-)

Nicolich, Nikolić (Agatin) Family Home, No. 194 Unije

Nicolich, Nikolić (Agatin) — Unije, Croatia

Martin Nicolich
- Martin Nicolich b. Onie, d. m: 14 Aug 1784
  - Andrea Nicolich b. 5 May 1785 Mali Losinj, d. 1871 Unije
  - Martin Nicolich b. 7 Sep 1788, d. 24 Jul 1871 Unije
    - Giovanni Nicolich b. 3 Dec 1822
      - Antonio Nicolich b. 13 Nov 1849 Unije, d. 4 Dec 1938 Unije
        - Andrew Nikolich b. 1865
        - Giovanni Andrea Nicolich b. 4 Dec 1875, d. 28 Mar 1961 Unije
        - Domenica Maria Nicolich b. 22 Jan 1878 Unije
        - Andrea Martino Nicolich b. 22 Aug 1880
        - Antun Nicolich b. 17 Apr 1882 Unije, d. 15 Jun 1975
      - Martin Giuseppe Nicolich b. 19 Mar 1857
        - Germana Nicolich b. 1890 Unije, d. 19 May 1980
        - Giacomina Nicolich b. 1904, d. 27 Oct 1997
      - Giovanni Patrizio Nicolich b. 16 Mar 1864, d. 1947
        - Giovanni Nicolich b. 6 Jun 1889,.d. 7 Feb 1912
        - Maria Nicolich b. 21 Apr 1891 Unije, d. 29 Aug 1977 Mali Losinj
        - Martin Nicolich b. 9 Aug 1895, d. 12 Dec 1978 Fairview,New Jersey
        - Oliva Nicolich
      - Andrea Giuseppe Nicolich b. 3 Sep 1865, d. 1942
        - Iosip Nicolich b. 6 Oct 1897, d. 28 Apr 1975
  - Antonio Nicolich (Palermo) b. 1791, d. 16 Nov 1859 Unije
    - Martino Nicolich b. 2 Mar 1825, d. 19 Nov 1907
      - [Andrea] Nicolich
        - Maria Nicolich
        - Martin Nicolich
      - Antonio Domenico (Paliermo) Nicolich b. 5 Mar 1864
        - Andric Nicolich b. 1901
        - Martin (Paljerma) Nikolic b. 14 May 1909, d. 25 Oct 1988 Hamilton,Ont.
        - Tony Nicolich
        - Maria (Palijermica) Nicolich b. Unije
      - Andrea Domenico Nicolich b. 8 Aug 1872 Unije, d. 5 Aug 1927 Unije
        - Ivan Nicolich b. 17 Oct 1903 Unije, d. 6 Feb 1989 Astoria,New York
        - Maria Nicolich b. 23 Nov 1909 Unije, d. 21 Jan 1991 Astoria,New York
      - Giovanni Nereo Nicolich b. 12 May 1856
  - Domenico Nicolich b. 1793, d. 19 Feb 1872 Unije
    - Domenico Nicolich b. 31 Jul 1834
      - Antonio Joannes Nicolich b. 12 Apr 1860 Unije, d. 19 Jan 1946 Unije
        - Antonia Nicolich b. 1893 Unije, d. 1978 Unije
        - Giuseppe Nicolich b. 26 Aug 1903 Unije
        - d. 20 Sep 1955 New York
      - Domenico Francesco Nicolich b. 3 Jun 1865, d. 1916
        - Lino Domenic Niccoli b. 23 Sep 1894, d. Mar 1964
        - Menigo Nicolich
        - Maria Nicolich b. 1907, d. Aug 1994 (near Venice),Italy
        - Giuseppe Nicolich
        - Franco Nicolich
        - Leone Nicolich b. 1914
      - Giovanni Eugenio Nicolich b. 29 Nov 1871
      - Ottavio Paolino Nicolich b. 22 Jun 1877, d. 6 May 1946
        - Domenico Nicolich b. 13 Mar 1908, d. 29 Sep 1943 Pula, Italy
        - Marica Nicolich
      - Zaccaria Leone Nicolich b. 19 Apr 1875, d. 15 Feb 1917
        - Domenica Nicolich b. 17 Feb 1899, d. 16 Jan 1983 Los Angeles, California
        - Harry Nicolich b. 14 Feb 1904, d. 29 Mar 1999 Freeport,New York
        - Tony Nicolich b. 6 Nov 1905, d. 26 Dec 1969 California
        - Osip Nicolich b. 11 Mar 1909, d. 4 Jul 1969
        - Maria (Marica) Nicolich b. 6 Nov 1913

1   2   3   4   5   6

NICOLICH, NIKOLIĆ   (Marketa)

The Marketa clan may trace their roots to Mali Losinj through the pre-1800 clan name 'Morich'. Marco Nicolich (1757-1837) the second generation in this genealogical tree carried the 'Morich' lineage name. By the fifth generation, Marcus Nicolich, carried the branch name 'Marketa'.

Several Nicolich (Morich) families are known from Mali Losinj. There was Tomaso Nicolich married Dunka before 1683 whose family eventually gave rise to the Marketa family in Unije. The Nicolich surname was written Mikolić in the church records for the 17th Century and early 18th Century.

Reverend Andrea Nicoli
(1919-1997)

Giuseppe Nicolich / Niccoli
(1858-1943)

Reverend Andrea Nicoli (Nicolich) (1919-1997) from Unije was ordained in 1942 and served in Ilovik and later in the United States.

Nicolich, Nikolić (Marketa) Home, No. 11 Unije

```
NICOLICH ─── Morcich ─── Marketa
```

Nicolich, Nikolić (Marketa) — Mali Losinj & Unije, Croatia

Tomic Mikolic b. 24 Feb 1686
+ Antona Lovretic m. 15 Aug 1706
    Gasparus Mikolic b. 8 Apr 1714
    + Domca. Bussanich m. 20 Sep 1746
        Marco Nicolich (Morich) b. 1757, d. 15 Dec 1837
        + Maria (---) b. 1760, d. 15 Mar 1840
            Gaspar Nicolich b. 10 Aug 1791, d. Dec 1880
            + Antonia Carcich b. 1795, d. 1880
                Marcus Nicolich b. 13 Feb 1820
                + Lucia Nicolich b. 18 Oct 1818, m. 1841, d. 11 Jun 1851
                    Gasparo Nicolich b. 11 Jun 1851
                    + Anna Emilia Villani m. 10 Feb 1880
                        Giovanni Nicolich

                        Nerina Nicolich
                        Silvio Nicolich
                    Alessandro Nicolich
                + Jacoba (Giacomina) Gliubcovich b. 2 Feb 1829, m. 30 Jun 1855, d. 18 Aug 1865
                  Giuseppe (Bepo) Nicolich b. 17 Apr 1858, d. 4 Jun 1943

                    Giacomina (Marcheto) Nicolich
                    + Giovanni (Jovanin) Pillepich b. 6 Jul 1886, d. 25 May 1948
                    Marco Nicolich
                    + Francia (Phyllis) Carcich
                        Nikolina Nicolich b. 2 Feb 1928
                        Michael Nicolich
                    Joseph (Bepo) Nicolich b. 20 Jul 1894, d. 6 Feb 1969
                    + Mary Claudia Radoslovich
                        Joseph Nicolich
                        Gloria Nicolich
                        Mary Nicolich
                    Piter (Peter) Nicolich b. 1903, d. 1927/37
                + Maria Verbora
                    Andrea (Don) Niccoli b. 26 Feb 1919, d. 18 Dec 1997
                Antonio Nico (Toneva) Nicolich b. 19 Dec 1863, d. 1944
                + Maria Antonia Radoslovich (Matesinica) b. 1 Sep 1863, d. 1960
                    Marco (Marketa) Nicolich b. 18 Oct 1887, d. 13 Mar 1968
                    + Maria Nicolich b. 21 Apr 1891, d. 29 Aug 1977
                      Antun (Tony) Nicolich b. Sep 1911, d. 1977
                      Marija Nikolich b. 22 Jan 1921
                      Giovanni (John) M.) Nicolich b. 4 Jan 1922, d. Feb 1962
                    Rosa Nicolich b. 11 Feb 1923
                  Marija Nicolich b. 1889
                  Agata Nicolich b. 1891, d. 1977
                  + Andrija Nicolich b. 1883, d. 1938
                    Maria (Andrica) (Martinica) Nicolich b. 28 Sep 1910, d. 6 Jan 1988
                    Martin Andrica Martinica Nicolich b. 23 Oct 1914, d. 26 Apr 1983
                    Andric (Martininica) Nicolich b. 14 Jan 1921, d. 18 Dec 1944
                    Filicita Nicolich
                    Antonia Jacomina (Agatin) Nicolich b. 13 Jul 1932
                  Ivan (John) Nicolich b. 31 Jan 1897, d. 5 Oct 1977
                  + Albina Carcich b. 26 Apr 1902, d. 27 Feb 1974
                    Dominic Nicolich b. 15 Jun 1925
                  + Marija (Mary) Cecco b. 1901, d. 28 Mar 1922
                    Marica (Mary) Nicolich b. 28 Mar 1922

1   2   3   4   5   6   7   8

NICOLICH, NIKOLIĆ   (Muscardin)

Joannes Antonio Nicolich was born in Mali Losinj in 1851 and died in Unije in 1920. Joannes' grandfather, also named Joannes carried the branch name of 'Muscardin'. The family traces descendency from the Mali Losinj Muscardin lineage back to Martin Mikolić who married in 1699. This lineage is shown in the accompanying genealogy.

Giovanni Nicolich (1851-1920) came to Unije from Mali Losinj, where his family originated. His son Antonio Nicolich (1879-) was involved in the capture of Nazario Sauro off the island of Galiola in 1916 during WWI. Later Giovanni moved his family to the newly formed Yugoslavia.

Mirto (Nick) Nicolich (1933-) owned the Star Press in Pearl River, Connecticut since 1958.

Giovanni Nicolich (1880-1939)

Antonio Nicolich (1879-1965)

Nicolich, Nikolić (Muscardin) Family Home, No. 119 Unije

Nicolich Family (Muscardin): Mirto (1929-) , Mariano (1930-), John (1933-) , Carlo (1926-1944), Dominick (1923-1998)

Nicolich, Nikolić (Muscardin) — Mali Losinj & Unije, Croatia

Martin Mikolić
+ Marija Busanic m. 7 Jan 1699
    Luka Mikolić b. 29 Aug 1720
    + Antonia Bussanich m. 9 Feb 1748
        Jseppo Nicolich b. 11 Nov 1752
        + Domenica Scopinich m. 11 Feb 1779
            Giovanni (Joannes) Nicolich (Muscardin) b. 25 Nov 1784, d. 1856
            + Girolama Nicolich b. 1797, d. 1867
                Antonio Silvestro Nicolich b. 31 Dec 1819
                + Maria Catharina Sablich b. 14 Nov 1824, m. 14 Jan 1850
                    Giovanni Antonio Nicolich b. 4 Dec 1851, d. 1920
                    + Lucia (Lucieta) Piccinich b. 9 Nov 1857, m. 1878, d. 2 Aug 1947
                        Antonio Giuseppe Nicolich b. 3 Mar 1879
                        + Marija Vjekoslava Nikolic (Stipana) b. 1889, m. 17 Apr 1907
                              Marija Nicolich b. 1908
                              Lucia Nicolich b. 1910
                              Antonia (Antica) Nicolich b. 1912/14, d. 1992
                              Sofia Nicolich
                              Krunoslava Nicolich
                              Ivo Nicolich b. 1919
                              Slavko Nicolich
                              Mira Nicolich
                              Sretko Nicolich
                        Giovanni Andrea Nicolich b. 24 Nov 1880, d. 7 May 1939
                      + Domenica Nicolich b. 25 Jan 1888, m. 1904, d. 17 Oct 1935
                              Iani (John) Nicolich b. 12 Sep 1905, d. Oct
                              1983
                              Lucia Nicolich b. 10 Apr 1910
                              d. 19 May 1987
                              Dominic Nicolich b. 17 Oct 1923, d. 20 Dec 1998
                              Karlo Nicolich b. 17 Sep 1926, d. 9 Oct 1944
                      Giuseppe Nicolich b. 18 Jun 1886, d. 25 Nov 1972
                      + Antonia Nicolich b. 1893, d. 1978
                              Giovanni Niccoli b. 26 May 1914, d. 20 Mar 1944
                              Antonia (Bepina) Nicolich b. 1919, d. 19 Jul 2001
                              Nori Nicolich b. 1928, d. Mar 1994
                      Rodolfo Nicolich b. 12 Jun 1888
                      + Antonia Gloria (Jevin) Carcich b. 9 Apr 1903, d. 25 Apr 1997
                              Rudolph Nicolich b. 3 Oct 1931
                              Charles Nicolich b. 14 Sep 1932
                              Edward Nicolich b. 15 Oct 1933, d. Oct 1969
                              Norbert Nicolich b. 17 Apr 1935, d. 11 May 2007
                      + Ana Tonova Matesinic Radoslovich b. 1894, m. 20 Nov 1923,
                      d. 27 Apr 1928
                              Ana Nicolich b. 31 May 1925
                              John Nicolich b. 27 Apr 1928
                      Domenico Nicolich b. 8 Jan 1890, d. 1966
                      + Agata (Ivana Matesinica) Radoslovic b. 10 Jun 1892, d. 7 Sep
                      1976
                              Lucia (Lucy)Nicolich b. 14 Jan 1920, d. 18
                              Aug 2001
                              Alice Nicolich b. 20 Mar 1922
                              Dominic Nicolich b. 5 Aug 1928
                      Carlo Nicolich b. 15 Jan 1892, d. Oct 1983
                      + Jennie b. 6 Jan 1901, d. Apr 1974
                              Viola Nicolich
                              Rakela Nicolich b. 1925
                              Charles Nicolich b. 1928
                              Gloria Nicolich b. 1930

1   2   3   4   5   6   7   8

NICOLICH, NIKOLIĆ   (Sancich)

The family origin for the lineage name of Sancich is unknown. The oldest known ancestor is Domenico Nicolich, son of Antonius and husband of Thomasina Nicolich (1807-1847).

The Sancich brothers, Mikula and Giovanni were born in house number 119 near the post office. Later they built their house where number 55 is today.

Giovanni Nicolich (1842-) Witnessed the naval engagement against Italy off the island of Vis (Lissa), in 1866. He was with the Austrian navy that came down from Pula to Vis which managed to sink several Italian ships in the ensuing battle.

Joseph Nicolich (1909-1993)

History of the Nicolich's / Nikolic's in Mali Losinj

This is a very common surname found throughout Croatia. Nikolić occurs in the parish records at least by the 16th Century in Losinj and probably dates back even earlier. The surname in the form of Mikolić appears in deeds from Veli Losinj for the period 1590 and 1602.

Nicolich, Nikolić (Sancich) Family Home, No.164 Unije

A birth record with the surname Nicolich occurs in Osor for Bartolomea, daughter of Nicolo born Nov. 14, 1609. In the earliest parish records for Mali Losinj Nicolich was spelled 'Mikolić'. Mikula in Croatian is Nicolaus which is rendered in Italian as Nicolo. Since Mikolić in English can be translated as 'son of Nicolaus' then Nicolich would be the Italian equivalent. The parish records in Mali Losinj were written in Croatian up to 1732 and thereafter they were written in Italian. Before 1732 the surname appears as Mikolić in the parish registers and afterwards as Nicolich. Several marriages of the Nicolich family from Unije are recorded from the 18th Century are listed in the Appendix.

Several lineages with this surname have been based in Mali Losinj. The lineages include Cicola, Morcich, Muskardin (Muscardin), and Salata. Some of these lineages have representative families in Unije. Also in Unije there is an additional Nicolich lineage named Kambera. This Kambera clan dates back to Simon Nicolich son of Andrea and born in 1826. See the following Nicolich family genealogies for details.

Nicolich, Nikolić (Sancich) — Unije, Croatia

Antonius Nicolich

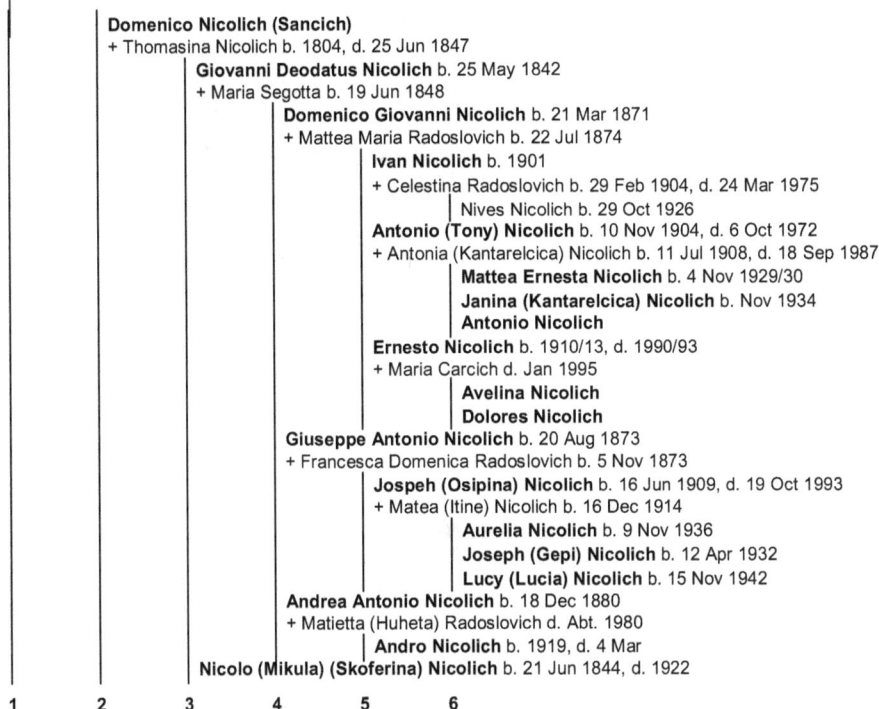

    Domenico Nicolich (Sancich)
    + Thomasina Nicolich b. 1804, d. 25 Jun 1847
        Giovanni Deodatus Nicolich b. 25 May 1842
        + Maria Segotta b. 19 Jun 1848
            Domenico Giovanni Nicolich b. 21 Mar 1871
            + Mattea Maria Radoslovich b. 22 Jul 1874
                Ivan Nicolich b. 1901
                + Celestina Radoslovich b. 29 Feb 1904, d. 24 Mar 1975
                  Nives Nicolich b. 29 Oct 1926
                Antonio (Tony) Nicolich b. 10 Nov 1904, d. 6 Oct 1972
                + Antonia (Kantarelcica) Nicolich b. 11 Jul 1908, d. 18 Sep 1987
                  Mattea Ernesta Nicolich b. 4 Nov 1929/30
                  Janina (Kantarelcica) Nicolich b. Nov 1934
                  Antonio Nicolich
                Ernesto Nicolich b. 1910/13, d. 1990/93
                + Maria Carcich d. Jan 1995
                  Avelina Nicolich
                  Dolores Nicolich
             Giuseppe Antonio Nicolich b. 20 Aug 1873
            + Francesca Domenica Radoslovich b. 5 Nov 1873
                Jospeh (Osipina) Nicolich b. 16 Jun 1909, d. 19 Oct 1993
                + Matea (Itine) Nicolich b. 16 Dec 1914
                  Aurelia Nicolich b. 9 Nov 1936
                  Joseph (Gepi) Nicolich b. 12 Apr 1932
                  Lucy (Lucia) Nicolich b. 15 Nov 1942
            Andrea Antonio Nicolich b. 18 Dec 1880
            + Matietta (Huheta) Radoslovich d. Abt. 1980
                Andro Nicolich b. 1919, d. 4 Mar
        Nicolo (Mikula) (Skoferina) Nicolich b. 21 Jun 1844, d. 1922

1   2   3   4   5   6

NICOLICH, NIKOLIĆ (Kambera)

The lineage origins are undetermined, but they may be linked either to the Agatin or Tomicev clans of the Nicolich/Nikolić families.

Nicolich, Nikolić (Kambera) -- Unije, Croatia

Andrea Nicolich
    Simeone (Sime) Nicolich b. 26 Jan 1826
        Giovanni Andrea Nicolich b. 2 Nov 1858
            Sime (Sam) Nicolich b. 4 Feb 1883, d. 1915
            Anton Nicolich b. 19 Dec 1899 Unije, d. 18 Nov 1945 Unije
            + Marija (Zvonora) Karcic b. 19 Oct 1902 Unije, d. Unije
                Tini Nicolich b. 1924, d. Jun 1989
                Ivan Nikolich b. 1926, d. 1981 New York,New York
                Katica Nicolich b. 30 Apr 1928, d. 5 Jul 1958 Unije
                Sime Nicolich b. 1933
                Josip Nicolich b. 1935
                Zora Nicolich b. 1940

1   2   3   4   5

NICOLICH, NIKOLIĆ (Tomicev, Tomicin)

This clan's genealogy extends back to Andrea Nicolich who died prior to 1837 and was married to Thomasina (1753-1840), who may have given her name to this branch of the Nicolich lineage. Other variations on the spelling of this surname include Nikolich and Niccoli. The lineage name was spelled two ways, either as Tomicev or Tomicin.

Originally this lineage name split into two with the addition of the Cincin lineage, probably dating from Andrea Nicolich (1874-1961).

Giuseppe Niccoli (1871-1949) was a contractor and builder, hence his name 'Osip Zidor'. He worked in Mali Losinj.

Valentino Nicolich (1907/08-1991)

Domenica Carcich (1873-) and Osip
Zidor Niccoli (1871-1949)

Nicolich Nikolić (Tomicnev) Family Home,
No. 190 Unije

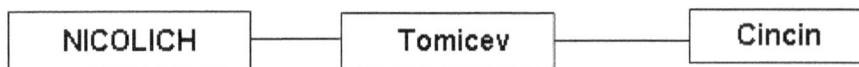

164

Nicolich, Nikolić (Tomicev) — Unije, Croatia

Andrea Nicolich
  Andrea Nicolich b. 1785, d. 23 Sep 1837
    Andrea Nicolich b. 1817, d. 14 Aug 1862
      Andrea Nicolich (Barba Rossa) b. 4 Apr 1846
        Andrea Giovanni Nicolich (Cincin) b. 2 Feb 1874, d. 25 Dec 1961
          Lucia Nicolich b. 1908
          Frane Nicolich b. 1910, d. 1991
          Laura Nikolic b. 1916, d. 4 Dec 2002
          Andrea Nicolich b. 15 Apr 1919, d. 29 Nov 2002
          Domenica Nicolich b. 1922
        Frane (Barbe Rose) Nicolich b. 21 Oct 1881, d. 16 Mar 1938
          Andrea Nicolich b. 1918
          Marija Nicolich
        Giuseppe (Bepo) Nicolich b. 1885/87, d. Feb 1939
          Joseph Nicolich b. 1921
          Palma Nicolich b. 28 Nov 1923
      Giovanni Nicolich b. 21 Nov 1852, d. 25 Jan 1892
        John (Zburke) Nicolich b. 17 May 1885, d. 30 Aug 1938
          Agata Nicolich b. 18 Sep 1921, d. 23 Nov 1990
        Andrew (Zburka) Nicolich b. 28 Mar 1889, d. 13 Jul 1972
          Andrea (Andrew) Matteo Nicolich b. 21 Aug 1922, d. 4 Jan 2004
          Mary V. Nicolich b. 23 Dec 1924
          Minnie Nicolich b. 9 Aug 1926
          Jenny Lucy Nicolich b. 9 Mar 1929
          Antonia Lucy Nicolich b. 9 Mar 1929
          John Nicolich b. 9 Dec 1935
          Helen Gloria Nicolich b. 9 Dec 1935
    Matte Nicolich b. 4 Feb 1827
      Andrea Calisto Nicolich (Rogoca) b. 14 Oct 1856
        Matteo (Matthew) Vincent Nicolich b. 1 Dec 1888, d. 13 Aug 1959
          Matthew Thomas Jr. Nicolich b. 8 May 1918
          Lawrence Vincent Nicolich b. 31 May 1921
        Andrea (Kalisto) Nicolich d. 1995
          Kalisto Nikolic
          Antonia (Tonica) Nikolic b. 1935
          Mary Nikolic
          Andric Nikolic
          Ivo Nikolic b. 1944
      Giovanni Domenico Nicolich b. 16 Sep 1860
        Jani Nicolich
          Ricardo (Tomicnev) Nicolich b. 1934
          Jani Nicolich b. 1920
      Tobia Domenico Nicolich b. 4 Feb 1866
        Matteo Nicolich b. 10 Nov 1894, d. 21 Dec 1968
          Tobia Nicolich b. 1920, d. 2000
          Ricardo Nicolich
          Salvatore Nicolich
        Valentino Nikolich b. 1907/08, d. 11 Jul 1991
          Dorando Nikolich
          Mario Nikolich
          Valentino Nikolich
          Milka Nikolich
      Matteo Gregorio Nicolich b. 16 Nov 1867, d. 13 Oct 1933
        Matteo Nicolich b. 6 Aug 1894, d. 26 Jun 1915
        Andrea (Pasametar) Nicolich b. 1901, d. 1988
          Matteo Nicolich b. 1925
          Zora Nicolich b. 1933
      Giuseppe Domenico(Osip Zidor) Niccoli b. 11 Dec 1871, d. 19 Nov 1949
        Matteo Niccoli
          Fabio Niccoli

1   2   3   4   5   6

PILLEPICH, PILEPIĆ

This surname appears in several parts of Croatia with the highest concentration in and around the region on Opatija and Rijeka.

The family in Unije originated with Mateo Pilepich, born in Rijeka in 1820 and who married Regina Mohovich. Around the same time other Pillepich's from Rijeka also settled in Mali Losinj. The Unije branch of this family can trace their lineage to Mateo Pilepich and Regina Mohovich. Two other Pillepich families married and settled in Mali Losinj. One of these was Giuseppe Pillepich born in Rijeka in 1851 and the other was Antonio Pillepich.

Spiridione Pillepich (1889-1959)

Matteo Pillepich (1891-1972)

Pillepich, Pilepić Family Home, No. 170 Unije

Pillepich, Pilepić — Unije, Croatia

Mateo S. Pillepich b. 24 Feb 1820, d. 1879
+ Regina Mohovich b. 7 Sep 1822
    Spiridione Pillepich b. 29 Apr 1857
    + Matea Caterina Carcich b. 19 Oct 1861, d. 1934/36
        Domenico (Menigo) Pillepich
        + Maria Carcich b. 23 Apr 1890, d. 31 Jul 1985
            Milan Pillepich b. 1919
            + Nina
        Giovanni (Jovanin) Pillepich b. 6 Jul 1886, d. 25 May 1948
        + Giacomina (Marcheto) Nicolich
        + Giacomina (Agatin) Nicolich b. 1904, d. 27 Oct 1997
        Spiridione (Spiro) Pillepich b. 23 Dec 1889, d. 28 Nov 1959
        + Elizabeta Jelisava Ana (Calcich) Radoslovich b. 22 May 1893, d. 6 Mar 1981
            Giuseppe (Bepi) Pillepich b. 16 Oct 1920, d. 21 Oct 2005
            + Anna (Simef) Rerecich b. 28 Nov 1924
                Josephine (Iosheta) Pillepich b. 12 May 1953
                Alex (Sandro) Pillepich b. 10 Oct 1955
            Marina Pillepich b. 24 Jul 1931
            + Ivan Carcich (Bravarof) b. 4 Mar 1928
                Claude Carcich b. 1953
                Jane Carcich b. 1956
                Elizabeth Carcich b. 1967
            Spiridione (Spiro) Pillepich b. 1916
    Matteo Pillepich b. 3 Aug 1891, d. 18 Mar 1972
    + Domenica Nicolich b. 20 Oct 1895, d. 18 Apr 1969
        Mateo Pillepich b. 1920, d. 14 Mar 1997
        + Jolanda (Racov) Carcich b. 1921
            Georgio Pillepich b. 1953
            Silvana Pillepich b. 1950
            Amalia Pillepich b. 1948, d. 1948
        Domenico (Meme) Pillepich b. 1921, d. 22 Aug 1992
        Giovanni (Jovanin) Pillepich b. 25 May 1927
        + Antonia Jacomina (Agatin) Nicolich b. 13 Jul 1932
            Andric Pillepich b. 14 Jan 1963, d. 16 Oct 1977
            Jovanin Pillepich
        Gina (Ina) Pillepich b. 1923
        + Andrea (Popich) Radoslovich b. 1921
            Mario Radoslovich
            Silvio Radoslovich
            Andrea Radoslovich
    Giuseppe (Bepo) Pillepich b. 6 Feb 1893, d. 3 Jan 1953
    + Anna (Sburcich) Carcich
    Alessandro Pillepich b. 5 Aug 1894, d. 7 Oct 1956
    + Germana (Agatin) Nicolich b. 1890, d. 19 May 1980
        Alessandro Pillepich b. 21 Nov 1925
        + Maria (Agatin) Nicolich b. 13 Feb 1931
            George Pillepich b. 22 Sep 1954
            Adrienne Pillepich b. 2 Aug 1957
        Georgio Pillepich

1   2   3   4   5

RADOSLOVICH, RADOSLOVIĆ – Early History

Šimunić claims *Radoslavić* is a compound surname (Rado-slavić) dating from the Middle Ages [58].

Besides Unije and Mali Losinj, this surname is also found on the island of Pag. The Radoslovich families in Mali Losinj are descendant from setters from Unije.

The name Radoslovich appears in Osor birth and marriage records from 1615 to 1749. Martin Radoslovich (nicknamed Grusloman) is listed as from Unije in 1624. This suggests that the Radoslovich families moved to Unije from the Osor area sometime in the 17th Century.

An early mention of this family in connection with Unije dates to 1680 and occurs in the Osor litigation document. In the document one of the plaintiffs was Anton Radoslovich.

Karstić Radoslovich son of Simun of Unije married in Osor on May 13, 1727. A number of Osor marriage and death records occur for those with the surname Radoslovich from Unije from 1765 to 1779. A number of these marriages are listed in the Appendix.

All the progenitors for the Radoslovich families from Mali Losinj have their origins in Unije during the first half of the 18th Century. Three early Radoslovich families are found in Mali Losinj which originated from Unije.

Karstić Radoslović married in 1727 was son of Simun of Unije; Simon of Simon married in 1749 also from Unije; and Martin of Unije married in 1712.

Several individuals with this surname were involved in the lumber trade between the islands of Losinj and Cres with transport to Venician markets. Christoforo Radoslovich son of Simon and Mattio Radoslovich son on Paolo worked in transporting lumber during the 1740's and 1750's. Later Nicolo Radoslovich was involved in the lumber trade during 1777 to 1794. A Nicolo Radoslovich was captain of the 'pielego *Beata Verine di Lussin* to Corfu in 1795. The following year Domencio Radoslovich son of Zuane captained the *Falcone* to Corfu.

The Mattessinich branch of this family returned to Unije in the 19th Century after settling in Mali Losinj in the early part of the 18th Century.

The Mencich branch of the Radoslovich family starts with Matteo Radoslovich (1879-1973) and is part of the Rosso clan, while the origins of the Sesturin lineage is unknown.

Mali Losinj 1938

Descendants of Martin Radoslović of Unije & Mali Losinj

Martin Radoslović b. Unije
+ Dunka Radosić m. 23 Jan 1712 Mali Losinj
     Mikula Radoslovich b. 10 Jan 1715
     Simon Radoslovich b. 1718
     + Manada Rasdosić b. 9 Feb 1724, m. 27 Nov 1751 Lussinpiccolo
         Romulus Radoslovich b. 17 Feb 1759
         + Nicolaa Haglich b. 1759, m. 8 Jan 1783
             Simon Radoslovich b. 2 Oct 1783
             Zuanne Radoslovich b. 11 Mar 1786
             Maria Radoslovich b. 14 Jul 1787
             Matteo Radoslovich b. 3 Dec 1788
         Tomaso Radoslovich b. 5 Nov 1752
         + Margarita Tarabochia m. 15 Nov 1773
             Simon Radoslovich b. 30 Jan 1775
             + Giacomina Piccinich b. 1777, m. 1798, d. 1853
                 Thomas Radoslovich b. 1798
                 + Matthea Picinich b. 1810, m. 5 Feb 1824
                     Petrus Radoslovich b. 1831, d. 1881
                     + Joanna Theresia Hoglievina b. 1833, m. 7 Jan 1856
                         Francesco Radoslovich b. 1861, d. 1928
                         Maria Petronilla Radoslovich b. 13 Nov 1863, d. 3 Apr 1954
                         Giovanna Antonia Radoslovich b. 1868
                         Petronillia Antonia Romila Radoslovich b. 6 Sep 1869, d. 29 Mar 1948
                 Joannes Radoslovich b. 1802
                 Alessandro Radoslovich b. 2 May 1815
                 + Giacomina Zorovich b. 1817, m. 6 Feb 1841
                     Michael Hieronymus Radoslovich b. 1851, d. 1932
                     + Antonia Natalina Mussalin m. 5 Jul 1873
                         Alesander Christophorus Radoslovich b. 1877
                         Giacomina Maria Antonia Radoslovich b. 16 Sep 1881, d. 15 Jun 1944
                         Antonio Matteo Radoslovich b. 1884
                 Dominicus Marcus Radoslovich b. 1820
              Antonius Radoslovich b. 24 Apr 1780
             + Cattarina Cosulich m. 23 Dec 1804
                 Joannes Radoslovich b. 1808
                 + Jacoba Picinich b. 1815, m. 2 May 1835
             Madalena Radoslovich b. 1782
             Tomaso Radoslovich b. 10 Dec 1784

1   2   3   4   5   6   7

RADOSLOVICH, RADOSLOVIĆ (Calcich, Kalčić)

This lineage goes back to Martin Radoslovich (1715-1750) son of Martin of Unije, though it is not known when the Calcich or Kalčić, lineage name came into use. Nicolo Radoslovich, born in 1841 carried this lineage name, while his brother, Andreja Radoslovich (1845-1935) carried the lineage name of Ghiriza (Girića). The lineage of Grovran or Gravran, also originates with the Calcich family and was first used by Mattheus Radoslovich, born in 1805.

Andrea Radoslovich (1845- 1935) called "Girica" or "Ghirica", minnow in English, was in the United States by 1885. His son Matij (Matthew) Radoslovich (1886-1972) was born in New York City. Another son, Gaudent Radoslovich (1891-1950) operated a restaurant in Greenwich Village of New York City between 1922 and 1950.

Radoslovich (Calcich / Kalcic) Family. Front: Stanislav (1922-1974), Andreja (1878-1948), Marija Karcic (1882-1955), Peter(1920-88) Back: Anton (1917-1972), Andreja (1912-1942), Keti (1914-).

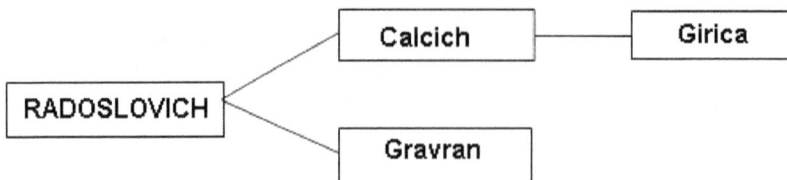

Radoslovich, Radoslović (Calcich) — Unije, Croatia

Martin Radoslovich
  Martin Radoslovich b. 1715, d. 1750
    Anto. Radoslovich (Calcich)
      Mattheus Radoslovich b. 1769, d. 1853
        Matteo Radoslovich b. 1806, d. 7 Sep 1850
          Carlo Radoslovich
          Nicolo (Mikula) (Calcich) Radoslovich b. 13 Sep 1841
            Matteo Angelo Radoslovich b. 26 Jan 1880
            Ivan Josip (Calcich) Radoslovich b. 18 Oct 1885, d. 26 Dec 1922
              John (Calcich) Radoslovich b. 5 May 1921, d. 5 Jan 1998
              Julio (Calcich) Radoslovich b. 8 Nov 1922, d. 10 Oct 1993
            [Mikula] Radoslovich
              Mirko Radoslovich b. abt 1925
          Andreja Ivan Radoslovich (Girica) b. 25 May 1845, d. 1935
            Caterina Anna Radoslovich b. 11 Feb 1875
            Andrea Giovanni Radoslovich (Calcich) b. 21 Jun 1878, d. 15 Aug 1948
              Katarina Radoslovich b. 12 Mar 1911, d. 1913
              Andreja Radoslovich b. 27 Nov 1912, d. 7 Apr 1942
              Keti (Kay) Apolonia Radoslovich b. 9 Feb 1914
              Maria Ana Radoslovich b. 9 Nov 1916
              Anton Lovro Radoslovich b. 28 Aug 1917, d. 1972
              Petar Simun Radoslovich b. 28 Feb 1920, d. Oct 1988
              Stanislav Josip (Stanley) Radoslovich b. 24 Jan 1922, d. 12 Aug 1974
            Matij (Matthew) Anthony Radoslovich b. 21 Sep 1886, d. 16 Jan 1972
              Matthew A. Radoslovich b. 20 Aug 1914, d. 6 May 1979
              Katherine Radoslovich b. 17 Aug 1916, d. 7 Aug 1936
              Mary Philomena Radoslovich b. 20 Sep 1917
              Ljubica (Laura) Leokadia (Caleich) Radoslovich b. 9 Dec 1918
              Florence Frances Radoslovich b. 27 May 1923
            Gaudent Sr. Radoslovich b. 1 Jun 1891, d. 7 Oct 1950
              Andrew J. Radoslovich b. 28 Nov 1921, d. 18 Jul 1940
              Katherine Antonia Radoslovich b. 20 Jan 1925
              Gaudent Jr. Andrea Radoslovich b. 17 Aug 1929
              Mike Radoslovich b. 8 Sep 1927, d. 7 Jan 2001
    Anto. Radoslovich (Calcich) b. 1760, d. 2 Oct 1817
      Mattheus Radoslovich (Grovran) b. 13 Jun 1805
        Matteo Radoslovich (Grovran) b. 13 Aug 1848
          Giuseppe Giusto Radoslovic b. 11 Oct 1879
            Giuseppe (Grovran) Radoslovich b. 27 Jul 1903, d. 3 Mar 1998
            Ernesta Radoslovich b. 13 Oct 1907, d. 2 Nov 1994
            Matteo Radoslovich b. 1910, d. 28 Jan 1991
          Giovanni Antonio (Grovran) Radoslovich b. 28 Mar 1880
            Romana Radoslovich b. 1910
            Matteo Radoslovich b. 1913
            Eta Radoslovich b. 1915
            Giovanni Radoslovich b. 1919, d. 15 Mar 1998
            Antonia Radoslovich
            Mafalda Radoslovich b. 1923
          Atanazio Radoslovich b. 1886
          Matietta (Huheta) Radoslovich d. Abt. 1980
            Andro Nicolich b. 1919, d. 4 Mar

1   2   3   4   5   6   7   8

RADOSLOVICH, RADOSLOVIĆ (Mattesinich, Matesinić)

This family has descendants in Unije and Mali Losinj. Its origins are with Simon Radoslovich, son of Simon of Unije who married Antonia Cosulich in Mali Losinj in 1749.

Several families descendant from Simon and Antonia Cosulich through their son Martin born in 1749. Martin married twice and had two sons named Nicolaus. These include the families of Simon Radoslovich, born in 1775 and his brother Nicolaus, born in 1779. A third brother Franciscus born in 1781 also had a large number of descendents, though his family is not shown in the accompanying genealogy.

Nicolaus Radoslovich who married in 1819, brought one branch of the family back to resettle in Unije. Nicolaus brought his son Joannes or Ivan born in 1829 in Mali Losinj to Unije as a young boy.

Ivan Radoslovich (1867-1957)

Ivan Radoslovich (1829-1903)

Radoslovich, Radoslović (Mattesinich)
Family Home, No. 131 Unije

Radoslovich, Radoslović (Mattesinch) — Mali Losinj & Unije, Croatia

Simon Radoslovich
　Simon Radoslovich m. 1749+ Antonia Cosulich
　　Joannes Radoslovich
　　　Joannes Radoslovich b. 1773, d. 21 Sep 1840
　　　　Antonio Radoslovich b. 14 Jan 1804
　　　　　Antonio Radoslovich b. 5 Mar 1849
　　　　　　Antonio Paolo Radoslovich b. 10 Aug 1871
　　Martin Radoslovich b. 1749, d. 21 Apr 1834 + Antonia Martinolich m. 1772, + Mattea Nicolich m. 1787
　　　Nicolaus Radoslovich m. 1819
　　　　Nicolo Radoslovich b. 1809
　　　　　Nicolo Radoslovich b. 1840
　　　　　Giovanni Antonio Radoslovich b. 19 Dec 1848 Mali Losinj, d. 8 Sep 1937
　　　　　　Matteo Cristoforo Giuseppe Radoslovich b. 3 May 1882
　　　　　　Mali Losinj, d. 21 Dec 1972 West New York, New Jersey
　　　　Joseph Radoslovich b. 22 Mar 1827
　　　　Joannes Josip Radoslovich b. 29 Mar 1829 Mali Losinj, d. 22 Oct 1903
　　　　　Antonio Giovanni (Balucin) Radoslovich b. 13 Nov 1854, d. 21 Sep 1950
　　　　　　Giovanni Anastasio Radoslovich b. 11 Dec 1879, d. 1973 Ilovik
　　　　　　　Giovanni Radoslovich b. 28 Nov 1904 Ilovik
　　　　　　　Anna Radoslovich b. 23 Dec 1905 Ilovik
　　　　　　　Giuseppe Radoslovich b. 25 Nov 1908
　　　　　　　Milka Radoslovich b. 11 Jun 1910 Ilovik
　　　　　　　Domenica Radoslovich b. 5 Feb 1912 Ilovik
　　　　　　Anton Radoslovich b. 18 Nov 1886, d. 5 Mar 1976 Unije
　　　　　　　Rejina Radoslovich
　　　　　　Petar Radoslovich b. 1 Mar 1897 Unije, d. 4 Feb 1993 Queens,N.Y.
　　　　　　　Anthony Radoslovich b. 9 Aug 1921 Unije, d. 10 Jul 1971
　　　　　　　Minnie Radoslovich b. 4 Nov 1933 New York
　　　　　Giovanni Giuseppe Radoslovich b. 14 Feb 1867 Unije, d. 9 May 1957
　　　　　　Ivanko Radoslovic b. 15 May 1893 Unije, d. 3 Sep 1985 Sun City,California
　　　　　　Martin Radoslovic b. 30 Mar 1899 Unije, d. 1925 New York
　　　　　　Josip Radoslovic b. 2 Oct 1905 Unije, d. Dec 2002 Unije
　　　　　　　Osip Radoslovic b. 15 Oct 1931 Unije
　　　　　　　Irene Radoslovich b. 3 Mar 1932
　　　Simon Radoslovich b. 11 Dec 1775
　　　　Martinus Radoslovich b. 1805
　　　　　Martinus C. Radoslovich b. 1836
　　　　　　Martino Simon Radoslovich b. 1867
　　　　　　Giovanni Radoslovich b. 25 Mar 1871
　　　　　　Marco Raffaele Radoslovich b. 16 Apr 1879
　　　　　　　Casimere Radoslovich b. 12 Mar 1912 Gregory, CO, d. 19 Aug 1930 Clayton, New Mexico
　　　Nicolaus Radoslovich b. 23 May 1779
　　　　Martinus Radoslovich b. Dec 1803
　　　　　Martino Antonio Radoslovich b. 1830
　　　　　　Giovanni Nicolo Radoslovich b. 1 Dec 1880 Mali Losinj
　　　　　Alexander Giovanni Radoslovich b. 1842
　　　　　　Giovanni Martino Simone Radoslovich b. 1 Mar 1862 Mali Losinj
　　　　　　　Giovanni Apolonio Domenico Radoslovich b. 9 Feb 1890

1　　2　　3　　4　　5　　6　　7　　8

RADOSLOVICH, RADOSLOVIĆ   (Papich, Popić)

This family can be traced back to Mateo Radoslovich (1775-1836) son of Mattheus. Mateo's sons, Andrea (1809-1873) and Antonio (1811-) carried the lineage forward. The derivation of this lineage name is a mystery.

Giovanni Radoslovich (1887-1973) worked in the United States and later returned to Unije. His son, Gianni Radoslovich (1920-1941) was sunk on the Italian ship *Lampo* out of La Spezia near the African coast.

Radoslovich, Radoslović (Popich) Family Home, No. 214 Unije

Giovanni Radoslovich
(1887-1973)

Radoslovich Radoslović (Popich), No. 129 Unije

Radoslovich, Radoslović (Popich) — Unije, Croatia

Mattheus Radoslovich
- **Matteo Radoslovich (Papich)** b. 1775, d. 16 Aug 1836 Unije
  - **Andrea Radoslovich** b. 30 Sep 1809, d. 17 Dec 1877 Unije
    - **Andrea Radoslovich** b. 31 Aug 1837
      - **Andrea Domenico Radoslovich (Gartljic)** b. 20 Jul 1871 Unije, d. 10 Feb 1947 Unije
        - **Joseph Radoslovich** b. 12 Jan 1905 Unije, d. 4 Aug 1989 Astoria,New York
          - **Joseph Radoslovich** b. 1930 Unije
          - **Andrew Radoslovich**
          - **Nelzi Radoslovich**
        - **Andrea Radoslovich** b. 1898 Unije d. 21 Mar 1950 Mali Losinj
          - **Andrea Radoslovich** b. 1921
          - **Anton Radoslovich** b. 1929, d. 2006
        - **Anton Radoslovich** b. 25 Jul 1901 Unije, d. 10 Jul 1971 New Jersey
      - **Domenico Antonio Radoslovich** b. 29 Aug 1878 Unije, d. 11 Jul 1929 Unije
        - **Andrea (Pioc) Radoslovich**
          - **Eleanora Maria (Norina) Radoslovich** b. 6 Nov 1929/30 Unije
          - **Andrea Radoslovich**
          - **Antonio Radoslovich** b. 1940
    - **Matteo Radoslovich** b. 1840, d. 1870 Unije
    - **Giovanni Radoslovich** b. 12 Nov 1842
      - **Andrea Domenico Radoslovich** b. 3 Aug 1878 Unije, d. 2 Jul 1938 Unije
        - **Andrea Radoslovich** b. 1921
          - **Mario Radoslovich**
          - **Silvio Radoslovich**
          - **Andrea Radoslovich**
      - **Giovanni Radoslovich** b. 11 Dec 1887 Unije, d. 3 Apr 1973
        - **Gianni Radoslovich** b. 20 Nov 1920, d. 18 Apr 1941
        - **Maria Radoslovich** b. 17 Feb 1922, d. 8 Sep 1942
  - **Antonio Radoslovich** b. 7 Nov 1811
    - **Matteo Radoslovich** b. 28 May 1839
      - **Antonio Andrea Radoslovich** b. 17 Dec 1879, d. 2 Jun 1965
        - **Mike Radoslovich** b. 26 Feb 1918 New York, d. 26 Jan 1994
          - **Michael Radoslovich** b. abt 1940 West New York, NJ
          - **Diane Radoslovich** b. abt 1940 West New York, NJ
        - **Robert Radoslovich** b. 24 May 1921 New York
          - **Susan Radoslovich** b. 9 Feb 1954 Jersey City,New Jersey
          - **Nancy Radoslovich** b. 18 Sep 1961 Jersey City,NJ
          - **Roberta Radoslovich** b. 18 Apr 1967 Jersey City,NJ
    - **Giovanni (Ivan Eduard) Radoslovich** b. 12 Oct 1844, d. 1920
      - **Antonio Marco Radoslovich** b. 12 Oct 1874, d. 1916
        - **Ivan (Piccolo Giovanni) Radoslovich** b. 13 Dec 1900 Unije, d. 1 Mar 1940 Normandy,France
          - **Maria Radoslovich** b. 1931
          - **Tony Randall** b. 1933
          - **Donata Radoslovich** b. 10 Feb 1934 Unije
          - **Luciana Radoslovich** b. 1938 Unije
        - **Antonio (Piccolo Toni) Radoslovich** b. 15 Feb 1905 Unije, d. Jun 1989 Cremona, Italy
          - **Wanda Radoslovich** b. 15 Mar 1931 Nerezine, d. 15 Mar 1938 Trieste, Italy
          - **Mafalda Radoslovich** b. 1 May 1932 Nerezine

1   2   3   4   5   6   7

RADOSLOVICH, RADOSLOVIĆ   (Rosso)

The family or clan name is Rosso. Matteo (1879-1973) also carried the family name of Mencich. Matteo's son Matteo (Mike) born in 1908 played accordion in the United States with famous players such as Carmen Carrozza. Carmen had a professional concert career playing with several American orchestras.

Carmen Carrozza (1921-) and Matteo (Mike) Radoslovich (1908-) second accordionist on the right.

RADOSLOVICH, RADOSLOVIĆ   (Sesturin)

Virgilio Radoslovich (1905-1998)

Radoslovich, Radoslović (Sesturin) Unije, Croatia

Matteo Radoslovich
  Martino Radoslovich b. 8 Nov 1828
  + Domenica Nicolich b. 1 Dec 1843
    Matteo Domenico Radoslovich b. 22 Sep 1867
    + Mattea Caterina Radoslovich b. 29 Oct 1867, m. Unije
      Virgilio Radoslovich b. 26 Jun 1905, d. 5 Nov 1998 New York
      + Minnie Rerecich (Jercich) b. 12 Nov 1908, d. 1 Nov 1986 New York
        Matteo (Mike) Radoslovich b. 25 Dec 1929, d. 26 Jul 1998
        Virgilio Redo b. 1931

    1   2   3   4   5

Radoslovich, Radoslovic (Rosso) — Unije, Croatia

Matteo Radoslovich (Rosso)
+ Gaudentia Carcich b. 1773, d. 26 Oct 1835
      Antonio Radoslovich b. 17 Jan 1803
      + Giacomina Nicolich b. 25 Oct 1801
          Antonius Radoslovich b. Apr 1829, d. 23 Aug 1850
      Matteo Radoslovich (Rosso) b. 20 Sep 1804, d. 22 Mar 1872
      + Tomasina Radoslovich b. 27 Feb 1811
          Maria Radoslovich b. 21 Oct 1840
          Domenico Andrea Radoslovich b. 31 May 1846
          + Nicolina Nicolich b. 6 Dec 1846
              Matteo Domenico Radoslovich (Mencich) b. 15 Jan 1879, d. 12 Nov 1973
              + Maria Margarita (Osuorka) Barburan b. 1880, m. 18 Jan 1904
                  Matteo (Mike) Radoslovich b. 30 Jan 1908
                  + Advisa (Luisa) (Jevin) Carcich b. 1905
                      Ana Radoslovich
                      Maria Radoslovich
                  Stella Radoslovich b. 24 Dec 1908
                  + John Picinic
                      Stella Picinic
                  Maria Radoslovich b. 9 Jan 1913, d. 18 Sep 2000
                  + Antonio Karcich b. 9 Aug 1907, d. Feb 1976
                      Anton Karcich b. 4 Jan 1936
                      Esterina Karcich b. 12 Feb 1941
                  Margerita Radoslovich b. 6 Jan 1914
                  + Toni Vidulich
                  Domenico Radoslovich b. 1918
                  Irma Radoslovich b. Sep 1918
                  + Pino Viscotti
                  Etta Radoslovich b. 1921
           Maria Radoslovich b. 30 Dec 1849, d. 1930
          + Andrea (Bukaleta) Carcich b. 26 Aug 1849, d. 7 Aug 1921
              Giuseppe Luciano Carcich b. 15 May 1875
              Carmela Andriana Carcich b. 22 Apr 1877
              Andrea Matteo Carcich b. 26 Nov 1880
      + Maria Segotta b. 1805, d. 5 Apr 1839
          Matteo Radoslovich (Rosso) b. 1 Jul 1831
          + Nicolina Steffanich b. 7 Apr 1842
              Nicolo Giovanni (Mikula) Radoslovich b. 2 Feb 1873, d. 26 Jan 1962
              + Regina Paolina Carcich b. 15 Jan 1877, m. 20 May 1896, d. 1948
                  Matti Radoslovich
                  + Regina Pillepich b. 1899
                      Nicolo (Niko) Radoslovich b. 19 Sep 1921, d. Feb 1945
                  Nicolo (Mikula) Radoslovich b. 10 Apr 1902, d. 3 Apr 1956
                  + Mattea (Bravarof) Carcich b. 7 Dec 1908, bu. 29 Jun 1991
                      Maria Radoslovich b. 1936
                      Matteo Radoslovich b. 15 Apr 1937
                      Regina Radoslovich b. 9 Jun 1949
                  Andrea Antun Radoslovich b. 22 May 1913, d. 5 Jan 1942
                  + Maria (Sburcich) Carcich b. 1915
                      Andrea Radoslovich b. 1937
                  Regina Radoslovich b. 1914
                  Nicoletta (Eta) Radoslovich b. 1919

1   2   3   4   5   6

RERECICH, RERECIĆ

The family of Rerecich (Rereka) had an appearance on Losinj by the 15th Century. Rereka is one of the original families that came to the island of Losinj in 1280. The surname in both forms (Rereka and Rerečić) appears in deeds from Veli Losinj for the period 1582-3 and 1587-1591.

An early mention of this family in connection with Unije dates to 1680 and occurs in the Osor litigation document. In the document two of the plaintiffs were Nicholas and Luke Rerecich.

This family is said to originally come from Veli Losinj and to be descended from two brothers, Sime from which the Simef clan comes from, and Jerko from which the Jercich clan originates. Unfortunately, the Status Animarum church records for Veli Losinj for the 19th Century, indicate that in the Rerecich families, Sime was a common name, but there is no record of two bothers Sime and Jerko. Several marriages of the Rerecich family from Unije recorded in the 18th Century are listed in the Appendix.

RERECICH, RERECIĆ (Jercich, Jerčić)

The earliest Rerecich (Jercich) for this family is Domenico Rerecich (1784-1854) whose father was Joannis.

Francesco Giuseppe Rerecich (1878-) worked in the United States in 1892 at the age of 14. He worked in Colorado, Washington, and New York.

Family of Paul (Paval) Rerecich (1882-1962) and Filictia Nicolich (1888-1979)

Rerecich, Rerečić (Jercich) Home No. 129 Unije

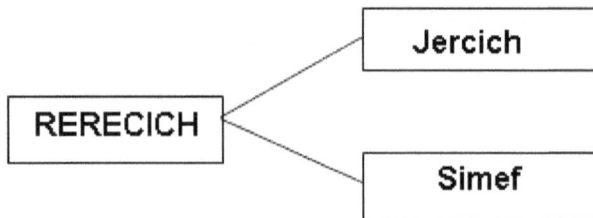

RERECICH — Jercich, Simef

178

Rerecich, Rerečić (Jercich) — Unije, Croatia

Joannis Rerecich

Domenico Rerecich b. 1784, d. 26 Dec 1854 Unije
+ Jacoba (Jacomina) Carcich b. 1777, d. 14 Jan 1852 Unije
    Domenico Rerecich b. 31 Aug 1816, d. 1878 Unije
    + Gasparina Nicolich b. 6 Jan 1818
        Anton Rerecich b. 21 Nov 1849
        + Tomasina Carcich b. 19 Jan 1854
            Paul Rerecich b. 18 Jan 1882 Unije, d. 30 May 1962 West New York,NJ
            + Filicita Dinka Nicolich (Martinica) b. 29 Oct 1888 Unije, m. 16 Feb 1913
            New York, d. 25 Apr 1979 West New York, New Jersey
                Tini Rerecich b. 1913
                Paul Rerecich b. 1917
                Martin Rerecich b. 1918
                Toma (Thomas) Rerecich b. 1921
                Mary Rerecich b. 1922
            Blaso Rerecich b. 3 Feb 1891, d. Mar 1966 Baltimore, Maryland
        Domenico Gregorio Rerecich b. 11 Mar 1856
        + Nicolina Francesca Segotta b. 4 Oct 1858
            Domenico (Pacencich) Rerecich b. 10 Dec 1880
            + Maria Karcic
                Marija (Marica) Rerecich b. 29 Aug 1909, d. 13 May 1980 Unije
                Anna Rerecich d. Mali Losinj
                Celestina Rerecich b. 1924, d. 17 Dec 1984 Mali Losinj
                Dominic Rerecich b. 1929
            Tony (Pacencich) Rerecich
            + **Milia** b. Miholjascica,Cres, d. 1994
                Rina Rerecich b. 1926
    Paolino Rerecich b. 13 Aug 1819
    + Maria Giovanna Karcic b. 25 Oct 1834, m. Cunski, d. Sep 1879 Unije
        Giovanni Martino Rerecich b. 16 May 1874 Unije
        + Maria Gasparina Carcich b. 4 Jan 1879
            Ivan Rerecich b. 1905 Unije, d. Unie
            Paolo Rerecich b. 1907 Unije, d. abt 1960 Genova, Italy
            + Maria Carcich b. 1908 Unije
                Rosa Rerecich b. 30 Aug 1930 Unije
                Maria Rerecich
                Paula Rerecich
                Sergio Rerecich b. 8 Feb 1943 Mali Losinj
                d. 22 Sep 1967 Genova,Italy
            Maria Rerecich b. 1912, d. 1947 Opatija
            + Ivo Galosich b. 30 Jun 1910 Unije, d. 23 Jan 1989 Unije
            Mariano Rerecich b. 11 Jan 1914 Unie,Austria, d. 25 Aug 1993
            + Julie Carcich b. 25 Jan 1920 Unije
                Ersilia Rerecich b. 11 Aug 1943
                Claudia Rerecich b. 16 Jun 1946
                Clara (Clareta) Rerecich b. 29 Sep 1952
        Francesco Giuseppe Rerecich b. 1 Feb 1878 Unije, d. 1964 Umag,Istria
        + Fiorina Adelajile Carcich b. 27 Sep 1880 Unije, d. 1961 Unije
            Mary Rerecich b. 1907, d. 1960
            Minnie Rerecich b. 12 Nov 1908, d. 1 Nov 1986 NY
            + Virgilio (Sesturin) Radoslovich b. 26 Jun 1905, d. 5 Nov 1998 New York
            Paolina Maria Rerecich b. 1910, d. Pola
            + Romolo Carcich b. 11 Apr 1908, d. 20 Jan 2002
            Fiore (Cvitko) Rerecich b. 19 Nov 1921 Unije, d. 2 Sep 1983 Eugene, Oregon
            + Bruna (Caroline) Nicolich b. 6 Dec 1925
            Lurdes Rerecich b. 1923 Unije
            + **Romolo Carcich** b. 11 Apr 1908, d. 20 Jan 2002

1   2   3   4   5

RERECICH, REREČIĆ (Simef)

Lineage name derives from the patronym for Sime (Simon). The ancestral chart begins with Simone Rerecich (1758-1838) son of Mattheus. But another Simone Rerecich existed in Unije born before 1740. Therefore, the original Sime who gave his name to this family lineage, remains unknown.

Two families of the Simef are descendant from a Simeon ancestor. This Simeon may be the same individual, though it has not been proven. There is a death record for a Simeon, born 1758, deceased March 11, 1838 who is a likely candidate for this ancestry. Simeon's (1758-1838) wife likely was Thomasina, born 1767, deceased 1833.

Antonio Rerecich-Simef (1930-) studied at the nautical school in Mali Losinj and completed his studies at Bakar. He became a merchant marine and passenger captain in Italy for the Lloyd Trestino Line worked on the route from Genoa to Sydney, Australia.

Lydia Rerecich (1914-) and Antonio Rerecich (1867-1954)

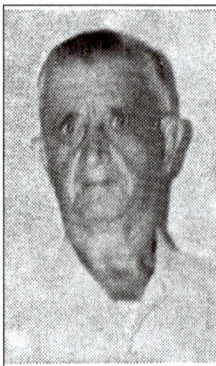

Giovanni Rerecich (1887-1970)

Rerecich, Rerečić (Simef) Home, Unije No. 175

Rerecich, Rerečić (Simef) — Unije, Croatia

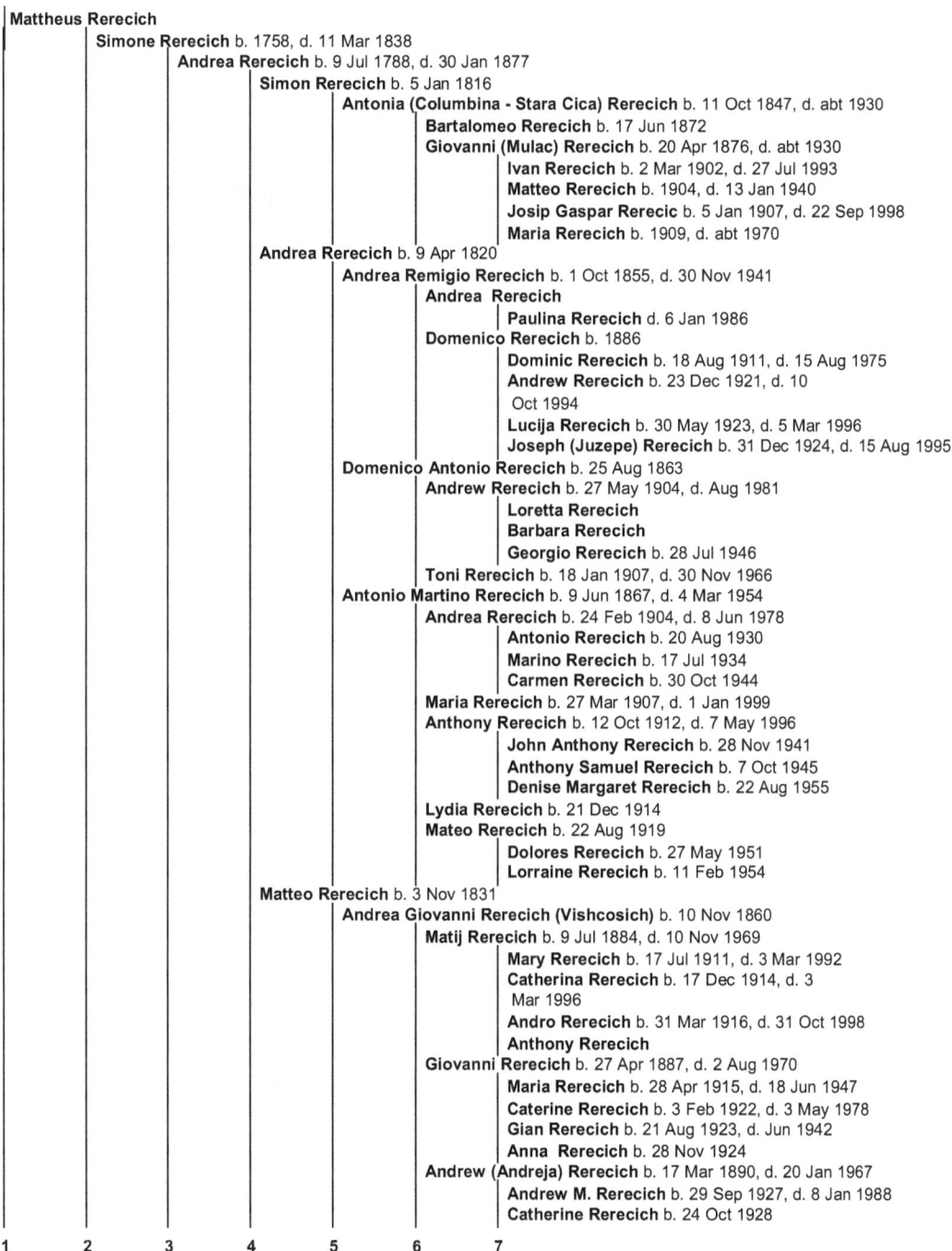

Mattheus Rerecich
    Simone Rerecich b. 1758, d. 11 Mar 1838
        Andrea Rerecich b. 9 Jul 1788, d. 30 Jan 1877
            Simon Rerecich b. 5 Jan 1816
                Antonia (Columbina - Stara Cica) Rerecich b. 11 Oct 1847, d. abt 1930
                    Bartalomeo Rerecich b. 17 Jun 1872
                    Giovanni (Mulac) Rerecich b. 20 Apr 1876, d. abt 1930
                        Ivan Rerecich b. 2 Mar 1902, d. 27 Jul 1993
                        Matteo Rerecich b. 1904, d. 13 Jan 1940
                        Josip Gaspar Rerecic b. 5 Jan 1907, d. 22 Sep 1998
                        Maria Rerecich b. 1909, d. abt 1970
            Andrea Rerecich b. 9 Apr 1820
                Andrea Remigio Rerecich b. 1 Oct 1855, d. 30 Nov 1941
                    Andrea Rerecich
                        Paulina Rerecich d. 6 Jan 1986
                    Domenico Rerecich b. 1886
                      Dominic Rerecich b. 18 Aug 1911, d. 15 Aug 1975
                      Andrew Rerecich b. 23 Dec 1921, d. 10
                      Oct 1994
                      Lucija Rerecich b. 30 May 1923, d. 5 Mar 1996
                      Joseph (Juzepe) Rerecich b. 31 Dec 1924, d. 15 Aug 1995
                Domenico Antonio Rerecich b. 25 Aug 1863
                  Andrew Rerecich b. 27 May 1904, d. Aug 1981
                    Loretta Rerecich
                    Barbara Rerecich
                    Georgio Rerecich b. 28 Jul 1946
                Toni Rerecich b. 18 Jan 1907, d. 30 Nov 1966
              Antonio Martino Rerecich b. 9 Jun 1867, d. 4 Mar 1954
                Andrea Rerecich b. 24 Feb 1904, d. 8 Jun 1978
                  Antonio Rerecich b. 20 Aug 1930
                  Marino Rerecich b. 17 Jul 1934
                  Carmen Rerecich b. 30 Oct 1944
                Maria Rerecich b. 27 Mar 1907, d. 1 Jan 1999
                Anthony Rerecich b. 12 Oct 1912, d. 7 May 1996
                  John Anthony Rerecich b. 28 Nov 1941
                  Anthony Samuel Rerecich b. 7 Oct 1945
                  Denise Margaret Rerecich b. 22 Aug 1955
                Lydia Rerecich b. 21 Dec 1914
                Mateo Rerecich b. 22 Aug 1919
                  Dolores Rerecich b. 27 May 1951
                  Lorraine Rerecich b. 11 Feb 1954
            Matteo Rerecich b. 3 Nov 1831
                Andrea Giovanni Rerecich (Vishcosich) b. 10 Nov 1860
                  Matij Rerecich b. 9 Jul 1884, d. 10 Nov 1969
                    Mary Rerecich b. 17 Jul 1911, d. 3 Mar 1992
                    Catherina Rerecich b. 17 Dec 1914, d. 3
                    Mar 1996
                    Andro Rerecich b. 31 Mar 1916, d. 31 Oct 1998
                    Anthony Rerecich
                Giovanni Rerecich b. 27 Apr 1887, d. 2 Aug 1970
                  Maria Rerecich b. 28 Apr 1915, d. 18 Jun 1947
                  Caterine Rerecich b. 3 Feb 1922, d. 3 May 1978
                  Gian Rerecich b. 21 Aug 1923, d. Jun 1942
                  Anna Rerecich b. 28 Nov 1924
                Andrew (Andreja) Rerecich b. 17 Mar 1890, d. 20 Jan 1967
                  Andrew M. Rerecich b. 29 Sep 1927, d. 8 Jan 1988
                  Catherine Rerecich b. 24 Oct 1928

1   2   3   4   5   6   7

SEGOTTA, SEGOTA

Also written as Šegota, this surname has a large concentration in Jablanac near Senj, a cluster of families in the Pula area, the city of Rijeka, and a few in the region from Senj to Zadar on the coast.

Several lineage names have developed for this surname in Unije, including Cikola (Cicula), and Habatar.

Laurentius Segota (1773-1828) who married Catharina Carcich is described as *Jablancensis*, indicating his place of origin as Jablanac to the east of Unije on the Croatian mainland.

Giuseppe Segota (1860-) from Unije worked as a sailor and afterwards worked in Colorado starting in 1889. Giuseppe was the youngest son of Andrea Segotta (1800-1875).

Catarina Segota (1852-), and sons Andreja (1878-1948), Matij (1886-1972), Godiento Radoslovich (1891-1950)

Segotta, Segota Home, No. 146 Unije

Segotta, Segota — Unije, Croatia

Gregorius Segotta
- Lovro Segotta (Bellusich) b. 1773, d. 31 Aug 1828
  - Andrea Segotta (Cicola) b. 9 May 1800, d. 1875
    - Giovanni Eduardus Segotta b. 11 Oct 1843
      - Bepo Segotta
      - Andrea Antonio Segotta b. 30 May 1873
        - Maria (Katonica) Segota b. 1892
        - Iva Segota b. 1910, d. 10 Jul 1987
      - Nicolo Matteo Segotta b. 15 Feb 1876
      - Giovanni Antonio Segotta b. 15 Feb 1876
      - Anton Agostino Segotta (Cicola) b. 27 Apr 1877, d. 27 Jan 1963
        - Ana Tomazina Segota b. 7 May 1902, d. 5 Jul 1981
        - Anton Segota b. 13 Aug 1910, d. 4 Nov 1968
        - Ivan Segota b. 28 Oct 1911, d. 15 Apr 1963
      - Ivan Mikula Segotta (Cicuola) b. 21 Sep 1882, d. 1953
        - John Segota b. 3 Oct 1921, d. 17 Apr 1987
        - Joseph Segota b. 27 Nov 1922
        - Anna Segota b. 7 Apr 1924
        - Thomas Segota b. 12 Jun 1925
        - Larry Segota b. 25 Jul 1926
        - Anthony (Cicuola) Segota b. 10 Oct 1927, d. Mar 1987
        - Dinka Segota b. 25 Nov 1930
        - Peter Segota b. 12 Feb 1932
        - Milan Segota b. 26 Sep 1933
      - Maria Segotta
        - Maria Galosich b. 16 Aug 1911, d. 26 Apr 1973
    - Nicolo Segotta b. 15 Jan 1852
    - Gregorio Segotta b. 19 Nov 1830
      - Giovanni Luca Segotta b. 18 Oct 1861
      - Domenica Giacomina Segotta b. 21 Nov 1865
      - Andrea Rocco Segotta b. 16 Aug 1869
      - Gregorio Domenico Segotta b. 3 Oct 1871, d. 11 Apr 1872
      - Antonio Andrea Segotta b. 16 Feb 1873
  - Gaudento Segotta
  - Antonius Segotta b. 1803, d. 21 Jul 1832
    - Maria Ant. Segotta b. Sep 1831, d. 14 Jan 1833
  - Domenico Segotta b. 1808, d. Aug 1856
    - Gaudenzio Segotta b. 10 Jan 1837
      - Giovanni Gaudenzio Segotta b. 17 Feb 1874
        - Toni Segotta
        - Anna Segotta b. 15 Nov 1893
        - Angelo Franjo Segotta (Habatar) b. 2 Oct 1895, d. 2 Oct 1972
        - Frona Segotta
        - Ivanka Segotta
    - Andrea Segotta b. 9 May 1845
      - Domenico Simone Segotta b. 22 Oct 1871
      - Maria Antonia Segotta b. 13 Nov 1873
  - Mattheus Segotta b. 1812, d. 8 Mar 1837
  - Laurentius (Lovro) Segotta b. 1 Jun 1819
    - Katarina Segotta b. 1852
  - Giovanni Segotta b. 22 Oct 1822
    - Giovanni Segotta b. 2 Aug 1849, d. Nov 1880
      - Giovanni Marco Segotta b. 23 Feb 1879
    - Gaudenzio Segotta b. 15 Jul 1852
    - Matteo Bonaventura Segotta b. 13 Jul 1858
    - Giacoma Pasquala Segotta b. 8 Apr 1855
    - Antonio Lorenzo Segotta b. 16 Jul 1862
    - Andrea Lorenzo Segotta b. 27 Aug 1867

1   2   3   4   5   6

VALLICH, VALIĆ

This surname appears in various places in Croatia including concentrations in the Pula and Rijeka regions. There were 18 families in 1945 at a settlement in the Rijeka area name Valići.

The Vallich surname begins to appear in 18th Century records for the Unije. The Valich family remained in Unije in small numbers. Jivan Valić of Anton married in 1722, and Maria Valić of Jivan married in 1726. The present day Valic family dates to Christophorus Valich (1753-1816). The small number of modern day Valić families from Unije can be attributed to the large number of females versus male births to families with this surname.

Andrea Antonio Vallich (1870-) moved to New York probably before the turn of the century, where he owned a grocery store. He accumulated money that he was called 'millionor' (millionaire). He returned to

Unije around 1926 or shortly thereafter and fixed his house up (house of present-day Magda Nadalin). Later he lost much of the investment he had made in shipping.

Domenic Valich (1882-1943)

Vallich, Valić Family Home, No. 123 Unije

Vallich, Valić — Unije, Croatia

Cristoforo Vallich b. 1753, d. 29 Jan 1816
+ Helena Radoslovich b. 1755, d. 30 Mar 1832
    Domenica Vallich b. 1794, d. 1865
    + Gni. Martinolich
    Domenico Vallich (Cagniza) b. 10 Aug 1796
    + Paulina Nicolich b. 1796, d. 20 Mar 1850
        Domenico (Menigo) Vallich b. 10 Apr 1827
        + Antonia Carcich b. 8 Aug 1826
            Domenico Andrea Vallich b. 14 Feb 1856, d. 11 Nov 1927
            + Domenica Filomena Carcich b. 10 Mar 1856, m. 11 Nov 1878, d. 4 Aug 1918
                Domenico Romolo (Dumic) Vallich b. 6 Sep 1882, d. 25 Dec 1943
                + Maria (Vlasic) Nadalin b. 15 Sep 1890, d. 26 Dec 1963
                    Maria Vallich b. 1913
                    Domenica (Meniga) Vallich b. 6 Jan 1916, d. 5 Apr 2007
                    Dominic Joseph Valic b. 21 Mar 1917, d. 30 May 1981
                    Antonia Vallich (Cagnize) b. 22 Mar 1926, d. 25 Feb 1978
                    Andrea Vallich b. 26 Sep 1920, d. Dec 1943
                Joseph Vallich b. 4 Jun 1885, d. 1960
                + Veronica Carcich b. 21 Apr 1890, m. 1909, d. 1957
                    Veronica Valich b. 31 Aug 1914
                    Domenica (Minnie) Valich b. 7 Jan 1916
                    Jacomina Valich b. 30 Jul 1918, d. Aug 1999
                    Josephina Valich b. 10 May 1920
                    Joseph J. Valich b. 8 Feb 1923
                    Mary Valich b. 4 Sep 1926
        Andrea Vallich b. 9 May 1837
        + Caterina Carcich b. 25 Jun 1838
            Domenico Gaudenzio Vallich (Kagniza) b. 29 Nov 1872
            + Maria Francesca Carcich b. 9 Mar 1876, d. 1940
                Katerina Valich d. Nov 1943
                + Diodoro (Zburkin) Carcich b. 1 Dec 1904, d. 7 Jan 1987
                    Catherina Carcich
                Andrew Valich

                Dominic Valich b. 19 Sep 1911, d. 4 Mar 1995
                + Flora b. 15 Jul 1909, d. 28 Nov 1997
                Julia Vallich b. 22 May 1913, d. 15 Jun 1998
                Lina Julia Valich b. 12 Sep 1915

1   2   3   4   5   6

APPENDICES

From Prehistory to the Roman Period

Recent archaeological work[59] has yielded evidence of the earliest farmers in the eastern Adriatic, including the area around the Kvarnar and Istria. Neolithic populations spread from the south up the Adriatic by 5750 B.C.

The Liburni, occupied sites on the islands of Cres and Losinj having settlements in present day Ustine, and Nerezine, all which may date prior to 1000 B.C. The nearby island of Veli Srakane is also reported to have contained a Liburnian site on the hill top of Straza. The Liburnians were a Venetic people, perhaps distantly related to the Latin and Roman people of Italy. The Venetics were a group of people who inhabited the northern end of the Adriatic stretching from the upper Adriatic islands to the Po valley in Italy.

The Liburni had settlements on Unije. The peak at Turan was a defensive fort, while the Kastel, a smaller peak, closer to the present-day town, was a settlement. Pottery and other archaeological evidence have been found at these sites.[60]

There was a Greek presence in the area in the form of traders who plied the waters of the eastern Adriatic. A Greek settlement in Dalmatia far to the south of Unije was established in 600 BC and Greek trade goods have been found on some of the Dalmatian islands, but it was the Romans who subdued the Liburnian pirates around Osor in the 1st and 2nd centuries BC and then settled on the islands. The island of Cres had several Roman settlements, at Osor, Cres, Beli, Prozina, Lubenice, Merag, Vrana, and Ustine.

The population that lived in the regions of Osor and Cres during the Roman period consisted mainly of Liburnian families with a small number of Italian families (Wilkes). It is probably during Roman times that the islands of Unije, Susak, and Srakane acquired

186

their respective Latin names of Nia, Sansacus, and Saracana. On Unije there are names for capes and coves which have Roman characteristics, like Lakunij (perhaps from Latin lucuna), the islet Samuncijel, Kambonara (Kambunion Krk), Arbit (cape and depth), Maracol and Limaran. Skok writes, "in Unije again one finds the names of capes and bays such as Glavina, Srednja, Vrulje, Art (rt), Stene [Stijene], Javore, Misnjak (capes and islands). The name Golima is unusual, if it is the same adjective golem, which is often found in Macedonian and Bulgarian toponomastic names. The name for the bay Ognjisca in regards to the toponomological nature goes in the same range as the name Kurila. Unusual are the names for capes such as Kujni, Vnetak, if it is like Mletak. Sibenska (the cove) certainly is the adjective of Silba, and not of Sibenik.

The cove Skopalj (perhaps it is from scopulus 'skolj', ispr. Skupjeli) is vague toponomically, Trestitelna and Jerina, like the name for depths of Pecni (perhaps the adjective is from pec 'spilja pecina'). In Unije there are names for capes and coves, which have Roman characteristics, like Lakunij (perhaps from Latin lucuna), the islet Samucel, Kambonara (Kambunion Krk), Arbit (cape and depth), Maracol and Limaran. Of all these names it is clear that Arbit is from the Latin arbutus as well as arbitus, which on the Adriatic is called ladonja (Istria), koscela, kopriva (Krk) 'arbutus unedo."[61]

Many loan words in the Unije dialect are acquired from the Latin derived language spoken on the Adriatic coast, called Vegliote or Dalmatian. Vegliote, whose last known speaker died at the turn of the last century, was the original language spoken by the Roman colonists who populated this region after its conquest of the Liburnian people.

Some Vegliote (v) derived words found in the Unijan dialect (u) are listed here. For instance 'beans', in Vegliote is *fasuol*(v) becoming *fasol* in the Unijan dialect; 'to finish', *fenait*(v) *finit*(u); 'onions', *kapul*(v) *kapula*(u); 'chair', *katraida*(v) *katrida*(u); 'kitchen', *kocaina*(v) *kuhina*(u); 'content', *kontiant*(v) *kuntiant*(u); 'breakfast', *marianda*(v) *marianda*(u); 'money', *monaita*(v) *munita*(u); 'soap', *sapaun*(v) *sapun*(u); 'mast', *yuarbul*(v) *iorbul*(u).

The closest Roman settlement to Unije was Apsorus, modern-day Osor. The population of Apsorus was probably composed of a native Liburnian substratum, with several Roman families from Italy, based on the frequency of native and Roman surnames attributed to Apsorus. Immediately to the south of Unije, on the island of Vele Srakane, in Roman times lived the Nunnuleia family, whose grave marker can still be found in the corner of one of the buildings on the island. The family was composed of wife and mother M. Petillio, who married a man by the name of Nunnuleia, and at least five of their children. The text of the marker follows with uncertain letters in square brackets, with English translation on the right :

      [D   M]   S

[PE] TILLIAE PRIMAE UXOR [I]	Petilliae first wife
Q. PETILLIO M(arci) F(ilio) [T]UTO[RI	Q. Petillio Marci son guardian e.g.
NUNNULEIAE M(arci) F(iliae) SECUNDAE]	Nunnuleiae Marcus second son
NUNNULEIO M(arci) F(ilio) CAP.	Nunnuleio Marcus son Cap.
N]UNNULEIO M(arci) F(ilio) LUCA	Nunnuleio Marcus son Luca
N]UNNULEIO M(arci) F(ilio) SENI[ORI]	Nunnuleio Marcus son Senior
SEX(TO) NUNNULEIO M(arci) F(ilio) LUC..	Sextus Nunnuleio Marcus son Luc[a]

Mirišće is due east of the present day lighthouse and next to the plain on the south coast of Unije. Remains of roof tiles and sheep bones are imbedded in the edge of the cliff face beyond the stone wall. Also, a grave was discovered in the 1990s on the shore near the stone wall, and other graves have been discovered to the north of Mirišće. That the people who stayed at Mirišće were shepherds is attested to by the numerous sheep bones and the small shelters located at the bottom of the bluffs at Mirišće may date to this period.

Mirišće wall

Mirišće grave

Records for Inhabitants from Unije 1624-1867 for Birth, Marriage or Death Records as Registered in Mali Losinj, Osor, and Cunski
(Record Type: b=Birth; m=Marriage; d=Death)

Date	Event	Surname	Given Name	Source	Relative	Relationship
18 Jun 1753	m	**Belanich**	Martin	M. Losinj	Jseppo	father
20 Nov 1765	m	Belanich	Anta.	M. Losinj	Biaso	father
28 Oct 1787	m	Belanich	Martin	Osor	Martin	father
22 Jun 1684	m	**Carcich**	Christofolo	Osor	witness	
6 Oct 1713	m	Carcich	Martin	M. Losinj	Antonia	
14 Jun 1722	m	Karčić	Karstic	M. Losinj	Pavl	father
25 Feb 1732	m	Karčić	Matia	M. Losinj	Pavl	father
13 Jul 1736	m	Carcich	Giacoma	M. Losinj	Zne	husband
24 Dec 1740	d	Carcich	Gioani	M. Losinj		
24 Apr 1747	m	Carcich	Christofolo	M. Losinj	Michiel	father
29 Jan 1749	d	Carcich	Andriana	M. Losinj	Michiel	husband
5 Feb 1755	m	Carcich	Martin	M. Losinj	Paolo	father
15 Dec 1757	b	Carcich	Christofolo	M. Losinj	Mattio	
25 Jun 1769	m	Carcich	Domco	M. Losinj	Christofo	father
26 Jan 1769	m	Carcich	Paolo	M. Losinj	Zuane	father
26 Jan 1771	m	Carcich	Paolo	M. Losinj	Zuane	father
9 Nov 1772	m	Carcich	Anto.	M. Losinj	Zuane	father
27 Oct 1774	m	Carcich	Zuane	Cunski	Cristoforo	father
6 Jul 1779	m	Carcich	Christofolo	Osor	Paolo	father
28 Oct 1787	m	Carcich	Andrea	Osor	Martin	father
11 Jul 1789	m	Karcich	Mattio	Cunski	Martin	father
1800	m	Carcich	Martin	Cunski	Martin	father
b.a. 1800	b	Carcich	Andrea	M. Losinj	Jacoba	wife
23 Jun 1812	m	Carcich	Christofolo	M. Losinj	Mattio	father
1820	m	Carcich	Antonio	M. Losinj	Antonio	father
9 Feb 1820	m	Carcich	Antonio	M. Losinj	Anto.	father
2 Feb 1822	m	Carcich	Andrea	M. Losinj	Andrea	father
27 Nov 1823	m	Carcich	Dominicus	M. Losinj	Andrea	father
15 May 1826	m	Carcich	Andrea	M. Losinj	Andrea	father
16 Oct 1829	b	Carcich	Maria Cath.	M. Losinj	Dominicus	father
4 Jul 1830	m	Carcich	Dominicus	M. Losinj	Andrea	father
16 Oct 1839	m	Carcich	Maria	M. Losinj	Andrea	father
15 Jan 1853	d	Carcich	Mattea	M. Losinj	Andrea	father
15 Feb 1853	b	Carcich	Antonius V.	M. Losinj	Andrea	father
14 Nov 1864	m	Carcich	Roco	M. Losinj	Gaudenzio	father
16 Oct 1865	m	Carcich	Martin A.	M. Losinj	Antonio	father
14 Jan 1867	m	Carcich	Giuseppe G.	M. Losinj	Antonio	father

Date	Event	Surname	Given Name	Source	Relative	Relationship
13 Feb 1736	m	**Giurich**	Ant.	M. Losinj	Matto	father
9 Oct 1743	m	Giurich	Matto	M. Losinj	Domca.	
23 Feb 1762	m	Giurich	Matio	M. Losinj	Matto	father
1798	m	Giurich	Matteo	M. Losinj	Anto	father
2 Dec 1747	m	**Mancich**	Franco.	Osor	Maria	Wife
2 Feb 1773	d	Mancich	Gasparo	Osor	nato Onie	anni 44
22 Jun 1684	m	**Nadalin**	Antonio	Osor	Zuana	wife
28 Dec 1748	m	Nadalinich	Matto	M. Losinj	Ellena NIC	wife
24 Jun 1782	m	Nadalin	Matto	M. Losinj		
7 Jan 1826	m	Nadalin	Dominica	M. Losinj	Mattheus	father
1 Apr 1852	m	Nadalin	Franciscus	M. Losinj	Matheus	father
15 Sep 1746		**Nicolich**	Anta		Marco	father
28 Nov 1748	m	Nicolich	Anta	M. Losinj	Tomaso	father
28 Dec 1748	m	Nicolich	Matto	M. Losinj	Anta NIC	wife
1751	b	Nicolich	Joannes	Unie	Giuseppe	father
24 Feb 1763	m	Nicolich	Zne.	M. Losinj	Gasparo	father
24 Feb 1764	m	Nicolich	Joannes	M. Losinj	Gasparo	father
26 Jan 1769	m	Nicolich	Martin	M. Losinj	Martin	father
16 May 1769	m	Nicolich	Zuane	M. Losinj	Martin	father
20 Jan 1774	m	Nicolich	Tomasina	Osor	Zuane	father
18 Sep 1783	m	Nicolich	Gasparo	M. Losinj	Gasparo	father
14 Aug 1784	m	Nicolich	Martin	M. Losinj	Martin	father
23 Jan 1800	b	Nicolich	Marco	M. Losinj	Gasparo	father
18 Oct 1801	m	Nicolich	Gian Pietro	M. Losinj	Zne	father
20 Aug 1809	m	Nicolich	Anna	M. Losinj	Tomaso	husband
17 Sep 1814	m	Nicolich	Martin	M. Losinj	qm Martin	father
10 Feb 1816	m	Nicolich	Domenico	M. Losinj	qm Martin	father
1837	d	Nicolich	Marco	Unie	Gasparo	father
16 Oct 1839	m	Nicolich	Joseph	M. Losinj	Joseph	father
21 Aug 1624	b	**Radoslovich**	Giovanni	Osor	Martin	father
13 June 1680		Radoslovich	Anton	Osor		
23 Jan 1712	m	Radoslovich	Martin	M. Losinj	Dunka	wife
5 May 1718	m	Radoslovich	Franic	M. Losinj	Gaspar	father
13 May 1727	m	Radoslovich	Karstic	M. Losinj	Simun	father
24 May 1738	m	Radoslovich	Anda.	Osor	Socolich	wife
5 Jul 1740	m	Radoslovich	Nicolina	M. Losinj	Matto	father
11 Sep 1743	m	Radoslovich	Gasparina	M. Losinj	Matto	father
9 Oct 1747	m	Radoslovich	Martin	Osor	Martin	father
29 Jan 1747	m	Radoslovich	Simon	M. Losinj	Mark	father

Date	Event	Surname	Given Name	Source	Relative	Relationship
5 Feb 1749	m	**Radoslovich**	Simon	M. Losinj	Simon	father
9 Nov 1765	d	Radoslovich	Martin	Osor		
16 Aug 1768	m	Radoslovich	Zuane	M. Losinj	Margta.	wife
1 Sep 1768	m	Radoslovich	Anto	M. Losinj	Anto	father
1 Mar 1769	d	Radoslovich	Giuseppe	Osor	Zuanne	father
14 Dec 1772	d	Radoslovich	Andriana	Osor	Gasparo	father
3 Jul 1776	m	Radoslovich	Domco	M. Losinj	Franco	father
10 Sep 1779	d	Radoslovich	Gerolimo	Osor	Gasparo	father
21 Aug 1774	m	Radoslovich	Girolomo	Osor	Gasparo	father
10 Oct 1787	m	Radoslovich	Antonius	M. Losinj	Anto	father
1 Feb 1826	m	Radoslovich	Antonia	M. Losinj	Matheus	father
19 Feb 1762	m	**Ragusin**	Agostin	Osor	Gasparo	father
13 Jun 1680		**Rerecich**	Luke	Osor		
23 Jan 1712	m	Rerečić	Augustin	M. Losinj	Mara	wife
23 Mar 1725	b	Rerečić	Osip	M. Losinj	Mattij	father
15 Jan 1729	b	Rerečić	Matij	M. Losinj	Unij	
11 Jan 1730	m	Rerečić	Martin	M. Losinj	Mikule	father
19 Jan 1780	m	Rerecich	Gerolima	Osor	Simon	father
28 Sep 1745	m	**Riezo**	Zorzi	M. Losinj	Pietro	father
19 Aug 1783	m	**Sepcich**	Matto	M. Losinj	Matto	father
26 Oct 1722	m	**Valic**	Jivan	M. Losinj	Antic	father
21 Aug 1726	m	Valcic	Mara	M. Losinj	Jivan	father
28 Dec 1748	m	Valic	Christofolo	M. Losinj	Nicolo	father

Names of Households in Unije for 1820

(Source: Death Register 1815-1880, Saint Andrew's, Roman Catholic Church, Unije, Croatia)

1	Zuliani, Joseph
2	
3	Nicolich, Dominicus
4	
5	Nicolich, Andrea (Tomicin)
6	Nicolich, Andrea (Tomicin)
7	Carcich, Andrea
8	Nicolich, Andrea
9	
10	
11	Carcich, Christopherus
12	
13	Radoslovich, Mattheus
14	Tarabochia, Martin
15	Nicolich, Dominica uxor Ant.
16	Radoslovich, Matthei (Calcich)
17	Radoslovich, Matthei (Rubez)
18	Carcich, Antonius
19	Carcich, Mariana
20	Nadalin, Dominica va Matheus
21	Carcich, Antonius
22	
23	Carcich, Michaelis
24	
25	Bellanich, Andrea & Mattheus Carcich
26	Carcich, Gaudentus
27	
28	
29	
30	
31	Stefanich, Antonia uxor Georgius
32	Carcich, Joannes & Dominicus
33	
34	
35	Carcich, Michaelis (Bardarinca)
36	Nadalin, Mattheus
37	Belllanich, Andrea
38	Radoslovich, Antonius & Joannis
39	Bussanich, Matthew
40	Rerecich, Andrea
41	Radoslovich, Johannis & Andrea Nicolich
42	Bellanich, Antonius
43	Bellanich, Thoma
44	Radoslovich, Antonius
45	Vallich, Domci.
46	Carcich, Anto. Dominicus
47	Radoslovich, Dominicus
49	Carcich, Cristophorus
50	Carcich, Antonius (Millich)
51	Carcich, Dominicus
53	Segotta, Laurentis
54	Carcich, Johannes
55	Nicolich (Sancich)

Names of Households in Unije for 1850

1	Radoslovich, Mattaeus (Papich)
2	Nicolich, Joannes (Muscardin)
3	Nicolich, Gioanni (Muscardin)
4	Carcich, Andrea
5	Nicolich (Tomicin)
6	Nicolich, Thomasina of Andrea
7	Nicolich, Andrea
8	
9	Radoslovich, Andreas & Joannis (Papich)
10	Radoslovich, Mattheus (Papich)
11	Carcich, Joannes (Bravarof)
12	Radoslovich, Andrea
13	Radoslovich, Nicolo (Calcich)
14	Radoslovich, Nicolo (Calcich)
15	Carcich, Andreas Jr. (Bravarof)
16	Carcich, Andreas Jr. (Bravarof)
17	Carcich, Andrea (Stari Bravar)
18	Carcich (Jevin) & Bellanich, Joseph
19	Bellanich, Mattea & Chr. Carcich (Balde)
20	Carcich, Vincenzo
21	Carcich, Paulus
22	Carcich, Nicolas (Prusian)
23	Carcich, Michaelis (Prusian)
24	Carcich, Andreas
25	Carcich, Matteus (Prusian)
28	Nadalin, Francesca
29	Cecco, Vincentius
30	Carcich, Antonia va Chyrstophorus
31	Radoslovich, Michaellinus
32	Radoslovich, Mattheus (Calcich)
33	Carcich, Andrea (Pasquich)
34	Segotta, Antonius
35	Carcich, Michael (Bardar)
36	Nadalin, Mattheus (Vlassich)
37	Carcich, Joannis
38	Carcich, Vincentus
39	Segotta, Mattheus
40	Carcich, Domenico (Pasquich) & Matteo Nadalin
41	Carcich, Michael (Bardar) & Rocco Carcich
42	Bellanich, Antonio
43	Carcich, Gaudenzio (Rocov)
45	Radoslovich, Mattheus (Papich)
47	Segotta, Domenico
48	Radoslovich, Mattheus (Rosso)
49	Rerecich (Jercich)
50	Cecco
51	Nicolich, Joannes (Mattesinich)
52	Nicolich, Nicolo (Sancich)
53	Radoslovich (Calcich) & Vuscovich
54	Carcich, Johannis
55	Nadalin, Antonius
56	Rerecich, Dominiucs (Gercich)
57	Nicolich, Joannes
58	Nicolich, Marco (Morich) & Antonius Radoslovich
59	Vallich, Dominicus (Cagniza)
60	Nicolich, Dominicus (Sancich)
61	Zuliani, Justus & Marco Carcich
63	Nicolich, Marcus
64	Gallossich, Joannis

Names of Households in Unije by House Number in 1880
(Source: Death Register 1815-1880, Saint Andrew's Roman Catholic Church, Unije, Croatia)

1	Radoslovich, Matteo (Sesturin)	58	Radoslovich, Matteo (Rosso) (Mencich)
2		59	---, Domenica and Giovanni Carcich
3	Giurich, Matteo and (Jevin)	60	Nicolich, Domenico
4	Carcich, Domenico	61	Nadalin, Francesco
5	Carich, Andrea (Andricevi)	62	Carcich, Tomasina and Giovanni Radoslovich
6	Martinolich, Andrea	63	Carcich, Bernardo
7	Martinolich, Mattea	64	Radoslovich, Antonio
8	Pillepich, Mateo	65	Bellanich, Tomasina and Antonion Nadalin
9	Carcich, Cristoforo	66	Bellanich, Andriana and (Rocovi)
10	Carcich, Andrea (Gevin)	67	Rerecich, Paolina (Jercich)
11	Nicolich Maria and. Andrea (Andricevi)	68	Carcich, Matteo (Pasquich)
12	--, Domenica and. Andrea (Tomicnev)	69	Carcich, Giuseppe (Pasquich)
13	Martinolich, Andrea		Carcich, Andrea
14	Radoslovich, Antonia	70	Bellanich, Martino
15	Radoslovich, Andrea (Popich)	71	Segotta, Gaudenzio
16	Radoslovich, Antonio	72	Nicolich, Gasparo
17	Radoslovich, Martino		Radoslovich (Sesturin)
18	Radoslovich, Maria	73	Carcich, Domenico (Zburkin)
19	Radoslovich, Matteo (Popich)	74	Carcich, Giacinto and (Sesturin)
20	Carcich, Maria and Vincenzo	--	Radoslovich, Mattea and Vincenzo
21	Nicolich, Domenico	75	Nicolich, Antonio (Muscardin)
22	Carcich, Matteo of Marianna	76	Nicolich, Giovanni
23	Radoslovich, Petronilla and Nicolo	77	Radoslovich, Matteo of Antonio
24	Carcich, Tomasina and Andrea	--	Radoslovich, Matteo of Matteo
25	Carcich, Martino (Bravarof)	78	Vallich, Andrea (Cagniza)
26	Carcich, Simone (Bravarof)	79	Carcich, Nicolo (Zburkin)
27	Carcich, Giuseppe (Bravarof)	80	Carcich, Gaudenzio (Zburkin)
28	Carcich, Antonio (Bravarof)	81	Carcich, Marco (Zburkin)
28	Carcich, Romolo (Bravarof)	82	Bellanich, Matteo (Tomovi)
29	Carcich, Domenico (Bravarof)	--	Bellanich, Tomasina of Tomaso
30	Haglich, Giacomina and Andrea	83	--, Maria va Tomaso Bellanich
31	Carcich, Domenico	84	Nicolich, Martino (Agatin)
32	Radoslovich, Giovanni of Matteo	85	Nicolich, Tomasina of Andrea
33	Radoslovich, Giovanni of Antonio	--	Andrea - Spiridione
34	Nadalin, Giovanni	86	Nicolich, Domenico (Agatin)
35	Nadalin, Andrea (Vlassich)	87	Nicolich, Martino (Agatin)
36	Nadalin, Pietro	--	Nicolich, Antonio
37	Rerecich, Giovanni (Simef)	88	Rerecich, Domenico (Jercich)
38	Nadalin, Maria and Giovanni	89	--, Maria qm Nicolo
39	Carcich, Antonio (Gevin)	90	Nicolich, Antonio
40	Nadalin, Matteo	91	Radoslovich, Giovanni
41	Rerecich, Andrea of Simone (Simef)	92	Nicolich, Matteo (Tomicnev)
42	Rerecich, Andrea of Andrea (Simef)	93	Radoslovich, Agostino
43	Rerecich, Simone (Simef)	94	Radoslovich, Antonio
44	Carcich, Maria and Andr. (Baldich)	95	Radoslovich, Matteo (Grovran)
45	Carcich, Paolo (Jercich)	96	Vallich, Domenico (Cagniza)
46	Carcich, Paolo	97	House of the Church of S. Andrea
47	Carcich, Andrea (Pasquich)	98	Nicolich, Simone
48	Segotta, Lorenzo and Martin (Agatin)	99	Nicolich, Carlo
49	Carcich, Marianna of Marianna	100	Gallosich, Giovanni of Ant.
50	Martinolich, Maria and Cristoforo	--	Gallosich, Giovanni of Giovanni
	Carcich & Cosulich	101	Segotta, Andrea and Gregorio
51	Nicolich, Andrea	102	Nicolich, Gasparo (Marketa)
52	Nicolich, Andrea (Sancich)	103	Baracca-patrini fondali di Unie
53	Carcich, Maria and Matteo Radoslovich	104	Casa Comunale ad uso curato
54	Carcich, Rocco	105	Carcich, Maddalena
55	Cecco, Elena	106	Segotta, Andrea
56	Segotta, Giovanni	107	Don Antonio Urarich
57	Segotta, Francesca and Lorenzo	110	Bellanich, Martino

Names of Households in Unije by Postal Number, 1937
(Source: Andrew Karcich, College Point, N.Y.,1996)

1	Radoslovich, Toni Mattessinich	62	Karcich,Toni Pasquich Storeh.
2	Nicolich, Ivan Muskardin	63	Rerecich, Dumingo
3	Segota, Toni Cikuola	64	Rerecich, Vicjenco
4	Nicolich -Papucine Storehouse	65	Karcich, Jani Losinke Rocof
5	Nicolich, Marko Marketa	66	Karcich, Lisandro Baldich
6	Storehouse	67	Karcich, Toni, Osuorke Storeh.
7	Karcich, Menigo Caroline	68	Rerecich, Romane Simef
8	Karcich, Andrea Zvonor	69	Rerecich, Matij SIme
9	Nicolich, Frona Spalaca	70	Karcich,Toni Zburk.
10	Karcich, Romolo	71	Karcich,Godento Zburkin Store.
11	Nicolich, Toni Caroline	72	Galosich, Iva Storehouse
12	Karcich, Costante Bravarof	73	Toncina Zanete Storehouse
13	Karcich, Toni Ilda Bravarof	74	Karcich, Emma
14	Karcich, Marija Carnoga	75	Rerecich, Ulcich
15	Deroja, Toni	76	Rerecich, Stari Jercich
16	Halich, Lovricov Storehouse	77	Nicolich, Stara Sburka
17	Radoslovich, Sesturin	78	Stare Kosirancike
18	Karcich, Toni Zaneto	79	Nadalin, Vlasich Matij
19	Rerecich, Marko Sime	80	Nadalin, Vlasich Marko
20	Karcich, Anjelincich	81	Cooperative/Store
21	Segota, Toni Luovre	82	Nicolich, Osip Sancich
22	Galosich, Zane	83	Radoslovich, Andrea
23	Karcich, Andrejin	84	Radoslov.,Andrea Storeh.
24	Karcich, Romano Bravarof	85	Tonica Andrejice
25	Karcich, Romano Bravarof	86	Radoslovich,Andrea Popich
26	Galosich, Menigo Lovic	87	Radoslovich,Filomencich Store.
27	Nadalin, Vicienco	88	Karcich, Jivicina
28	Nicolich, Toni Zrapoce Agatin	89	Radoslovich,Filomencich Store.
29	Galosich, Jelena	90	Belanich, Martin
30	Karcich, Iva Zrapoce	91	Nicolich, Cincin
31	Karcich, Andrejica	92	Nicolich, Haracich
32	Nicolich, Ivan Zmulina	93	Andrice Jelice
33	Nicolich, Toni Haracich	94	Karcich, Luca Andricevi?
34	Karcich, Zvonora Storehouse	95	Butchers-Verbora, Frane (Cres)
35	Karcich, Andreja Zvonor	96	Fishing Storage
36	Cecco, Toni	97	Olive Press-Italian Group
37	Karcich, Giusepina	98	Halich, Menigo Lovrich
38	Karcich, Jovanin's Storehouse	99	Verbora, Frane (Cres)
39	Karcich, Andrejica	100	Karcich, Marije Luke Andricevi
40	Cecco, Toni Arnesta	101	Nicolich, Mate
41	Karcich, Mota	102	Carcich, Matteo Jevin-Pacuha
42	Karcich, Jovanin Bravarof	103	Tonke Zidora
43	Karcich, Menigo Zbalature	104	Karcich, Coto Juric Jevin
44	Karcich, Osip Cote	105	Karcich, Anjelincich
45	Karcich, Menige Zbalature	106	Karcich, Anjelincich Store.
46	Galosich, Ivo	107	Fishery
47	Karcich, Benjaminka	108	Olive Press-Croatian Group
48	Matij Sime Storehouse	109	Carcich, Matteo Jevin-Pacuha
49	Karcich, Benjaminka	110	Nicolich, Kota Splasice
50	Karcich, Menigo Marianice	111	Radoslovich,Popich Govani
51	Bussanich, Veronica	112	Radoslovich,Popich-MarijeRosse
	nee Karcich Rocovice	113	Karcich,Jani Losinke-Racof
52	Segota, Jelenicica	114	Nicolich, Oliva
53	Anete Skonali's Storehouse	115	The Military
54	Nicolich, Guobicina	116	Nicolich, Toni Marketa
55	Nicolich, Menigo Sancich-Pand.	117	Gargurica
56	Nicolich, Paljermo	118	Martin's Storehouse
57	Karcich, Mariancich	119	Segota, Andreje Cikuola
58	Ferluga, Erena	120	Nicolich, Perina
59	Nicolich, Itina	121	Nicolich, Toni Kamer
60	Nicolich, Martin Martinica	122	Church's Storehouse
61	Karcich, Toni Pasquich	123	Valich, Dumich

124	Segota, Toncich	175	Rerecich, Toni Sime
125	Radoslovich, Nikola Jurovice	176	Baradarinke
126	Mihovila	177	Nicolich, Menigo Muskardin
127	Radoslovich, Petar	178	Yurovich's Storehouse
128	Nicolich, Tubia Tomicnev	179	Karcich (Zburkin)-Konceta
129	Rerecich, Milija Jercich	180	Radoslovich, Ana Grovran
130	Karcich, Kalebincich	181	Karcich, Menigo Uljane
131	Radoslovich, Ivan Mattessinich	182	Valich,Andrea Kanjica
132	Nicolich, Morkovac	183	Karcich, Preturic
133	Radoslovich, Nicolo-Jurovice	184	Rerecich, Menigo Doroteje
134	Pilepich, Jovanin	185	Karcich,Godjento Zburkin
135	Radoslovich, Mulecich	186	Bellanich-Padovice
136	Bepa Zaneva	187	Bellanich-Preruc
137	Rerecich, Jivan Jercich	188	Karcich, Zburkin-Mikulica
138	Karcich, Judita	189	Rerecich, Frane Jercich
139	Karcich, Jovane Pasquich	190	Nicolich, Tomicnev-Skija
140	Bellanich, Martin-Kintela	191	Filomenta
141	Filomenta	192	Nicloich, Stipan Agatin
142	Nicolich,Tom.Margerita Pover.	193	Nicolich, Zaharinke Agatin
143	Rerecich, Balarin	194	Jivanicina Agatin
144	Nadalin, Delajdich Lucija	195	Nicolich, Bepo Marketa
145	Nadalin, Delajdic Osip	196	Priest's House
146	Segota, Anjelo	197	Karcich, Andr.Judite
147	Bellanich, Coto Belich	198	Rerecich, Jercich-Pacencich
148	Bellanich, -Boca	199	School
149	Belanich,Martin-KinjeraStoreh.	200	Church, St. Andrija's
150	Radoslovich, Girica	201	Police
151	Karcich, Rokovica	202	Nicolich, Tomicnev-Cunscak
152	Cecco, Frane	203	Nicolich, Agatin-Pistularo
153	Bellanich, Martin Toma Kinjerica	204	Karcich, Toni Nerije Bravarof
154	Karcich, Susca Osip Sburcich	205	Nicolich, Jani Tomicnev
155	Karcich, Ivan Sburcich	206	Benardo
156	Seganich, Antonia	207	Radoslovich, Mulecich-Anvira
157	Karcich, Ambrosio	208	Radoslovich-Precizinke
158	Nicolich, Musa	209	Nicolich,Andrea Pasametar
159	Karcich-Kote Roka	210	Karcich,Maria Kalebincic
160	Karcich, Ambrosia Storehouse	211	Rerecich, Bepa Simich
161	Martin Paljerma	212	Rerecich, Bepa Simich
162	Nicolich, Andric	213	Nicolich, Otavio Agatin
163	Nicolich, Jermane Marketa	214	Radoslovich, Popich-Galtirich
164	Nicolich,Toni(San.)-Kantarelcich	215	Rerecich, Simef-Signora marija
165	Radoslovich,Old Nadale nee Sablic	216	Luca Skonoli
166	Radoslovich, Atanazio	217	Karcich, Andiceve
167	Cecco, Menigo	218	Karcich, Dragotin
168	Segota, Angelo-Mikeletti	219	Radoslovich, Pelago Popich
169	Nadalin, Bepina	220	Agaticine
170	Pilepich, Matejina	221	Radoslovich Romana Skonoli
171	Pilepich, Spira	222	Radoslovich, Stari Grovran
172	Pilepich, Spirinke	223	Romula Zbalature (Derencinovi)
173	Karcich, Bepo Zburkin	224	Radoslovich, Andrea-Piljoca
174	Karcich, Ivancina Zburkin		

Croatian Mill Members in 1900

Name	Clan/Family	Name	Clan/Family	Name	Clan/Family

1. Ivan Radoslović of. Ivan
2. Anton Radoslović of Ivan
3. Ivan Radoslović od Ivana
4. Anton Radoslović pok. Antona
5. Anton Radoslović od Antona
6. Matij Jurić pok. Matija
7. Andrija Karčić (Andrić)
8. Dinko Kozulić of Jeronima
9. Ivan Ferluga
10. Martin Nikolić (Agatin)
11. Andrija Radoslović (Girica)
12. Andrija Radoslović (Girica)
13. Ivan Karčić (Evin)
14. Andrija Nikolić (Agatin)
15. Nikola Haljić of Anton
16. Ivan Radoslović of Matij
17. Josip Karčić of Anton
18. Anton Karčić of Matij
19. Ivan Nikolić of Simun
20. Marko Nikolić of Anton
21. Anton Galošić of Ivan
22. Ivan Karčić (Bravarof)

23. Ivan Karčić (Gabrijel)
24. Andrija Karčić (Gabrijel)
25. Gaudent Karčić of Ivan
26. Pavao Karčić (Evin)
27. Anton Nikolić of Mark
28. Matija Karčić of Matij (Evin)
29. Andrija Karčić (Rokof)
30. Ambroz Haračić
31. Anton Šegota of Ivan
32. Anton Šegota of Ivan
33. Stipan Nikolić of Andrija
34. Ivan Karčić of Ivan
35. Matij Karčić (Evin)
36. Anton Jurić of Matij
37. Izidor Karčić of Matij
38. Anton Nikolić of Ivan
39. Konstantin Karčić of Martin
40. Ivan Karčić of Andrija(Andrić)
41. Ivan Karčić of Ivan (Ivanina)
42. Ivan Karčić of Nikola (Kalebinčić)
43. Anton Galošić of Antona

44. Andrija Šegota of Andrija (Čikolic)
45. Matija Karčić of Dominika
46. Gavde Nadalin of Petar
47. Andrija Šegota of Ivan
48. Gaudent Karčić of Ivan
49. Lovro Nikolić of Martin
50. Marko Rerečić of Mark
51. Antun Karčić of Andrija
52. Antun Belanić of Antun
53. Romono Karčić of Martin
54. Martin Nikolić of Martin
55. Anton Karčić of Anton
56. Andrija Karcić of Dinko (Preturić)
57. Anton Šegota of Ivan (Čikola)
58. Andrija Nikolić of Andrija (Agatin)
59. Andrija Karčić of Anton (Paskvić)
60. Ivan Karčić of Andrija (Andrić)
61. Ivan Galosić of Ivan
62. Andrija Nikolić of Martin

Source: *Unije: kuzelj vaf sarcu* by Margita Nikolic, pages 195-196.

Italian Mill Members

Name	Clan/Family	Name	Clan/Family	Name	Clan/Family

1. Domenico Carcich (Čarieni)
2. Domenico Carcich
3. Domenico Carcich (Čarni)
4. Antonio Carcich (Tončina)
5. Giovanni Carcich (Bravarof)
6. Giovanni Carcich (Romula)
7. Andrea Carcich (Zburčich)
8. Domenico Carcich (Sudac)
9. Andrea Carcich (Andrić)
10. Domenico Carcich (Andrić)
11. Antonio Carcich (Andrić)
12. Gaudenzio Carcich (Saldotovice)
13. Gaudenzio Carcich (Julijane)
14. Domenico Carcich (Mariajanice)
15. Ambrogio Carcich (Ambruoz)
16. Begnamo Carcich

17. Giovanni Carcich (Skonoli)
18. Bellanich (Kvaščic)
19. Domenico Cecco
20. Giovanni Nicolich (Muškardin)
21. Domenico Nicolich (Spolaza)
22. Antonio Nicolich (Pištularo)
23. Zaharia Nicolich
24. Antonio Nikolich (Haracich)
25. Giovanni Nicolich (Agatin)
26. Andrea Nicolich (Činčin)
27. Giuseppe Nicolich (Bepić)
28. Tobia Nicolich
29. Giovanni Nicolich (Poverić)
30. Matteo Nikolich (Matijskonoli)
31. Giuseppe Nicolich (Zidor)
32. Antonio Nicolich (Paliermić)
33. Domenico Nicolich (Musa)
34. Antonio Nicolich (Kantarielčić)

35. Matteo Radoslovich (Šešturin)
36. Matteo Radoslovich (Grovran)
37. Giuseppe Radoslovich (Grovranić)
38. Giuseppe Nicolich (Sančić)
39. Antonio Radoslovich (Popić)
40. Antonio Radoslovich (Filomienčić)
41. Andrea Radoslovich (Tačić)
42. Giovanni Radoslovich (Rošo)
43. Andrea Rerecich (Simić)
44. Domenico Rerecich (Dumingo)
45. Antonio Rerecich (Sime)
46. Andrea Rerecich (Viciozo)
47. Antonio Rerecich (Jerčić)
48. Givoanni Rerecich (Balarin)
49. Romolo Carcich
50. Domenico Valich (Kanjica)

List compiled by Virgilio Radoslovich in New York and later copied by Josip Nikolić in 1991. Members of the mill at the head of the dock in Unije.

Entry to the United States of Residents from Unije up to 1900

Entry to U.S.	Address	Given Name	Surname	Birth	Sources
1874		Antonio	Carcich	1860	Naturalization Record
1885		Andrea	Carcich	1855	Ship Records
1885		Andrea (Ghiriza)	Radoslovich	1845	
1885		Andrea Gio.	Radoslovich	1878	
1885		Andrea Giov.	Radoslovich	1878	
1885		Dca.	Carcich	1874	
1885		Giovanni	Carcich	1863	
1885		Ivan Carlo	Carcich	1863	Ship's Record
1886		Domenici	Carcik	1857	
1886		Giov.	Carcich	1850	
1886		Matj. Anthony	Radoslovich	1886	
1887		G.?	Galosich	1859	Ship Records
1887		Matteo	Carcich	1838	Ship Records
1887		Michele	Carcich	1851	
1887		Paolo	Carcich	1845	Ship Records
1888		Antonio	Carcich	1853	Ship's Record
1888		Antonio Lorenzo	Bellanich	1865	Ship's Record
1888		Giov. Anto.	Carcich	1869	
1888	New York	Giov. Anto.	Gallosich	1864	
1888		Giov. Nicolo.	Carcich	1866	
1888		Giov. Nicolo.	Carcich	1866	
1888		Giovanni	Radoslovich	1842	
1888		Giovanni	Radoslovich	1843	Ship's Record
1888		Marco	Carcich	1843	Ship's Record
1888		Marco	Carcich	1846	Ship's Record
1888		Tomas	Radoslovich	1861	Ship's Record
1889		Giuseppe	Segota	1860	
1889		Giuseppe	Segota	1860	Ship Records
1890	Delta, B.C.	Andrew	Gallosich	1866	d. Calif.
1892		Anton	Carcich	1861	
1892		Francesco Gius.	Rerecich	1878	
1894		Anton	Carcich	1867	
1894		Constante	Carcich	1872	Ship's Record
1895	537 W. 59th St.	Bonaventura	Carcich	1860	1900 Census
1895	547 W. 39th St.	Frank	Verbora	1872	1900 Census
1896	537 W. 59th St.	Antonio		1875	1900 Census
1896	537 W. 59th St.	Domenico	Carcich	1862	1900 Census
1896	537 W. 59th St.	Lorenzo	Nicolich	1876	1900 Census

Entry to U.S.	Address	Given Name	Surname	Birth	Sources
1897	537 W. 59th St.	Andrea	Nicolich	1874	1900 Census
1897	547 W. 39th St.	Andrew	Karcich	1869	1900 Census
1897	547 W. 39th St.	Andrew	Radish	1878	1900 Census
1897	547 W. 39th St.	Anton	Rerecich	1862	1900 Census
1897	547 W. 39th St.	Antonio	Gallosich	1870	1900 Census
1897	547 W. 39th St.	Antonio	Segotta	1877	1900 Census
1897		Cherubino	Carcich	1872	
1897	Seattle	Giovanni Andrea	Nicolich	1875	
1897		Giov. Gaud.	Carcich	1875	
1897		Giovanni Marco	Segotta	1879	Ship Records
1897	547 W. 39th St.	John	Carcich	1869	1900 Census
1897	547 W. 39th St.	John	Segota	1879	1900 Census
1897		John	Radoslovich	1881	Roll 226
1897	547 W. 39th St.	Matja	Karcic	1869	1900 Census
1897	547 W. 39th St.	Nicolo	Radoslovich	1871	1900 Census
1897	Br. In U.S.	Romolo	Carcich	1878	
1898	537 W. 59th St.	Antonio	Bellanich	1871	1900 Census
1898	537 W. 59th St.	Antonio	Cecco	1871	1900 Census
1898	537 W. 59th St.	Antonio	Segota	1864	1900 Census
1898	547 W. 39th St.	Giacomo	Gallosich	1879	1900 Census
1899	547 W. 39th St.	Anton	Nikolic	1863	1900 Census
1899	547 W. 39th St.	Domenico	[Valich]	1872	1900 Census
1899	547 W. 39th St.	John	Segotta	1882	1900 Census
1899	537 W. 59th St.	Marco	Radoslovich	1872	1900 Census
1899	537 W. 59th St.	Marco	Rerecich	1876	1900 Census
1899	537 W. 59th St.	Paul	Carcich	1844	1900 Census
1900	New York	Andrea	Segotta	1873	
1900		Domminic Gaudenzio	Valic	1872	1900 Census
1900		Isidoro	Carcich	1874	
1900	Delta, B.C.	Tomasina Maria	Nicolich	1869	

Note: Street addresses are for Manhattan, New York. B.C. is British Columbia.

Unije Islanders in New York City with Year of Residency 1895-1950

MANHATTAN, N.Y.

East 3rd, 242
NIKOLIC, Peter (Sophie) **(1933)**

West 16th St., 241
RERECICH, Frank **(1940)**

West 18th St., 411-13
RERECICH, Frank (Helen) **(1933)**

36 St., [198] + 11 Ave.
CARCICH, Constantino **(1902)**

West 40 St., 609
CARCICK, Domenico **(1902)**

42 St., 65
CARCICH, Giovanni **(1902)**

West 39th St., 543 at 106
VERBORA, Frank **(1900)**
GALLOSIC, Anton **(1900)**
RADOSLOVICH, Nicolo **(1900)**
KARC[IC], Matja **(1900)**
NIKOLIC, Anton **(1900)**
KARCICH, Andrew **(1900)**
SEGOTA, John **(1900)**
GALOSSICH, Giacomo **(1900)**
CARCICH, John **(1900)**
SEGOTTA, John **(1900)**
SEGOTTA, Antonio **(1900)**

West 44th St., 454
CARCICH, Martin **(1920)**

West 44th St., 510
CARCICH, Matthew **(1920)**

West 44th St., 559
CARCICH, Martino **(1902)**

West 45th St., 427
NICOLICH, Anthony **(1933)**

West 45th St., 454
CARCICH, Martin **(1920)**

West 45th St., 532
CARCICH, Andrew apt 10 **(1933)**
CARCICH, Andrew Jr. **(1933)**
CARCICH, Jos., apt. 14 **(1933)**
CARCICH, John, apt 6 **(1933)**

West 45th St., 534
RERECICH, John **(1933)**

West 45th St., 536
CARCICH, John **(1931)**
CARCICH, Romolo **(1931)**
RADOSLOVICH, Andrew **(1920)**
RERECICH, Antonio **(1933)**
RERECICH, Domenick A. **(1933)**

West 45th St., 538
CARCICH, Ambroso **(1933)**
CARCICH, Dominick **(1933)**

West 45th St., 552
RADOSLOVICH, A.A. **(1931)**
CARCICH, Romolo **(1917)**

West 45th St., 555
CARCICH, Domenico **(1902)**
CARCICH, Gaudenzio **(1902)**

West 45th St., 557
CARCICK, Maria **(1902)**
CARCICK, Andrea Ga[ud.] **(1902)**
RADOSLOVICH, Domnick **(1915)**

West 46th St., 414
NICOLICH, Mike **(1933)**

West 46th St., 444
RADOSLOVICH, A. **(1950)**
RADOSLOVICH, Anton **(1933)**
RADOSLOVICH, Marion **(1933)**
RERECICH, John **(1933)**

West 46th St., 464
NICOLICH, Peter (Anna) **(1933)**

46th St., 627
CARCICH, Antonio **(1902)**
CARCICH, Andrea **(1902)**

West 47th St., 503
CARCICH, Andrea **(1933)**
CARCICH, Anthonio **(1933)**
KARCICH, Jos. (Anna) **(1933)**
RERECICH, Michl. **(1933)**

West 47th St., 513
NADALIN, Andrew **(1931)**

West 47th St., 515
BELLANICH, John **(1925)**
KARCICH, Andrew **(1925)**
KARCICH, Andrew **(1920)**
KARCICH, Andrew (Mary) **(1933)**
CARCICH, Antonio **(1925)**
CARCICH, John **(1917)**
KARCIC, Nicholas **(1920)**
CARCICH, Nicholas **(1920)**
CARCICH, Nix. **(1925)**
KARCICH, Nickolas **(1925)**
KARCIC, Nicolas **(1924)**
KARCICH, Nicholas **(1933)**
NADALIN **(1925)**
NICOLICH **(1920)**
NICOLICH, John **(1920)**
NICOLICH, Rudolph (Antonio) **(1933)**
RADOSLOVICH, Minnie **(1933)**

West 47th St., #517
CARCICH, Anthony **(1920)**
CARCICH, Antonio **(1918)**

47th St., 557 at 11th Ave.
CARCICH, Anthonio **(1902)**

West 48th St., 413
CARCICH, Anthony J. (Mary) **(1933)**

West 48th St., 418
NICOLICH, Andrew (Mary) **(1933)**

West 48th St., 420
NICOLICH, Martin **(1924)**

West 48th St., 422
CARCICH, Luke **(1931)**

West 48th St., 515
NICOLICK, Dominick **(1933)**

West 48th St., 527
RERECICH, Lawrence **(1950)**

West 49th St., 512
KARCIC, Andro **(1934)**

West 49th St., 523
NICOLICH, Jos. **(1933)**

West 49th St., 524
KARCICH, John **(1931)**
KARCICK, John **(1933)**
NICOLICH, John. **(1933)**
NICOLICH, Steve **(1933)**
RADOSLEVICH, John **(1933)**
RERECICH, Andrew **(1933)**
RERECICH, Antony **(1933)**
RERECICH, Laurence **(1933)**

West 49th St., 526
RADOSLOVIC, Martin A. **(1924)**

West 49th St., 528
CARCICH, Frank **(1933)**
CARCICH, John **(1933)**
CARCICH, John B. **(1933)**

West 49th St., 531
NIKOLICH, Andrea **(1933)**
NIKOLICH, Anthony **(1933)**
NIKOLICH, Guisippi **(1933)**
NIKOLICH, John **(1933)**

NIKOLICH, Marko **(1933)**
NIKOLICH, Martino **(1933)**

West 49th St., 533
CARCICH, John (Annie) **(1933)**

West 49th St., 543
RERECICH, Matthew **(1950)**

West 49th St., 726
CARCICH, Dominic/Peter **(1950)**
NICOLICH, Andrea/Anna **(1950)**

West 51th St., 550
CARCICH, John **(1924)**

West 50th St., 532
NICOLICH, John Y. **(1924)**

West 51th St., 554
NADALIN, John **(1931)**

West 58th St., 57
NICHOLICH, LouiseT Mrs. **(1931)**
NICOLICH, Antonio **(1933)**
NICOLICH, Louise **(1933)**

59th St., #537
BELLANICH, Antonio **(1900)**
CARCICH, Antonio **(1902)**
CARCIK, Domenici **(1902)**
[CARCICH], Domenico **(1900)**
CARCICH, Andrea **(1902)**
CARCICH, Anto. **(1902)**

59th St., #537
CARCICH, [Paul] **(1900)**
CARCICK, Giovanni **(1902)**
CECCO, Antonio **(1900)**
NICOLICH, Andrews **(1900)**
NICOLICH, Lorenzo **(1900)**
RADOSLOVICH, Marco **(1900)**
[RERECICH], Marco **(1900)**
[SEGOTA], Antonio **(1900)**

West 60th St., #244
CARCICH, Giuseppe **(1902)**

East 66th St., 411
RADOSLOVICH, Dominic **(1950)**

West 68th St., 260
CARCICH, Dominick **(1933)**

72rd St., 1462
NICOLICH, John **(1933)**

73rd St., 426
KARCIK, Jos. (Anna) **(1933)**

East 78th St., 232
NICOLICH, John A. **(1924)**

West 109th St., 102
RADOSLOVICH, Andrew **(1931)**
RADOSLOVICH, Andrew **(1933)**

West 115th St., #549
CARCICK, Giovanni Roco **(1902)**
CARCICH, Andrea **(1902)**

West 177th St., 655
CARCICH, Nicholas **(1931)**

4th (Fourth) Ave., #1147 rear, New York, Queens
RADOSLOVICH, Matthew **(1920)**

10th (Tenth) Ave., 440
KARCICH, Andrew M. **(1950)**

10th (Tenth) Ave., 488
RERECICH, John **(1933)**

10th (Tenth) Ave., 643
CARCICH, Anthony **(1933)**

10th (Tenth) Ave., 645
RADOSLOVICH, Gavdent **(1918)**

10th (Tenth) Ave., 649
NICOLICH, Audrea[sic] **(1924)**

10th (Tenth) Ave., 688 NYC
RADOSLOVICH, Matteo **(1950)**

10th (Tenth) Ave., 699
NICOLICH, Steve **(1933)**

11th (Eleventh) Ave., #547 at 59th St.
CARCICH, Andria Domenico **(1902)**
CARCICH, Ambrose **(1917)**

11th (Eleventh) Ave., #604
CARCICH, Andrew **(1920)**
CARCICH, Andrew **(1917)**

11th (Eleventh) Ave., #706
KARCICH, Andrew **(1920)**

11th (Eleventh) Ave. #898
CARCICH, Antonio (1895)

Amsdm Ave., 70
RADOSLOVICH, John **(1933)**
RERECICH, Dominic **(1933)**

Broadway, 3409
CARCICH, Anthony D. **(1950)**

22 Harbor St.
CARCICH, Andrea **(1902)**

Gwich (Greenwich), 807
RADOLSLOVICH, G. **(1950)**

145 Washinton St.
CARCIH, Antonio **(1902)**

? St., #647
CARCICH, Andrea **(1902)**

QUEENS (N.Y.)

23rd, 22-21
RADOSLOVICH, D. **(1942)**

30th, 2621
RADOSLOVICH, Gaudetn **(1933)**

33rd Street, 2311
NICOLICH, Andrew **(1930)**

34th, LIC 30-35
RADOSLOVICH, Peter **(1942)**

47th St.,
LIC Astoria 25-39
NICOLICH, Elsie R. **(1942)**

Sources for Unije Islanders in New York City 1895-1950:

Marriage Register 1921, Saints Cyril and Methodius Roman Catholic Church, New York City, NY
New York. 1900, 1920, 1930 U.S. census, New York City
New York. 1915, 1925 New York State census
New York City Directory 1918/1919; 1922/1923; 1924/1925; 1933/1934
New York City. Manhattan & Bronx City Directory 1931
New York City. Manhattan Telephone Directory 1940/1941; 1950
New York City. Queens Telephone Directory 1942/1943
New York City. U.S. District Court (Naturalization Records
Passenger Ship Record. New York City 1904
Port of New York City 1897-1902 Index, G.S. film #543476
U.S. Military Registration Cards 1917-1918

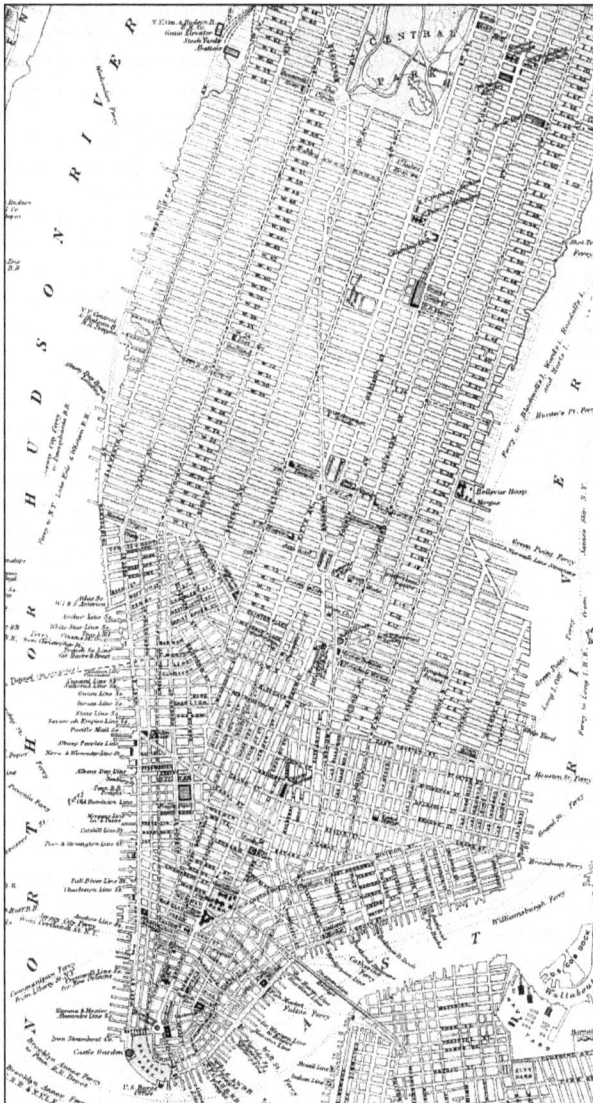

Manhattan, New York, 1885

INDEX TO NEW YORK CITY NAMES & YEAR OF RESIDENCY 1895-1950

CARCICH, John, born May 1869 (1900) West 39th St., 543 at 106

CARCICH, John (1931) West 45th St., 536

CARCICH, John, born 1880; Occupation: Deckhand (Tugboat) NYCRR (1917) West 47th St., 515

CARCICH, John B. pntr (1933) West 49th St., 528

CARCICH, Jos., apt. 14 (1933) West 45th St., 532

KARCICH, Jos. (Anna) deckhand (1933) West 47th St., 503

KARCIK, Jos. (Anna) (1933) 73rd St., 426

CARCICH, Luke (1931) West 48th St., 422

CARCICH, Martin, age 46, born 1874 Austria, 1916 (1920) West 45th St., 454

CARCICH, Martin, age 46, born 1875 Austria, living alone 1920. (1920) West 44th St., 454

CARCICH, Martino, age 23, born 1876, arrival 5/21/1899; [cousin] Franco Giov. (1902) West 44th St., 559

KARC[IC], Matja, born Sept 1869 (1900) West 39th St., 543 at 106

CARCICH, Matthew, age 45, born 1875, wife Jinnie age 46, children: Emno, Matthew (1920) West 44th St., 510

CARCICK, Maria, age 21, born 1880 Lussin; sister Antonia C[ecco] (1902) West 45th St., 557

CARCICH, Nicholas (1931) West 177th St., 655

KARCIC, Nicholas, age 41, born 1869, wife Lucy, age 46, born 1864 (1920) West 47th St., 515

CARCICH, Nicholas, age 42, wife Catherine age 40, children: Lewis, Jennie, Anna (1920) West 47th St., 515

CARCICH, Nix., age 47, New Nor. Ctr. R.R.; wife Kate, children Louis, Jinnie, Anna, (1925) West 47th St., 515

KARCIC, Nicolas (1924) West 47th St., 515

KARCICH, Nicholas (Lucy) rigger (1933) West 47th St., 515

KARCICH, Nickolas, age 46, Occ: Build Trade; wife Lusie, age 50 (1925) West 47th St., 515

CARCICH, [Paul] born 1844 (1900) 59th St., #537

CARCICH, Romolo (1931) West 45th St., 536

CARCICH, Romolo, born 1890 (1917) West 45th St., 552

CECCO, Antonio, born 1871 (1900) 59th St., #537

GALLOSIC, Anton, born May 1870 (1900) West 39th St., 543 at 106

GALOSSICH, Giacomo, born Aug 1879 (1900) West 39th St., 543 at 106

NADALIN, Andrew (1931) West 47th St., 513

NADALIN, John (1931) West 51st St., 554

NADALIN, John, age 31, Occ: Capt. Boat.; wife Anna, age 23; dau. Mary, age 3 yrs (1925) West 47th St., 515

NICOLICH, Andrea-1120 and Anna (1950) West 49th St., 726

NIKOLICH, Andrea longshoremn (1933) West 49th St., 531

NICOLICH, Audrea[sic] (1924) 10th (Tenth) Ave., 649

NICOLICH, Andrews born [1874] (1900) 59th St., #537

NICOLICH, Andrew, age 41, wife, children: Andrew, Mary, Minnie, Antonia (1930) 33rd Street, 2311 (Queens)

NICOLICH, Andrew (Mary) (1933) West 48th St., 418

NIKOLIC, Anton, born Dec 1863 (1900) West 39th St., 543 at 106

NICOLICH, Anton, age 27 born 1893, enumerated with Karcic,Nicholas, boader (1920) West 47th St., 515

NICOLICH, Antonio singer. (1933) West 58th St., 57

NIKOLICH, Anthony longshoremn (1933) West 49th St., 531

NICOLICH, Anthony (1933) West 45th St., 427

NICOLICK, Dominick (1933) West 48th St., 515

NIKOLICH, Elsie R. (1942) 47th St., LIC Astoria 25-39 (Queens)

NIKOLICH, Guisippi longshoremn (1933) West 49th St., 531

NICOLICH, John A. carp (1924) East 78th St., 232

NICOLICH, John computer Title Guarantee & Trust Co. (1933) 72rd St., 1462

NICOLICH, John, age 33, born 1887,enumerated with Karcic, Nicholas, boarder (1920) West 47th St., 515

NICOLICH, John Y. boatmn (1924) West 50th St., 532

NICOLICH, John, plstr. (1933) West 49th St., 524

NIKOLICH, John longshoremn (1933) West 49th St., 531

NICOLICH, Jos. (1933) West 49th St., 523

NICOLICH, Lorenzo, born 1876 (1900) 59th St., #537

NICHOLICH, Louise T Mrs. (1931) West 58th St., 57

NICOLICH, Louise singer (1933) West 58th St., 57

NIKOLICH, Marko longshoremn (1933) West 49th St., 531
NICOLICH, Martin (1924) West 48th St., 420
NIKOLICH, Martino longshoremn (1933) West 49th St., 531
NICOLICH, Mike longeshoremn. (1933) West 46th St., 414
NICOLICH, Peter (Anna) (1933) West 46th St., 464
NIKOLIC, Peter (Sophie) (1933) East 3rd, 242
NICOLICH, Rudolph (Antonio) deckhd (1933) West 47th St., 515
NICOLICH, Steve (1933) 10th (Tenth) Ave., 699
NICOLICH, Steve longshoremn. (1933) West 49th St., 524

RADOSLOVICH, A. (1950) West 46th St., 444
RADOSLOVICH, A.A. (1931) West 45th St., 552
RADOSLOVICH, Andrew (1931) West 109th St., 102
RADOSLOVICH, Andrew J. (Marie K.) supt (1933) West 109th St., 102
RADOSLOVICH, Andrew,age 40, wife Mary, children: Catherine, 5, Mary, Anthony, (1920) West 45th St., 536
RADOSLOVICH, Anton (1933) West 46th St., 444
RADOSLOVICH, D. (1942) 23rd, 22-21 (Queens)
RADOSLOVICH, Dominick (1950) East 66th St., 411
RADOSLOVICH, Domnick, lodger, age 37 (born 1878) Austria, [19]15 Al, Porter (1915) West 45th St., 557
RADOLSLOVICH, G. (1950) Gwich (Greenwich), 807
RADOSLOVICH, Gaudent (Gaudent Coffee Pot) Astoria (1933) 30th, 2621 (Queens)
RADOSLOVICH, Gavdent, confr. (1918) 10th (Tenth) Ave., 645
RADOSLOVICH, John pntr (1933) Amsdm Ave., 70
RADOSLEVICH, John longshoremn (1933) West 49th St., 524
RADOSLOVICH, ML (1942) Burns, Frst. Hls. Boulvard [3]04 (Queens)
RADOSLOVICH, Marco born 1872 (1900) 59th St., #537
RADOSLOVIC, Martin A. deck hd (1924) West 49th St., 526
RADOSLOVICH, Matthew, wife Mary, child. Matthew, Katherin, Mary, Ljubica (1920) 1147-4th Ave., Queens
RADOSLOVICH, Marie A. (1942) Booth, Frst. Hls. 65-41 (Queens)
RADOSLOVICH, Marion (1933) West 46th St., 444
RADOSLOVICH, Matteo (1950) 10th (Tenth) Ave., 688 NYC
RADOSLOVICH, Minnie drsmkr (1933) West 47th St., 515
RADOSLOVICH, Nicolo, born June 1871 (1900) West 39th St., 543 at 106
RADOSLOVICH, Peter (1942) 34th, LIC 30-35 (Queens)
RADOSLOVICH, Stanley (1942) Nrthrn. Bl Jk Ht 82-11 (Queens)

RERECICH, Andrew busboy (1933) West 49th St., 524
RERECICH, Antonio longshoremn (1933) West 45th St., 536
RERECICH, Antony longshoremn (1933) West 49th St., 524
RERECICH, Dominic longshoremn (1933) Amsdm Ave., 70
RERECICH, Domenick A. longshoremn (1933) West 45th St., 536
RERECICH, Frank (1940) West 16th St., 241
RERECICH, Frank (Helen) (1933) West 18th St., 411-13
RERECICH, John (1933) West 45th St., 534
RERECICH, John pntr (1933) 10th (Tenth) Ave., 488
RERECICH, John longshoremn (1933) West 46th St., 444
RERECICH, Laurence fismn (1933) West 49th St., 524
RERECICH, Lawrence (1950) West 48th St., 527
[RERECICH], Marco, born 1876 (1900) 59th St., #537
RERECICH, Matthew, pntr. (1950) West 49th St., 543
RERECICH, Michl. (1933) West 47th St., 503

[**SEGOTA**], Antonio, born 1864 (1900) 59th St., #537
SEGOTTA, Antonio, born April 1877 (1900) West 39th St., 543 at 106
SEGOTA, John, born May 1879 (1900) West 39th St., 543 at 106
SEGOTTA, John, born Sept 1882 (1900) West 39th St., 543 at 106

VERBORA, Frank, born May 1872, cook (1900) West 39th St., 543 at 106

NOTES

1 Julijano Sokolić, "Neki prilozi za sintezu novije povijesti otoka Losinja (1918-1945)", in *Otocki ljetopis Cres-Losinj* 5, 1984: 259.

2 Leo Kosuta, "Glagoljas i glagojica na Cresu i Losinju", in *Otocki LjetopisCres-Losnij*, 1975, 250.

3 Ivana Miletić, "Arheoloska topografija otoka Unije (Archaeological topography of Unije island)". *Histria Archaeologica* (September 2004), 33/2002: 195-263.

4 Miletić, Arheoloska topografija otoka Unije (Archaeological topography of Unije island), 263.

5 Tullio Pizzetti, *Con la bandiera del protettor San Marco: la marineria della Serenissima nel Settecento e il contributo di Lussino*, 3 volumes (Pasian di Prato, Italy: Campanotto Editore, 1999), 1: 230.

6 Pizzetti, *Con la bandiera del protettor San Marco*, 1: 246.

7 Nikola Crnković, Franjo Velčić, Julijano Sokolić, Goran Ivanisević, *725 godina Veloga Lošinja* (Zagreb: Interprint, 2005), 85.

8 Pizzetti, *Con la bandiera del protettor San Marco*, 1: 230.

9 *Glagokjski Losinjski protokoli notara Mikule Krstinica i Ivana Bozicevica (1564-1636).* Radovi Staroslavenskog Zavoda, volume 9 (Zagreb: Ognjen Prica, 1988), 54, 90, 114, 135, 178, 188.

10 Pizzetti, *Con la bandiera del protettor San Marco*, 1: 247.

11 Pizzetti, *Con la bandiera del protettor San Marco*, 3: 72.

12 Pizzetti, *Con la bandiera del protettor San Marco*, 3: 76.

13 Rudi Francin, *The turbulent history of the north Adriatic archipelago: an account of the enigmatic islands.* New York, s.n.,1984.

14 *Glagokjski Losinjski protokoli notara Mikule Krstinica i Ivana Bozicevica (1564-1636).* Radovi Staroslavenskog Zavoda, volume 9 (Zagreb: Ognjen Prica, 1988), 188.

15 Birth register 1609-1673, Saint Mary's Roman Catholic Church, Osor, Croatia, microfilm no. 2099981 – item 1, Family History Library, Salt Lake City, Utah, February 15, 1629, and January 7, 1633.

16 Anton Bozanić, Iseljenici cresko-losinjskog otocja u New Yorku i okolici: jedno stoljece organiziranog drustvenog zivota nasih otocana u New Yorku, (Cres-Mali Losinj-New York: Katedra Cakavskokg sabora), 228. and Ivan Kukuljevic Sakcinski, 1852. *Arkiv za povestnicu Jugoslavensku.* Volume 2, (Zagreb: Tiskom Dra. Ljudevita Gaja,1852), 2: 293.

17 Mihovil Bolonić, 1975. Prezimena i nadimci u Vrbniku. *Krkci Zbornik* 6: 209-256

18 Luca Lovrečić, Similjana Ristić, Bojana Brajenović, Miljenko Kapović, Borut Peterlin. Human Y-specific STR haplotypes in the Western Croatian population sample. *Forensic Science International* 149: 257-261.

19 Margita Nikolić, *Unije: kuzelj vaf sarcu* (Mali Losinj: Katedra cakavkog sabora Cres-Losinj, 2000), 66-82.

20 Ricardo D'Erco, *O Ribolovu na istocnom jadranu : historijsko-prvna, ribarstoveno-politicka i ekonomska grada* (Zagreb: n.p. 1973), 49, 52.

21 Confirmation Register 1592-1754, Saint Mary's Roman Catholic Church, Mali Losinj, Croatia, microfilm no. 2199340 – items 2 and 3, Family History Library, Salt Lake City, Utah,
1715.

22 Francin, *The turbulent history of the north Adriatic archipelago: an account of the enigmatic islands.* New York, s.n.,1984, 32-33.

23 Branko Fucić, *Glagoljski Natpisi*, (Zagreb: Jugoslavenske Akademije Znanosti i Umjetnosti, 1982), 393.

24 *Memoria Liturgiae Slavicae in Dioecesi Auxerensi,* ([s.l.]: [s.n.], [19__]), 55.

25 Confirmation Register 1592-1754, Saint Mary's Roman Catholic Church, Mali Losinj, Croatia, microfilm no. 2199340 – items 2 and 3, Family History Library, Salt Lake City, Utah, 1677.

26 Marriage Register 1704-1745, Saint Mary's Roman Catholic Church, Mali Losinj, Croatia, microfilm no. 1738833 – item 1, Family History Library, Salt Lake City, Utah.

27 Death Register 1753-1791, Saint Mary's Roman Catholic Church, Osor, Croatia, microfilm no. 2099983 – item 1, Family History Library, Salt Lake City, Utah.

28 Marriage Register 1746-1821, Saint Mary's Roman Catholic Church, Mali Losinj, Croatia, microfilm no. 2084820 – item 2, Family History Library, Salt Lake City, Utah.

29 Fortis, *Travels into Dalmatia,* 466.

30 Pizzetti, *Con la bandiera del protettor San Marco*, 3: 449.

31 Pizzetti, *Con la bandiera del protettor San Marco*, 2: 371, 375-378, 381-382.

32 Fortis, *Travels into Dalmatia,* 408-9.

33 Fortis, *Travels into Dalmatia,* 412

34 Fortis, *Travels into Dalmatia,* 409

35 Fortis, *Travels into Dalmatia,* 424.

36 Fortis, *Travels into Dalmatia,* 425.

37 Fortis, *Travels into Dalmatia,* 468.

38 Fortis, *Travels into Dalmatia,* 395, 398.

39 Fortis, *Travels into Dalmatia,* 399

40 Fortis, *Travels into Dalmatia,* 417

41 Census 1815, 1819, Haupt Auswies, (Historical Archives Rijeka), 20, 28

42 I. Rudan et al. Cancer incidence in eastern Adriatic isolates, Croatia: examples from the islands of Krk, Cres, Losinj, Rab, and Pag. *Coll. Antropol.* 23(2): 547-556.

43 Božo Milanović, *Hrvatski Narodni Preporod u Istri.* Knijga Druga (1883-1947) (Istarsko Knijževno Drugštvo Sv. Jirilia I Metoda, 1973), 280.

44 Nikolić, *Unije: kuzelj vaf sarcu,* 66-82.

45 Antun Turčić, *Susak otok pijeska, trstike i vinograda; the island of sand, reed and vineyards.* Susak: Župni ured, 1998.

46 Fortis, *Travels into Dalmatia*

47 Lovrečić. Human Y-specific STR haplotypes in the Western Croatian population sample. *Forensic Science International* 149: 257-261.

48 Turčić, *Susak otok pijeska, trstike i vinograda; the island of sand, reed and vineyards.*

49 Josip Bratulić, Petar Šimunović, *Prezimena i Naselja u Istri: Narodnosna statistika u godini oslobodenja* (Pula/Rijeka: Čakavski sabor, 1985), volume 2, 177.

50 Durdica Bartolić, *Otok Unije* (Diplomski rod), (Zagreb, Geografski Zavod, 1989), 27, 33.

51 Neera Hreglich Mercanti, Ricordando Lussino: I Velieri, [s.l.]: [s.n.], 2001, 2: 74, 85.

52 Istrian Benevolent Association booklet, 1922

53 Bozanić, *Iseljenici cresko-losinjskog otocja u New Yorku i okolici*, 71.

54. Petar Šimunović. *Hrvatska Prezimena*. Zagreb: Golden Marketing-Tehnička Knjiga, 2006, 393.

55. Šimunović. *Hrvatska Prezimena*.425.

56. Šimunović. *Hrvatska Prezimena*, 215.

57. Šimunović. *Hrvatska Prezimena*, 80.

58. Šimunović. *Hrvatska Prezimena*, 395.

59 Staso Forenbaher and Preston, T. Miracle (2005). The spread of farming in the Eastern *Adriatic. Antiquity.* 79: 1-15.

60 Miletić, *Arheološka topografija otoka Unije (Archaeologicaltopography of Unije island)* p. 195-263.

61 Petar Skok, *Slavenstvo i Romanstvo na Jadranskim Otocima : Toponomasticka ispitivanja.* Zagreb: Jugoslavenske Akademije Znanosti i Umjetnosti, 1950, 50.

BIBLIOGRAPHY

100 Godina Turizma Cres-Losinj. Zagreb: Turistkomerc, [1985].

Bartolić, Durdica. *Otok Unije* (Diplomski rod). Geografski Zavod, Zagreb, 1989.

Bolonić, Mihovil. 1975. Prezimena i nadimci u Vrbniku. *Krkci Zbornik* 6: 209-256

Bozanić, Anton. *Iseljenici cresko-losinjskog otocja u New Yorku i okolici: jedno stoljece organiziranog drustvenog zivota nasih otocana u New Yorku.* Cres-Mali Losinj-New York: Katedra Cakavskokg sabora, 1997.

Bratulić, Josip and Petar Šimunović. *Prezimena i Naselja u Istru: narodnosno statisika u godini oslovodenja.* 3 volumes. Pula, Rijeka, s.n., 1985.

Budinich, Melchiade. *L'Abolizone della Liturgia Glagolitica nellaParrocchia di Lussingrande ne 1802 con documenti.* Lussinpiccolo: Giadrino Infantile Italiano di Lussingrande, [1905].

Crnković, Nikola, Franjo Velčić, Julijano Sokolić, Goran Ivanisević. *725 godina Veloga Lošinja,* Zagreb: Interprint, 2005.

D'Erco, Ricardo. *O Ribolovu na istocnom jadranu : historijsko-prvna,ribarstoveno-politicka i ekonomska grada.* Zagreb: n.p. 1973.

Dumancić, Dragutin. Island of Unije: sustainable agricultural development

Finka, Božidar, Pero Budak (editors). *Leksik Prezimena Socijalističke Republike Hrvatske.* Zagreb: Nakladni zavod Matice Hrvatske, 1976.

Forenbaher, Staso, and Preston, T. Miracle (2005). The spread of farming in the Eastern *Adriatic. Antiquity.* 79: 1-15.

Fortis, Alberto. *Travels into Dalmatia.* New York: Arno Press & the New York Times, 1971. Orignally published as *Viaggio in Dalmatia* (1778), and also published in English as *Travels into Dalmatia,* London: J. Robson, 1778, and in Croatian as *Put po Dalmaciji.* Zagreb: Globus, 1984.

Francin, Rudi. *The turbulent history of the north Adriatic archipelago: an account of the enigmatic islands.* New York, s.n., 1984.

Fucić, Branko. *Apsyrdites.* Mali Losinj: Narodno sveuciliste, 1990.

Fucić, Branko. *Glagoljski Natpisi*, Zagreb: Jugoslavenske Akademije Znanosti i Umjetnosti, 1982

THE HISTORY AND FAMILIES OF UNIJE

Glagokjski Losinjski protokoli notara Mikule Krstinica i Ivana Bozicevica (1564-1636). Radovi Staroslavenskog Zavoda, Volume 9. Zagreb: Ognjen Prica, 1988.

Hreglich Mercanti, Neera. Ricordando Lussino: I Velieri, volume 2. [s.l.]: [s.n.], 2001.

Istrian Benevolent Association booklet, 1922.

Kosuta, Leo. Glagoljas i glagojica na Cresu I Losinj. *Otocki Ljetopis Cres-Losnij*, 1975, p. 249-253.

Lovrečić, Luca, Similjana Ristić, Bojana Brajenović, Miljenko Kapović, Borut Peterlin. (2005). Human Y-specific STR haplotypes in the Western Croatian population sample. *Forensic Science International* 149: 257-261.

Memoria Liturgiae Slavicae in Dioecesi Auxerensi [s.l.]: [s.n.], [19___].

Milanović, Božo. *Hrvatski Narodni Preporod u Istri*. Knijga Druga (1883-1947). Istarsko Knijževno Drugštvo Sv. Jirilia I Metoda, 1973.

Miletić, Ivana. *Arheološka topografija otoka Unije (Archaeological topography of Unije island)*. Histria Archaeologica: časopis Arheološkog muzeja Istre, rujan 2004, 33/2002, p. 195-263.

Nikolić, Margita. *Unije: kuzelj vaf sarcu*. Mali Losinj: Katedra cakavkog sabora Cres-Losinj, 2000.

Pauzin, Ljubo. O dobrim i slabim vremenima. *Nia ljetopis otoka Unije*. Broj 1, godina 1 [1991], p.6-7.

Petrinović, Kruno. Finci zaljubljeni u Unije i maline. *Gloriju*. No. 13. ozulak 1998, p. 44-47.

Pizzetti, Tullio. *Con la bandiera del protettor San Marco: la marineria della Serenissima nel Settecento e il contributo di Lussino*. 3 volumes. Pasian di Prato, Italy: Campanotto Editore, 1999.

Rudan, I., Campbell H., Ranzani G.N., Strnad M, Vorko-Jovic A., John V., Kern J., Ivankovic D., Stevanovic R., Vuckov S., Vuletic S., Rudan P. (1999). Cancer incidence in eastern Adriatic isolates, Croatia: examples from the islands of Krk, Cres, Losinj, Rab, and Pag. *Coll. Antropol.* 23(2): 547-556.

Sakcinski, Ivan Kukuljevic. 1852. *Arkiv za povestnicu Jugoslavensku.* Knijiga II. Zagreb: Tiskom Dra. Ljudevita Gaja.

Skok, Petar. *Slavenstvo i Romanstvo na Jadranskim Otocima : Toponomasticka ispitivanja.* Zagreb: Jugoslavenske Akademije Znanosti i Umjetnosti, 1950.

Sokolić, Julijano. Neki prilozi za sintezu novije povijesti otoka Losinja (1918-1945). *Otocki ljetopis Cres-Losinj* 5, 1984, p. 258-259.

Stanesić, Sanja. *Iseljenici i povratnici : Unije.* Bilten Minstarstva Povratka i Useljenistva. Broj 21. Listopad 1998, p.22-25.

Starc, Nenad. Nia u 21.stoljecu. *Nia ljetopis otoka Unije.* broj 1, godina 1 [1991], p. 10-13.

Šimunović, Petar. *Hrvatska Prezimena.* Zagreb: Golden Marketing-Tehnička Knjiga, 2006.

Turčić, Antun. *Susak otok pijeska, trstike i vinograda; the island of sand, reed and vineyards.* Susak: Župni ured, 1998.

Wilkes, J.J. *Dalmatia.* London: Routledge & Kegan Paul, 1969.

Zlatić, Danko. Dva Mala Otoka u sjeni vec ih. In: *Matica IsleljenickiKalendar* 1965, p. 175-179.

www.ingramcontent.com/pod-product-compliance
Lightning Source LLC
Chambersburg PA
CBHW080610270326
41928CB00016B/2994